Finding History

Research Methods and Resources for Students and Scholars

Christine Bombaro

THE SCARECROW PRESS, INC.
Lanham • Toronto • Plymouth, UK
2012

Published by Scarecrow Press, Inc.
A wholly owned subsidiary of The Rowman & Littlefield Publishing Group, Inc.
4501 Forbes Boulevard, Suite 200, Lanham, Maryland 20706
www.rowman.com

10 Thornbury Road, Plymouth PL6 7PP, United Kingdom

British Library Cataloguing in Publication Information Available

Library of Congress Cataloging-in-Publication Data

Bombaro, Christine, 1971–
    Finding history : research methods and resources for students and scholars / Christine
Bombaro.
          p. cm.
    Includes bibliographical references and index.
    ISBN 978-0-8108-8379-6 (cloth : alk. paper) — ISBN 978-0-8108-8380-2 (ebook)
    1. History—Methodology—Study and teaching. 2. History—Research—Study and
teaching. I. Title.
    D16.B693 2012
    907.2—dc23   2012012751

∞™ The paper used in this publication meets the minimum requirements of American
National Standard for Information Sciences—Permanence of Paper for Printed Library
Materials, ANSI/NISO Z39.48-1992.

Printed in the United States of America

To the history majors of Dickinson College:
past, present, and future.

Above all things, in our historical investigations let us be exact. Here there is no justification of haste and lack of precision. So far as practicable, let us go to original sources of information. If we are obliged to receive information at second-hand, let us insist on knowing where our informant received his knowledge and his impressions. . . . There is no atonement for carelessness. If the historical student is unwilling to seek for the truth, even in the remotest recesses of darkness, he will have to be content to see his work lightly esteemed.

—Charles Kendall Adams, *A Manual of Historical Literature*, 3rd ed.
New York: Harper & Brothers, 1888

Contents

Acknowledgments

This book would not exist without the help of many colleagues, friends, and loved ones.

Finding History was generously supported by two important sources of funding. The first was a Carnegie-Whitney Grant from the American Library Association, which funded my travel to Boston, Massachusetts, and Washington, DC, and also paid part of my interns' salaries. The second was two Dana Research Assistantships from Dickinson College, which allowed me to hire two remarkably talented and indispensable interns. I thank the review boards of both committees for providing me with the extra support I needed to complete the project.

This book could never have been finished without the help of my two Dana interns. My first intern, W. John Monopoli, class of 2011, was responsible for testing my research methodology by investigating reasons for John A. J. Creswell's apparent change of name. Though not a history major, John developed as much interest in John A. J. Creswell as I had. His essay reveals both the frustrations and successes that come with any historical research project, and it filled me with a great sense of pride to have observed John learning the process under my tutelage and enjoying it. My second intern, Colin Macfarlane, class of 2012, was a history major genuinely interested in the usefulness of this book to his fellow students. He was not in any way reticent with the constructive criticism that shaped the organization and flow of this book, thus making the final project far superior to what I would have produced without his input. It would have taken me at least an additional year to complete this book without the help of both John and Colin, and I can only hope that the work they did with me on this project benefits them in some small way as they pursue their own careers.

I must wholeheartedly thank the professors of Dickinson College's Department of History for sharing their inexhaustible knowledge, and for offering humorous but always thorough and thoughtful critique of my work. Of particular help were Marcelo Borges (Latin American history) and Karl Qualls (Russian history). Professors David Commins (Middle East history) and Steve Weinberger (Middle Ages and Renaissance history) not only contributed their knowledge and offered constructive criticism, but also taught me as an undergraduate history major at Dickinson College. Professor Matthew Pinsker (U.S. Civil War era) generously allowed me to use numerous examples from his House Divided project throughout this book and additionally put me in touch with his knowledgeable and helpful colleagues at Harvard University. All of the history professors at Dickinson who teach historical research methods courses agreed to assign early drafts of this book as required reading.

I also owe a debt of gratitude to my colleagues in the Waidner-Spahr Library at Dickinson College. My director, Eleanor Mitchell, is without question is the finest leader I have ever had the privilege to work for and has always encouraged me to share my knowledge with a wide audience. She fully supported this project from its inception. Dickinson's cataloging librarian, Kirk Doran, retains an unbelievable knowledge of cataloging practices and over the years has helped me figure out the best ways to navigate library catalogs and databases; some of the advice that appears in this book I learned from him. James Gerencser, Dickinson's archivist and fellow graduate from the Dickinson College Class of 1993, offered publication leads and ever-patient assistance with the John A. J. Creswell files. He and Dickinson's special collections librarian, Malinda Triller, also spent quite a bit of time helping my interns and me identify helpful files and out-of-copyright maps in Dickinson's collection. Dickinson's GIS specialist James Ciarrocca created the maps of the Pine Grove Furnace area in chapter 4, and emeritus professor of geology Noel Potter provided the explanation and historical context of the region.

I say thank you also to the staff members at the Houghton Library of Harvard University who showed me the inner workings of university-sized libraries and archives: Tom Horrocks, associate librarian for collections; Rachel Howarth, associate librarian for public services; Leslie Morris, curator of modern books and manuscripts; Hope Mayo, curator of printing and graphic arts; Christina Davis, curator of the Woodsberry poetry room; and John Overholt, assistant curator of the Donald and Mary Hyde Collection of Dr. Samuel Johnson and early modern books and manuscripts.

In Washington, DC, I am particularly grateful for the help of William Davis at the National Archives, who spent quite some time pulling records and documents relating to John A. J. Creswell. As I later described the experience to my intern, Mr. Davis "spent more time helping me than I would have spent on myself."

The employees and volunteers at the Historical Society of Cecil County in Elkton, Maryland, were particularly enthusiastic about this project and helped me to retrieve materials on Creswell both on site and remotely. Special thanks go to Billie Todd, Carol Donache, Mike Dixon, and Gary Burns.

At Scarecrow Press, I say thank you to my editor Martin Dillon for his patience in seeing this project through to its completion. I am also grateful to Michael Hermann for his initial interest in my proposal and for ensuring that it was reviewed by Scarecrow's editorial board before he moved on to work for a different publisher.

I thank some of my earliest supporters with great affection. My parents and grandparents encouraged my academic success throughout my life and ensured that I received the best possible education. My friend George Rhyne, emeritus professor of history at Dickinson College, became my mentor and surrogate parent while I was a student at Dickinson and hired me for an internship that introduced me to the standards of professional writing and editing.

I would be greatly remiss if I did not offer a special word of thanks to my dearest friend, emeritus professor John M. Osborne (English history), for introducing me to A. J. Creswell, as well as his steady encouragement, most excellent advice, and painstakingly thorough proofreading. Before his retirement, John quite liberally allowed me to conduct assessments on the students in his research courses, thus greatly improving my teaching methodology. He spent generous amounts of his time reviewing my drafts, talking me through writer's block over tea, and making sure that I did not omit any important advice to future historians.

Finally, I thank Anne Marie Sargent, my best friend of a quarter century (and counting), for supporting me through my life's darkest days and for celebrating my brightest ones.

Preface

If there is anything that a historian can rely on, it is that everything changes over time. Culture, technology, geography, government, people's opinions, and indeed anything concerning humanity change with the passage of years, decades, and centuries. So too do the tools we use to study history.

Researchers have always had to adapt to changes in the dissemination and collection of information. What originally was recorded on handmade scrolls of papyrus or sheets of calfskin is now viewable as points of light on a computer screen. Historians have adapted the study of history to include the use of such revolutionary technological advances as the printing press, the typewriter, the mimeograph, the fax machine, the digital camera, and satellite technology. Despite technological innovation, however, the act of seeking information that helps historians understand why and how events have come to pass has remained essentially the same for centuries. As Sherman Kent of Yale University wrote in 1941: "[Research] consists of gathering facts—old and well-known ones at first, and later, with the help of deeper knowledge . . . new ones. It consists of forming hypotheses on the basis of these facts, of testing these hypotheses for traces of one's own ignorance or bias, of cleansing them if possible."[1] This fundamental summation of research holds true today and would have held true hundreds of years before Kent wrote those words.

Although the goals of historical research remain the same, the methods we use to discover and obtain knowledge have changed drastically since Kent's day. Much of the research we need to study history can be discovered online, downloaded, or reproduced instantly with a scanner or digital camera, and physically mailed or electronically delivered to the researcher who needs it. Technology has made information easier than ever to obtain. It has not, however, made information easier to discover. The explosion of information on the Internet has actually made the process of searching for relevant information more difficult than it ever was for prior generations of historians. The historical research process once consisted of poring over large tomes containing lists of materials printed in tiny fonts; checking out a few books from one's local library; making photocopies of articles; ordering a few items from other libraries that may have taken weeks to receive by mail; and, if the funds, time, and interest were favorable, traveling to the places where historical events took place. Now, with proper access privileges, much of this work can be done on a home or office computer.

Yet to a person who has never had to perform academic research, the process can be daunting. Studies have shown that the proliferation of information in the late twentieth and twenty-first centuries has actually made the research process seem more difficult for undergraduate students than it had in the past.[2] Because items of personal curiosity are relatively easy to find and the tolerance for error on the open Internet is large, the lines between scholarly research and "everyday life research"—the search for news, jobs, price comparisons, health information, friends and family members, and so on—have become blurred.[3] Nonetheless, the unprecedented amount of scholarly information now easily accessible in libraries puts a lot of pressure on college and university students to find the highest quality information that is directly relevant to the topic being explored. Because information seems so easy to obtain compared to days of the recent past when it existed only on paper, college and university professors will not accept an excuse that relevant information cannot be found.

This book aims to help new students of history adapt to the ever-changing and ever-expanding world of historical research. Internet search engines like Google have conditioned us to think that all of the information one could ever need can be found with one simple search. The reality is that no single source can ever be relied upon to provide all the information necessary to create a comprehensive and compelling research project. There is, in fact, a method behind the research process that is followed by history professionals and librarians every day, but it is perhaps not explained clearly or often enough to students new to the process. Standards in research methodology have been laid out by the American Historical Association (AHA) and the Association of College and Research Libraries (ACRL), two organizations responsible for helping people to learn how to research effectively and efficiently.[4] Based on those standards, the goals of this book are to help students of history

- know when academically oriented information is required;
- identify the different types of tools that are available to help locate required sources;
- use research tools efficiently and effectively;

- determine which types of sources are most appropriate for each project;
- include a balanced mix of source types in the project;
- physically acquire research materials;
- make evaluative judgments about the scholarly value of any given source;
- integrate the materials into the research project; and
- use sources responsibly.

Historians must be the most mentally flexible of researchers because of the constant changes in research technology and because of the many possible places in which historical documentation can be found. Though research is an intellectually challenging and rewarding experience, it is rarely easy and never a fast process. If it were, libraries would not spend literally millions of dollars to provide the resources described throughout this book and thousands of hours developing programs to teach people how to research effectively.

The research process can become easier and more efficient when you take the time to learn from others how to use the tools necessary to complete the job. Research skills are best perfected when you do not treat the research process as a solitary exercise but rather take advantage of the knowledge you can gain from the experienced professionals at your college or university. History by its nature is a discussion, and as such, you should take full advantage of all the study and effort of those who have researched before you, as they would certainly have wished you to do. Never be afraid to ask questions of those available to help you, and be sure to allow yourself enough time during the process to use their advice. You never know where research will lead you, and the direction you initially choose will inevitably change during the course of your project, just as history itself does.

Many guides on the theory of how to write a research paper in history have preceded this book and are available through reputable academic presses. Most of them contain useful advice about how to write a history paper or how to pass a history class, but many do not devote much space to the research process. Fewer still provide specific instruction on how to manipulate those sources to find relevant research material. Students who do not have the benefit of professional advice from a librarian or careful monitoring from their professors probably will use few, if any, of the quality scholarly sources devoted to historical inquiry that their professors should and do expect of them. Most students entering college have a vague recognition that the research process should begin at their college or university library, but they cannot acquire effective research skills without deliberate instruction. The intent of this book, therefore, is to compensate as much as possible for gaps in formal research instruction.

Once instructed in proper research methods, many students of history find the research process to be an enjoyable experience of exploration and discovery. In order to maximize the chances of that happening, this guide describes the appropriate sources needed for college and university level history projects, explains in specific detail where and how to look for scholarly research material, and provides instructions and examples illustrating how to manipulate information sources to expedite the search process without sacrificing quality of the sources. This book will provide history researchers with transferable skills needed to complete research projects in most other disciplines and to demonstrate to their readers that they have used the sources they found both thoroughly and appropriately.

NOTES

1. Sherman Kent, *Writing History* (New York: Appleton-Century-Crofts, Inc., 1941), 29–30.

2. Alison J. Head and Michael B. Eisenberg, "What Today's College Students Say about Conducting Research in the Digital Age," *Project Information Literacy Progress Report* (4 February 2009), 2.

3. Ibid., 3.

4. For the standards of the American Historical Association, see http://www. historians.org/teaching/policy/CriteriaForStandards.htm. For the standards of the Association of College and Research Libraries, see http://www.ala.org/ala/mgrps/divs/ acrl/standards/informationliteracycompetency.cfm.

Chapter One

Introduction to Historical Research

Some students mistakenly believe that they cannot start a research project without a clear topic or thesis in mind. Actually, the opposite is true. Students who are struggling to form specific and focused ideas can and should engage in exploratory research before committing to a topic. Exploration is not only a good way to refine a potential topic, but it also reveals how modern scholars think about historical topics and how the research on a topic has evolved over the years of its study. Exploratory research can help you figure out if your project is viable and original and whether you will be able to find enough material to support and enhance your argument.

Thesis: A statement within a book or article that defines the author's argument and main points.

You should always allow yourself several weeks at minimum to conduct research for a project that is expected to be longer than ten pages or is to be presented in front of a group. It will probably take you days if not weeks to gather all the material you will need to complete your project. If you need to borrow some material from other libraries, you have to allow time for it to arrive so that you can use it effectively. You must also take into account the time it will take you to read closely and process all the information you gather so that you can form your own opinions about the topic you are studying. Additionally, researching early will give you time to ask appropriate questions about your sources and, if necessary, adjust the focus of your topic. Research projects almost always evolve at least slightly away from the writer's original intention during researching and writing. Finally, if you have a draft of a paper prepared early, you can ask a professor, a librarian, or a writing tutor to read it and make constructive suggestions for improvement. You cannot be a successful historian until you understand that research is *never* a quick process, even with all of the modern technological innovations in information access at our disposal.

Most researchers should begin looking for historical sources in their own college or university library or local public library. There is also quite a bit of research material available at no cost on the Internet. Although a wealth of perfectly acceptable information can be found on the Internet, there are still many important pieces of evidence available through specialized sources found only in libraries that have the mandate and the funds to pay access fees for these often-expensive products. In short, all potential sources of research material should be investigated; no single source will provide you with all the evidence required to complete a research project successfully. This book provides tips on how to access and use all available sources for a history project efficiently and effectively.

While many historical topics have been well researched, it is possible that you may ask a historical question for which little directly related research material is available. Although such topics may take extra time to research, they should be considered good opportunities to investigate an original question that professional historians have not yet fully considered. Indeed, it is often more difficult to add original thoughts to topics about which much has been written. If you find that you are asking a new or underresearched historical question, your research might focus upon comparing and contrasting similar situations or events and applying conclusions from other situations to your own theories. Such a topic may be more challenging to research than topics for which an abundance of material is available, but in the end, as your curiosity and knowledge increase and as your topic begins to take shape, it will be a rewarding experience.

Whatever your topic, if you feel that you are not finding enough material about your project, or if you are finding too much and are having difficulty zeroing in on the material that is most relevant, be sure to ask a librarian for help and advice. Librarians will be able to help you think about your topic in ways you had not considered, as well as help you find useful sources of information. Among your professors, librarians, and the thousands of historians who have come before you, your network of support is vast.

There are many ways to begin accessing historical research material and numerous methods you can use to acquire material. This book will help you learn the best ways to find the historical evidence required to produce a well-researched and successful history project.

A NOTE ABOUT PLAGIARISM

Plagiarism is the act of copying another person's ideas and presenting them as if they were your own work. It is a serious breach of scholarly ethics. Plagiarism has been exposed as a problem in colleges and universities and beyond. Plagiarism scandals have occurred at respected institutions of higher learning, some of which resulted in graduates having their degrees revoked months or years after they left school and subsequently losing their jobs. Professional writers found guilty of plagiarism have suffered public embarrassment and also been fired.[1] Put simply, plagiarism is theft.

Attempting to patch your writing with phrases and paragraphs written by others can seem like an attractive option when you are facing project deadlines and rushing to complete a project. However, students who try to cut corners by cobbling together strings of quotes, by forcing quotes into a paper that has been essentially already written, or by mashing up a bunch of ideas from different authors in an attempt to make a "new" paper will likely receive a bad grade at best and find themselves facing formal plagiarism accusations carrying the risk of suspension or expulsion at worst.

Fortunately, plagiarism is easy to avoid. You must simply respect the research material you uncover as the property of others. You may, and are in fact encouraged to, use those ideas as the foundation upon which to develop your own ideas, but not without formally acknowledging the work of those who inspired and informed yours. By taking the time to conduct and process your research as suggested in this book, you will easily develop your own opinions and arguments about the topic, at which point you can responsibly use the work of other historians to support your own assertions.

Plagiarism is most easily avoided when you acknowledge the ideas of other historians by creating a bibliography of the sources you consult and using footnotes to indicate when you are including a direct quote or paraphrasing another historian. Information about how to properly cite research material by means of bibliographies and footnotes can be found in appendixes A and B.

HOW TO USE THIS BOOK

The quest for information need not necessarily to follow the same path each time, and not all types of sources are appropriate or necessary to use for every history project. Reading this entire book will give you a complete picture of the research process and help you locate and select the sources that will benefit your project the most. This book is designed so that each section can be consulted at the point of need and used independently of one another. The sections cross-reference one another when additional explanation may be needed.

This book is best used as a guide to researching large-scale projects that require sustained work, an original thesis, and many sources of information. The advice in this book does not address reaction or opinion papers, or projects for which the sources you need to use are prescribed by your classroom instructor. Like any other book of this nature, this one guide cannot possibly anticipate every research conundrum that you might encounter. The aim, rather, is to get you used to the process of researching, using certain staples of historical research as examples, so that you can naturally begin to find material on your own.

The research process is similar for most academic libraries in the United States, although specific available products will vary from library to library. Much, although not all, research can be done via the Internet, particularly for those who are students or faculty members in an academic community. This guide will be most useful for researchers working in the United States and other countries with western-style libraries, where access to library materials is generally open and unrestricted. Nonwestern libraries may not contain the same material and may not allow open-access privileges to material. Although every attempt has been made to provide examples of research material in languages other than English, and from all eras and geographic areas of world history, this guide will be most useful when researching historical topics that can be examined primarily in the English language.

NOTE

1. See, for example, Paula Wasley, "The Plagiarism Hunter," *The Chronicle of Higher Education*, 6 April 2007, A8–A11; Marc Santora, "Columbia Professor in Noose Case Is Fired on Plagiarism Charges," *The Chronicle of Higher Education*, 24 June 2008, 1; and Luke Slattery, "Plagiarism Plagues an Australian University," *The Chronicle of Higher Education*, 1 November 2008, A36.

Chapter Two

Getting Started

LEARNING YOUR LIBRARY

Before starting a research project, you should take some time to familiarize yourself with your library's online research services and its physical space. Since every library's building space and bookshelves are arranged differently, you should consult a library map, usually available at the service desks or on the library's website, and take a walk around the building the first time you use it. Pay particular attention to the sections of the library where the history books are shelved.

It is crucially important for you to talk with a librarian about your needs and expectations before embarking on a research project, especially for the first time, because college and university libraries are vastly different from public and high school libraries in terms of size, organization, and range of resources. Even if it is not a specific requirement of your class, it is a good idea to make an appointment to discuss your project with the specific librarian who works with your school's history department, so that you will know what to expect from the research process at your particular library. When you request a consultation with a librarian prior to beginning a topic, he or she can direct you to appropriate sources and help you navigate your library's physical layout. Librarians are there to answer your questions about library resources and best research practices, and they will welcome the opportunity to teach you how to research efficiently, use your sources ethically, and help you find that one elusive bit of information that will bring your project to a successful conclusion.

EVIDENCE

Evidence is the knowledge upon which we base our beliefs and interpretations about past events. Whether it comes in the form of documents or artifacts, evidence provides a basis upon which to prove a point or help form opinions about the past and to demonstrate the validity of beliefs and assertions.

Evidence: Knowledge and artifacts used to demonstrate the validity of beliefs and assertions.

Original sources of evidence are critical to any historical research project, and every researcher must take reasonable care to ensure that all evidence used in a paper or project is relevant and reliable. Historical evidence exists in numerous formats, including but not limited to books, journal articles, newspaper articles, handwritten pages, photographs, video files, and sound recordings. Evidence can be stored on paper or may be available electronically by way of free, public websites or on websites that require payment for access.

The documents and artifacts needed for historical research can be found in many places, but your local college, university, or public library is usually the first place you should look to begin gathering information. If you are working on a project for a college course, your professors will expect you to use the relevant research materials at your disposal, not only material that is available for free on the Internet, but also material that is available only through subscriptions that you must access from your library's website.

You must use three categories of evidence for most history projects: tertiary sources, secondary sources, and primary sources. Tertiary sources, such as *Encyclopedia Britannica* and the *Dictionary of American Biography*, are quick reference materials that briefly describe biographies, events, places, and eras by condensing facts and figures into a few pages or paragraphs. Secondary sources provide summaries, analyses, commentaries, or criticism of historical events; most of the secondary sources you will use are books such as Paul Fussel's book *The Great War and Modern Memory* (1975) or articles such as Frederick Jackson Turner's "The Significance of the Frontier in American History" (1893). Most of the secondary sources you use should be scholarly, meaning that they are written by experts in their respective fields of history. Primary sources are documents, artifacts, and other evidence of an event produced by firsthand witnesses at the time the event occurred; a primary source may be *The Domesday Book* or the United States' *Bill of Rights*. These three categories of sources will be addressed in greater detail in later chapters of this book.

EVALUATING SOURCES

Evaluating sources for their scholarly value and relevance to your project is a crucial part of the research process. No matter where you find a source, it is your scholarly and ethical responsibility as a historian to determine that the sources you use to support your arguments are accurate, appropriate for the type of work you are doing, and not themselves plagiarized from other sources. Even though many of the sources you will find in an academic library can be considered scholarly, you should always verify the value of the works you choose as they relate specifically to your own arguments and assertions. It may not be immediately obvious to you whether a source is scholarly and appropriate for your project. Determining the validity of a source is an evaluative process that may ultimately require you to make informed judgments about the nature of the material.

When seeking research material for a project, keep in mind that it is unacceptable to "pad" a bibliography with sources that are only marginally related to your topic or to try to force a document to work in your favor. Rather than reading the entire text of every source you find, you can make a preliminary determination of its value to your project by subjecting each source to a series of questions as noted below. For any source you find, you should consider how specifically an item could be helpful to your project and decide how it might add depth to your assertions. Because of the differences between tertiary, secondary, and primary sources, each type must be evaluated against a specific set of questions.

Tertiary Sources

You can assess the scholarly value of a tertiary source work by considering it against the following questions.

Who produced the source? Entries in tertiary sources may not be attributed to specific authors, but you can usually at least find a list of contributing authors by scanning the introduction or first few pages of the item. You also should look for material produced by scholarly presses that specialize in history such as Columbia University Press and Routledge.

Can you verify the information? The information you find in tertiary sources should be consistent with the information you find in other sources of evidence. Dates, names, places, spellings, and other pieces of verifiable information should be accurate.

Does the source provide additional sources for reading? A good tertiary source should provide a list of primary and secondary sources that you can use to gather more information about the topic.

Secondary Source Books and Articles

You can assess the scholarly value of a secondary work by considering it against the following questions.

What are the author's credentials or authority to write on this topic? A good secondary source should be written by a person with academic credentials in history or by someone who has demonstrated a commitment to the field by teaching history and writing about it in journals and books produced by respected publishers. Appendix C provides a list of well-known and well-respected scholarly journal and book publishers.

Does the work have a thesis? You should be able to identify in early sections of the work what historical question the author is trying to answer. A good secondary source should add new perspective to your topic, even if it largely verifies the arguments of other historians whose sources you are also using. In addition to the nature of the argument, the thesis should indicate whether the author is incorporating new evidence, evaluating sources based on a different paradigm, or analyzing the argument from an alternative point of view. In short, the author should state a compelling reason for writing about the topic.

How is the source written? Academic books and articles tend to have a formal, serious, straightforward tone, and are written using language specific to the subject area. The author may assume that his or her audience has some basic knowledge about the topic.

How and from where did the writer obtain the sources used to support the argument? The author should provide footnotes and/or a bibliography of related sources you can use to gather additional information for your own topic. A good scholarly bibliography provides a breadth of sources representing the various historical arguments that have been published about the topic since historians started writing about it. You can and should use the author's sources to supplement your own bibliography, provided, of course, that you examine these additional sources as carefully as you did the one that cited it.

How does the material support or challenge your own ideas and the other sources you have examined? You should be able to use the source to help answer your own questions about your topic and to help you consider your topic from a different perspective. A source that simply reiterates information from other sources may be less helpful than one that offers new information or examines known information in new ways.

Secondary Source Websites

Websites require extra criteria for evaluation. Upon first glance, some websites may appear to be scholarly because they often are peppered with factual historical information and statements by scholars who are interviewed and have their comments parsed and used in sound bites as convenient to the story. The History Channel's website, for example, might appear initially to be a scholarly site, but upon closer examination, you would find that the website is owned by the company A&E (Arts & Entertainment) Television Networks. As A&E Television Networks is a profit-making company, the content of the History Channel is motivated largely by profit even though the focus of the television channel and the website is history. However, the fact that the History Channel is part of an entertainment enterprise does not necessarily mean that all the information provided on the website or in the television programs is nonscholarly and not useful; on the contrary, the producers often interview the world's top-noted historians for their historical documentaries. Before using information from such a website though, you must make sure that the source is scholarly, or at least that the specific bits of information you draw from the site are credible. In addition to the questions you should ask of secondary source books and articles as noted above, you should consider websites against the following additional questions.

Why was this page created? The thesis of a website may be difficult to determine, or there may not be a thesis that seeks to argue a position. However, the website should include, at least, some sort of mission statement or About page explaining why it was created and what type of audience it seeks to inform.

Is the site's information current? There should be a copyright date or update date indicating when work was last done on the site. In the absence of a recent update, the material provided on the website should be unaffected by the passage of time, and all links should be functioning.

What type of organization sponsors the web page? A website containing scholarly information usually is sponsored and maintained by a college or university, nonprofit organization, or government entity rather than a commercial business. You can tell what type of organization maintains the website by the domain indicator at the end of the web address:

.edu: An educational institution, such as a college or university; also used for elementary and high schools
.com: A commercial business
.gov: A government organization
.org: A nonprofit organization

Primary Sources

Although documents produced at the time of an event are crucial for historians to understand what motivated people's actions and events, you must also learn to recognize why the original material itself was created. The following questions will help you determine this.

What is the author's connection to the events described in this document? The author should have firsthand knowledge of the events he or she is describing. Statements regarding historical events should be reasonably informed and accurate. Mentions of dates, people, and places should be consistent with other sources of evidence.

What is the author's purpose for creating this piece of evidence? Most primary sources are directed to a specific individual or audience. You must determine whenever possible who was originally intended to see the source. The tone and significance of the document may take on different meanings depending on the intended recipient. You should determine whether the author was trying to sway opinion or inform, and what the intended outcome of the document was.

Did the creator of this piece of evidence accomplish what he or she hoped? You should try to determine if there was a response or reaction to the creation of the source and what that was.

Nonscholarly Secondary Sources

Though much of the material you use to support a history research project should be scholarly, you may have occasion to use nonscholarly, or popular, materials during the course of your research. Cultural and media studies are important elements of historical knowledge. You may, for example, need nonscholarly sources to gauge popular opinion or determine how the media influenced collective thinking on current events. Just keep in mind that nonscholarly works cannot be used as a substitute for the in-depth and critical analysis that scholarly sources offer.

You can determine whether a work is nonscholarly by subjecting it to the following questions.

Who is the author? For nonscholarly works, the author usually is not a trained historian or other academic specialist. For some nonscholarly works, you may not be able verify the author's qualifications. The author may have credentials in the field of journalism, but may not have an advanced degree in academic studies like history or political science.

Does the work contain a bibliography or works cited list? A telltale sign of a nonscholarly work is the absence of a bibliography, footnotes, or other references to the origin of the information presented.

What tone does the author take? The language used in nonscholarly sources tends to be informal, entertaining, and widely appealing.

Does the source include consumer advertisements? Nonscholarly works may be for-profit publications that use advertising as a major source of revenue. Advertisements in nonscholarly sources typically promote items such as household goods, pharmaceuticals, automobiles, or other consumer products. The companies that buy advertising space in a nonscholarly source may have some influence over the source's content, thereby injecting bias into it.

Who publishes the source? Nonscholarly sources are usually published by profit-making publishers such as Conde Nast, Hearst Communications, and Time Inc.

Where can you obtain this source? Nonscholarly sources are relatively inexpensive compared to scholarly sources and can found in popular booksellers, grocery and drugstores, and street corner newsstands.

This section provided a brief overview of how to categorize sources and evaluate them for scholarly value. With practice, you will learn to quickly determine the scholarliness and usefulness of any source you uncover during the course of your research. If, after subjecting your source to the appropriate evaluative criteria, you are still in doubt about whether to use it, ask a professor or a librarian for a professional opinion.

KEEPING TRACK OF YOUR RESEARCH AND CITING

Before beginning the research process, it is important to formulate a plan for keeping track of the material you find. It is easy to forget where you found important material if you do not keep careful track of what it is and where you found it. If you let your research become lost or disorganized, you might end up repeating much of your work in a rush and under pressure. When you are working under a deadline, your final product can suffer significantly if you have to waste time attempting to re-create your original work. For this reason, it is a good idea to also keep track of any *potentially* useful source you find even if you are not completely sure that you will use it in your final project. A source that does not initially seem useful suddenly may become crucial as your research progresses. It is easier to record what you find and where you find it as you go along rather than try to recreate your research path long after your initial efforts.

There are many options available for keeping track of your sources, some traditional and some modern. One method is to write down the information about each source you find on individual note cards or to type the information into a word processing document. You could also keep a research diary, recording in narrative form the steps you take to find sources and the results of each step.

Another easy way to manage your sources is to use a web-based biblio-graphic management program. These products allow you to import citations of books, articles, book chapters, websites, and other sources from databases, organize the sources, and quickly create correctly formatted bibliographies. You also can use these products to share your sources for group projects. Some of these products are free, and some require a fee because of the extra features they offer, such as the ability to link to your library's sources and integration with word processing programs. Examples of free bibliographic management programs include those listed below:

BibMe at http://www.bibme.org/
CiteULike at http://www.citeulike.org/
Zotero at http://www.zotero.org/

Your librarian can tell you if any fee-based products are available at and supported by your college or university, and show you how to use them. Examples of fee-based bibliographic management programs include these products:

EndNote at http://www.endnote.com/
NoodleBib at http://www.noodletools.com/
ProCite at http://www.procite.com/
Reference Manager at http://www.refman.com/
RefWorks at http://www.citeulike.org/

Web-based bibliographic management programs allow you to access your bibliography from anywhere with an Internet connection. If you are interested in using a bibliographic management program, it is a good idea to take some time to learn how to use it before you begin a long research project. Most of these programs have help pages or tutorials and take half an hour or less to learn.

Scholarly websites, described in more detail in chapter 3, are an important part of the research process, but because there are so many of them, they can be difficult to organize. Some of the bibliographic management prod-ucts listed above will allow you to enter websites into your account. You might also keep track of helpful websites by bookmarking them in your web browser; however, this method requires you to use the same computer all the time. Another option is to use a social bookmarking website. Social book-marking sites allow you to save, organize, and search a list of websites that you find useful or entertaining and allow you to assign tags, or descriptive words and phrases, to the items in your account so that you can find them easily if your lists become long. Some examples of bookmarking technology include Google Bookmarks (http://www.google.com/bookmarks) and Faves. com (http://faves.com/home).

Anytime you uncover a source that proves relevant to your project, you should record all the information about the item that you need to find it again. For each source you find, you should record

- A complete citation (appendix A provides information about writing citations);
- The database, index, book, or website you used to find it;
- The search terms you used to find the item;
- A brief summary of the item or a note about how it supports your thesis; and
- Key quotes with page numbers.

Of all the information you should record about your sources, a complete citation is the most crucial.

Citation: A reference to a source that includes all the information a reader would need to find it.

A citation, much like an address, is a reference to a book or article that provides all of the information necessary to locate the item, such as author, title, and year of publication. A citation that is incorrect or incomplete may prevent a researcher from finding the evidence needed for a project; a single mistyped letter or digit will hide a source deep in a forest of data, never to be seen again. Most research resources are edited heavily to prevent mistakes that would make it difficult to locate important sources.

Though there are many citation styles used in academia, the history profession usually recommends that citations be written in the Chicago style, which employs the use of footnotes for quotes in addition to a bibliography at the end of a work. This Chicago style is explained in detail in the book *The Chicago Manual of Style*, which is produced in both print and online versions and likely is available at your library. The fundamentals of the Chicago style of citation are addressed in appendix A, and information about footnoting is addressed in appendix B.

Chapter Three

Overview of Historical Information

The evidence needed to embark upon a history project can be found in many places, such as libraries, archives, the Internet, museums, and even in people's attics. Often the most difficult part of a research project is figuring out where to look for appropriate evidence. Some evidence is available in books or on websites and can be easily found and shared. Some evidence is unique, rare, valuable, and irreplaceable and cannot be obtained by anyone except specially trained researchers.

The best way to begin historical research is by gathering all relevant materials available at your college or university library. Your library provides access to many essential research materials required for historical research, some of them available only by subscription. These subscription-based research tools provide access to material that is widely recognized as scholarly by professionals who study history for a living. In addition, the librarians at college and university libraries are available to advise you on what specific sources are best suited to your individual research project, to show you how to use those sources most effectively, and to help you redirect your search if you encounter difficulty.

Because no library owns everything that exists on any particular topic, they must rely on borrowing partnerships with other libraries to obtain some materials necessary to supplement students' and faculty members' long-term and intensive research projects. These services, often referred to as *interlibrary loan*, greatly expand the breadth of material that you can obtain. If you are unfamiliar with your college's or university's interlibrary loan service, ask a librarian or check the library's website for off-campus borrowing procedures and policies. There are few research topics that a college or university library cannot help you complete, even if the sources you need are not available the moment you discover them. Your librarians probably can help you obtain additional books that you require within a week or two; many articles may be obtained even faster.

The following sections describe the most frequently used types of research sources that contain historical evidence. The bibliography of a well-rounded and well-researched history project should contain a balanced mix of all the types of sources described in the following sections.

BOOKS

Books are a longtime staple of academic inquiry and continue to remain among the best sources to use for a history project. Books in the historical profession sometimes are referred to as *monographs*, meaning that they are long scholarly studies of one topic by one or more authors.

> **Monograph:** A detailed scholarly work of writing, usually on one topic and in the form of a book.

Another type of book you may encounter is an *anthology*, which is a book that examines a topic from the perspectives of multiple authors, each of whom contributes one or two chapters. In addition to their traditional print format, books are available in electronic format (eBooks), which you can read on your laptop or desktop computer, tablet, or smart phone.

Why Use Books in a Research Paper?

Most libraries, especially those of colleges and universities, own scholarly books on many topics in United States and world history. The importance of books in the research process should not be underestimated. As the traditional medium for the dissemination of information in history, they allow authors to examine a topic in detail, thereby providing the reader with a greater perspective of the issues and the nuances of the scholarly arguments surrounding the subject. The authors of scholarly historical works may spend months or years researching the topic and normally consult many sources during the course of investigating the questions they choose to address. Books about history usually are extensively edited and critiqued by other scholars for their scholarly merit prior to publication. Using books for a research topic may at first seem daunting because they are lengthier than other types of sources; however, they often serve as the foundation of scholarly debates and discussions. The in-depth information available in books cannot easily be replicated in other types of sources. In short, books are an essential element in any historical research project.

Library Catalogs

Thanks to the Internet, it has become easy to search for books that contain material relevant to most research projects. Most libraries make this possible by allowing free access to their online catalogs. A *catalog* is a searchable database, or in some cases, a physical list, of all the items a particular library owns.

Catalog: A database or physical list of items kept in a library.

The catalog provides you with all the information you need to access any title available in the library, including its title, author, publisher information, and the item's location within the library. The catalog descriptions for modern books also may provide bonus information about research material, such as summaries and reviews of books. Increasingly, you will even find complete copies of electronic books that can be read online through library catalogs.

The link to a library's online catalog usually is featured prominently on the library's website and will look similar to the example in figure 3.1. More information about searching library catalogs for books and other materials can be found in chapter 5.

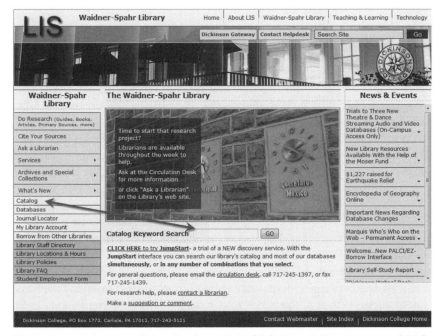

Figure 3.1.   Access to a Library Catalog with Multiple Entry Points. Courtesy of Dickinson College.

JOURNALS AND JOURNAL ARTICLES

A *journal* is a regularly printed publication containing articles or short studies of topics, each written by different authors.

Journal: A publication released on a regular basis containing short writings by different authors. Journals are also known as periodicals, serials, or magazines.

A scholarly journal is a publication containing research on academic topics, usually intended to be read by professionals in the field or students learning about the topic. Most articles in a journal will be related by the theme, event, time period, or person. One issue of a journal typically contains several articles. Journals also are known as periodicals because they are published on a periodic basis, which may be weekly, monthly, several times per year, or annually.

Like newsstand magazines, most professional journals are not free and require a paid subscription to obtain. With highly specialized topics and somewhat expensive subscriptions, certain history journals may be found only in libraries. Individual journal articles can be particularly difficult to obtain without using a library.

Why Use Journal Articles in a Research Paper?

Journal articles are vitally important sources of historical information, often containing the most recent findings and interpretations of history. Many notable history scholars publish their research regularly in journals and often use them to explore ideas that they later develop more fully in a monograph. Readers can find differing opinions and see changing interpretations about a historical topic by reading studies from different time periods in a variety of journals.

Journal Formats

Journals may be published on paper or online, or simultaneously in both formats. Increasingly, journals are being published in both formats and many are now moving toward exclusive online publishing. Content-wise, there is no difference between a journal article that is published in print and the same article online, although the pages may have a slightly different appearance. Many libraries choose to subscribe to journals online because the online version may be read by several people at the same time, whether they are in the library building or not. Usually at colleges and universities, online journals may be read only by those who can authenticate themselves as current faculty members or students with a password that the library or campus provides.

Whether published in print or online, journals are easily identified by certain defining characteristics. The articles in history journals are written by history scholars including professors with masters degrees and doctorates. Information describing the journal's scope and mission, subscription information, and submission information for potential authors should be available inside the front cover of the journal or on an About link on its website. Additionally, look for information about the journal's publisher. Most history journals are published by colleges, universities, or scholarly organizations such as the American Historical Association (http://www.historians.org/) and the Organization of American Historians (http://www.oah.org). An individual issue of a journal should have a table of contents, a volume and/or issue number, and a date of publication including the year and month or season, as illustrated in figure 3.2.

Some newer journals started publication as online-only journals and were never published in print format. Such journals are sometimes referred to as *born digital*. An example of online-only journal is the *E-Journal of Portuguese History*, which can be found at http://www.brown.edu/Departments/Portuguese_Brazilian_Studies/ejph/.

INTERNATIONAL REVIEW OF SOCIAL HISTORY, VOLUME 56 - ISSUE 02

A Consumers' International? The International Cooperative Alliance and Cooperative Internationalism, 1918–1939: A Nordic Perspective
Mary Hilson
International Review of Social History, Volume 56, Issue 02, August 2011, pp 203-233
doi: 10.1017/S0020859011000150, Published online by Cambridge University Press 06 May 2011

Revolutionary Rhetoric and Labour Unrest: Liège in 1886 and Seville in 1901
Custodio Velasco Mesa
International Review of Social History, Volume 56, Issue 02, August 2011, pp 235-266
doi: 10.1017/S0020859011000174, Published online by Cambridge University Press 21 Jul 2011

Migration Systems in Nineteenth-Century North-Western Portugal: The Case of Vila do Conde
Cristiana Viegas de Andrade
International Review of Social History, Volume 56, Issue 02, August 2011, pp 267-299
doi: 10.1017/S0020859011000186, Published online by Cambridge University Press 21 Jul 2011

The Road to Democracy: The Political Legacy of "1968"
Marianne Maeckelbergh
International Review of Social History, Volume 56, Issue 02, August 2011, pp 301-332
doi: 10.1017/S0020859011000162, Published online by Cambridge University Press 21 Jul 2011

Figure 3.2.   Title Page of the International Review of Social History. Copyright 2002 Internationaal Instituut voor Sociale Geschiedenis. Reprinted with the permission of Cambridge University Press.

As noted, journals may require a subscription fee to view the content. If you find an online journal by searching the Internet and cannot access the content without a subscription, you may be able to get a copy from your library at no direct cost to you. To find out whether your library owns a subscription to a particular journal, check its subscription list, which is described in more detail below, under Library Journal Subscription Lists.

Locating Appropriate Journal Articles

There are thousands of scholarly journals available in print and online, but it would be futile to page aimlessly through every issue of every journal for articles that might be relevant to your research topic. Researchers require special finding aids to help locate the articles in journals that are most relevant to their research projects. These finding aids, known as indexes, essentially are lists of articles arranged by topic that enable you to search for relevant articles simultaneously across many journals.

Index: A printed list of journal citations arranged by topic.

Indexes were once produced exclusively in paper format as large books that would be updated a few times per year. Today, most are produced as online databases that are updated monthly, weekly, or daily. Most scholarly journals include an information page that indicates which indexes or databases monitor that journal's content. Two of the most important indexes used for finding journal articles in history are America: History and Life and Historical Abstracts, both of which are available in paper and online format.

More information about using databases and indexes to locate journal articles can be found in chapter 5.

Library Journal Subscription Lists

Most academic libraries carry hundreds or thousands of subscriptions to journals on all subjects and will make available updated lists of those journal titles in paper binders or on their websites. Such lists may be called Journal Locator, Journal Finder, Journal List, E-journal List, Subscription List, or some similar variation in terms. Journal lists usually are arranged in alphabetical order by title and are searchable by title. You also may be able to browse the list by subject so you can see what journal titles your library subscribes to in the field of history—or any other subject. Figure 3.3 illustrates an example of a journal subscription list.

Journal Locator

Search here to find out if we have print or online access to particular journals, newspapers, or magazines.

Example searches:

- New York Times
- Nature
- Journal of Philosophy

Find journals by title or ISSN

| Title contains all words ▼ | | | Search |

Browse journals by title

0-9 A B C D E F G H I J K L M N O P Q R S T U V W X Y Z Other

Browse journals by subject

| -- Please select a subject category -- ▼ | Search |

Dickinson College, PO Box 1773, Carlisle, PA 17013, 717-243-5121

Figure 3.3. Dickinson College's Journal Finder. Courtesy and © of Dickinson College and Serials Solutions.

When you are reading a book or journal article that provides a citation to an article that you would like to read, you can use your library's subscription list to find out if the article is available in your library. Before consulting a subscription list, it is important to record the complete citation of the article you are seeking. Your library may own certain issues of a journal but not every issue that has ever been published. The library may not have started a subscription until several years after the journal first started publishing, or it may have stopped a subscription at some point in the journal's publication history. It is much easier to determine whether your library has the issue you need when you have a full citation including author, title of article, year of publication, volume number, issue number, and page numbers. You will need all of this information to order a copy of an article from another library if your library does not have it and also to cite the article when you quote it in your project.

If you have a citation for an article you need and you do not see a subscription list on your library's website, ask a librarian for help.

NEWSPAPERS AND OTHER NEWS SERVICES

Newspapers are daily or weekly records of current events. Modern newspapers appeared in the mid-fifteenth century after Johannes Gutenberg invented the printing press and were published regularly in colonial America in the late 1600s. Many modern newspapers are published both on the Internet as well as in traditional paper newsprint. Titles of newspapers in English often include words such as "times," "post," or "tribune." Examples of newspapers are the *New York Times*, the *Guardian*, and the *San Francisco Chronicle*.

Newspaper: A daily or weekly publication that reports local, national, and/or international news.

Although many newspapers continue to be published in their traditional print format, most newspaper publishers make a condensed version of recent issues available for free on their websites. Access to older and complete issues from the newspapers' websites may require a subscription fee, and you can usually get a personal subscription to either the print or online version, or both. You also can obtain copies of many recent and historical newspaper articles without charge through a public, college, or university library.

Though the print versions of newspapers are easily recognizable, it may be more difficult to tell whether an online article is from a newspaper or another type of source such as a magazine or scholarly journal. An online newspaper should have the same distinguishing characteristics as a print version of the paper. The website should prominently display the newspaper's title and logo with the date. You should see current news headlines and links to the full stories on the paper's home page. You should also see links to different sections for local and world news, political opinion, the arts, sports, and other features. Some online versions of newspapers include audio and video feeds in addition to the photographs normally found in the print versions.

News is also available on websites that are extensions of radio, television, and other news networks such as the following:

- www.ap.org (The Associated Press)
- bbc.co.uk (British Broadcasting Corporation)
- www.cnn.com (Cable News Network)
- www.npr.org (National Public Radio)

Although online access to newspaper articles is convenient, it is sometimes preferable to read older copies of newspapers in their original print format. Online versions of older newspapers may include only partial access to articles or may exclude other information that may be of significant historical or cultural value, such as images, advertisements, announcements, and obituaries. Strategies for finding newspaper articles are discussed in greater length in chapter 5.

Why Use Newspaper Articles in Research Papers?

Newspapers are invaluable sources of information for researchers investigating how prior generations recorded and interpreted their own experiences. Forms of regular news communication have existed since the Roman Empire, and they are important research tools precisely because they have been keeping record of human history for so long. Newspapers can help you determine the factors that may have influenced a historic event such as an election result, public dispute, or even the weather. They are important sources of political opinion, small town news, biography, draft records and war casualties, interviews, and in-depth, firsthand descriptions of events.

Newspaper Bias

When reading newspapers you should be aware that some of them are supporters of political ideologies. Current and historical newspapers and other news outlets on the radio, television, and the Internet may lean toward conservatism, liberalism, or some other political ideology, and this bias may affect how information is presented to the reader. This is particularly true of nineteenth-century newspapers in the United States, many of which, from the national to the local level, were founded explicitly to support one political party or another. A newspaper's political bias may be obvious when the articles regarding politics clearly favor one side, but more often the bias is not quite so easy to discern. To determine a newspaper's bias, you should carefully consider the way stories are covered and decide whether the news source provides equal consideration to opposing viewpoints. Often the easiest way to decide is to identify an issue or incident that has clear political motivation and read the paper's opinion section and political cartoons to see what stance the editors take. You may also be able to research the newspaper's ownership, history, and political allegiance in an encyclopedia or dictionary. Keep in mind too that newspapers with long histories may change political affiliations along with changes in ownership and the political landscape.

Newspapers as Primary or Secondary Sources

Newspaper articles may be considered to be either primary sources or secondary sources, depending upon the context in which they are used. They may be considered to be primary when they are used to examine events from the point of view of those who lived through them or when they contain eyewitness accounts of an event. Newspaper articles that report facts compiled from other sources or provide analysis usually are considered to be secondary. It is important that you establish the context of any newspaper article you intend to use for a history project so that your interpretation properly reflects the article's point of view.

DATABASES

A *database* is a computer file that stores records of specific kinds of information and then allows a researcher to search for the information stored in it. Databases record all the information necessary to locate useful material that has been published in books, journals, newspapers, and other sources. The information stored in a research database usually includes the item's title, author, publication date, subject, and other information necessary to locate the item. The database may also include a brief summary or evaluation of each item.

Database: A searchable collection of data typically stored in electronic format.

Though available online, many of the most important history research databases are accessible only with a paid subscription. Subscription-only databases are designed for use by the populations of colleges and universities, and many do not offer subscription options to individuals. Consequently, you must access subscription-based databases from your library's website in order to be able to search them. Links to your library's available subscription databases are probably featured prominently on your library's website; if not, ask a librarian to help you find them.

Why Use Databases for a Research Paper?

It is practically impossible to find journal and newspaper articles without the aid of a database or index. Individual issues of journals and newspapers may publish articles related to specific time periods, themes, people, or events, but the specific subject matter of individual articles in one issue may not be related. Without a database, you would be forced to spend hours looking through the table of contents of each of the journal's issues to find relevant articles. Databases help you to find not only relevant articles, but also journals that are most likely to publish articles related to your topic. Databases can help you examine the way scholars' opinions about your topic have developed and changed over time. Additionally, certain databases can help you find images, sound recordings, maps, and videos of historic events or news regarding events.

Many databases are specialized by subject, meaning that all of the content relates to a particular topic or theme. A library catalog, for example, is simply a database allowing a researcher to find all the material that one particular library owns. No database is large enough to hold all of the world's scholarly information, nor would that be practical. Therefore, many databases on many subjects exist. Some databases are multidisciplinary, meaning that they cover a broad range of topics. Specialized databases contain information about only one topic or discipline, usually in greater depth than a multidisciplinary database may be able to do. The researcher's challenge is to seek out databases that are likely to be the most useful for each research project. Generally, the more specialized and focused a database is, the easier it will be for you to find the most relevant information contained within it. Most libraries provide descriptions of all the databases to which they subscribe. Before using a database, you should read its description carefully to be sure that it covers the historical topic or era you are researching.

Although some multidisciplinary databases are helpful for historical research, you should concentrate most of your research efforts initially on databases that collect scholarly material specifically about history. This will help to keep irrelevant sources out of your search. History databases may contain primary, secondary, and/or tertiary information and may be further subcategorized by time period or by geographic location covered.

The companies that collect and organize scholarly journals must make important and difficult decisions about how many titles of books, journals, newspapers, and other documents to include in each database. There are thousands of scholarly history books and hundreds of scholarly history journals, some of which have been published regularly for decades. In the case of journals, database companies must decide not only which titles to cover, but also how much of the journal's publication history to include. Sometimes a database may include every issue of a journal, and sometimes it will include only a selected range of issues.

Database Selection

There is no greater disappointment in the research process than spending hours looking for information only to find out that you have been searching in the wrong places. As noted above, not all of the databases your library provides are appropriate for every search. Some databases cover many different subjects by indexing only a small selection of the most widely read books and journals in that field. Some databases cover specific topics in great depth. For that reason, not even all of the history databases available at your library are appropriate for every history project. The database Historical Abstracts, for example, covers world history from the year 1450 to the present, excludes coverage of North America, and provides citations to secondary source articles published since 1955. Therefore, this database would not be useful for the study of historic events that took place prior to 1450, for the history of North America, or for finding articles published prior to 1955. You would be able to fill in those gaps by using, for example, the database Iter, which covers secondary sources published between 1784 to the present related to the history and culture of the Middle Ages and Renaissance. Even more databases are available to cover areas of history beyond the scope of Historical Abstracts and Iter.

Before beginning your research with any database, find its description and be sure you know the answers to the following questions:

- Does the database cover the time period you are researching?
- Does the database cover the country or region you are researching?
- Does the database include the type of source you need (i.e., primary, secondary, or tertiary sources, or some combination of the three)?
- If the database covers primary sources, what specific kinds? Newspapers? Personal documents? Images?

Taking a few moments to answer these questions will make your searches much more productive. You will be able to search with the confidence of knowing that the database you are using adequately covers the specific subject matter you are researching.

Citation-Only vs. Full-Text Databases

Databases may be described as citation-only or full-text. A citation-only database provides only the citation information necessary to locate the book or article. For a book, a citation normally includes the book's title, the names of the author(s) or editor(s), the book's publisher, the city in which the book was published, and the year it was published. For a journal article, a citation normally includes the author(s), the title of the article, the title of the journal, the volume and issue numbers of the journal, and the year the article was published. Other important identifying information such as a translator and edition number also may be included in a citation. Citation-only databases include lists of important keywords mentioned in the article and may or may not include a summary of each item listed. Conversely, a full-text database will provide complete copies of articles, books, or documents in addition to the citation and any associated subjects, keywords, or summaries.

Despite the drawback of not providing immediate full-text access, the benefits of citation-only databases must not be overlooked. The two most important history databases, Historical Abstracts and America: History and Life, which are described in detail in chapter 5, do not provide automatic direct full-text access to all of the articles and books that they cite. However, just because a database does not itself automatically provide full text does not mean you cannot access the item at your library in other ways.

If you search a database and find a book you would like to use, you should check your library's catalog to see if there is a copy in the book stacks. More information about searching library catalogs can be found in chapter 5. If you search a database and find an article you would like to read, your library may have it available online from another provider. Once you find an article that looks promising, click on the title of the article and see if there is a .pdf or .html link to the full text. If not, there may be a button called a Link Resolver, which will tell you whether or not your library owns a subscription to the journal you need and will provide you with a link to the article if it is an online version. A link resolver is often customized and may have a different appearance from library to library. A link resolver should look similar to the example in figure 3.4. If you do not see a .pdf link, an .html link, or a link resolver on the database screen, you can check your library's subscription list for availability, as described earlier in this chapter. Your library may have the journal from a separate online provider or in print format.

Although databases are indispensible sources for primary and secondary historical information, they may not be easy or free to access. Students at colleges and universities usually will have access to specialized history databases in their libraries. Visitors to such institutions may have to obtain special permission to use the library's resources. Since subscriptions to databases can be expensive, no library will own every single helpful database; however, students taking classes in a particular subject can be assured that their college

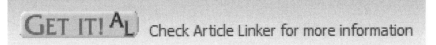

Figure 3.4. Example of a Link Resolver. Courtesy and © of Dickinson College and Serials Solutions.

or university library provides access to databases that will prove helpful for any topic taught at their school.

MICROFORMS

Libraries have always struggled with space issues. The constant acquisition of new books and journals puts libraries at perpetual risk of running out of shelf space. One way libraries attempted to solve space issues in the twentieth century, before modern digitization, was to collect material on microforms. Microforms are rolls or sheets of photographic tape that store images of documents. The images are greatly reduced in size and can be read only on special viewing machines. If material is held in your library on microform, you will see a notation in the library's catalog record that looks similar to that in figure 3.5.

Microform: Reels or sheets of photographic film used to store serial publications at a greatly reduced size to save library shelf space. Microforms can be read only with specialized machines.

Microforms were popular storage mediums for magazines, scholarly journals, and newspapers in the last half of the twentieth century because they stored much more information using less shelf space than the printed versions of the same materials. Many libraries even discarded the print versions of the material if they collected a duplicate in microform. Research material usually is no longer published on microfilm or microfiche, but as a historian, you probably will have occasion to consult historical materials that were reproduced on microform and have not since been made available in a modern format.

Microforms typically are available in one of two types: microfilm, which is a roll of transparent photographic tape on a circular reel, as illustrated in figure 3.6; and microfiche, which is a flat, transparent, plastic card, as illustrated in figure 3.7. Microforms must be read using special machines designed to

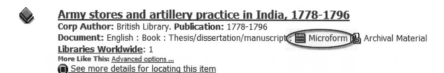

Figure 3.5. Microfilm as Indicated in WorldCat. Copyright 2011 OCLC Online Computer Library Center, Inc. Used with Permission. FirstSearch, OCLC, WorldCat, and the WorldCat logo are registered trademarks/service marks of OCLC.

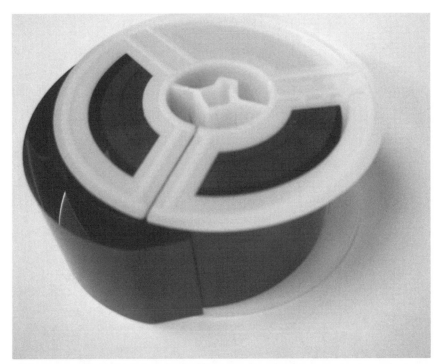

Figure 3.6.　Microfilm Reel. Courtesy of Dickinson College.

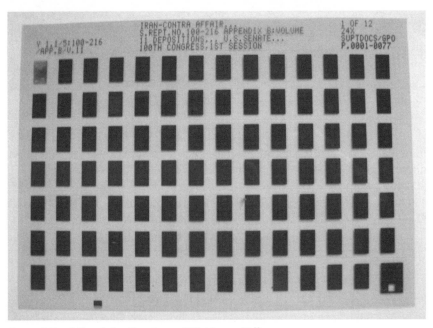

Figure 3.7.　Microfiche. Courtesy of Dickinson College.

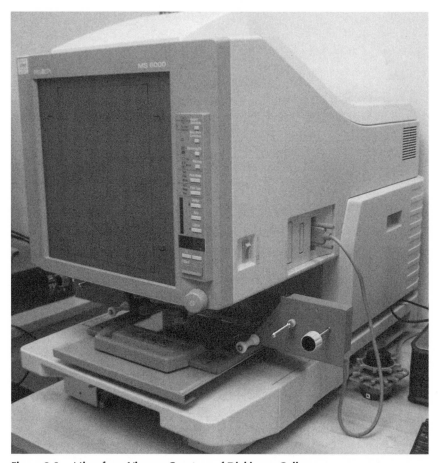

Figure 3.8. Microform Viewer. Courtesy of Dickinson College.

illuminate and magnify the film. Libraries and archives that have materials on microforms provide special viewers, such as the one illustrated in figure 3.8, that allow you to read the material on a screen. Some microform viewers can be connected to computers so that you can make digital scans of the film and then save or email those scans. Before using microforms for the first time, ask a library staff member to show you how to use the machines.

INDEXES

Indexes are the book versions and predecessors of databases. Essentially, they are alphabetically arranged lists providing citations to hundreds or thousands of sources relevant to topics in history. Index volumes usually are published once or twice per year and include articles on each topic that were published since the last volume was printed. Most indexes that were once found exclusively in paper format, before online options existed, have been converted to online databases.

Databases are becoming more common in libraries than indexes because they are convenient to use, offer many different search options, and multiple researchers can use them simultaneously. Though many indexes now have online counterparts, you still may have occasion to use the printed versions in many libraries, particularly when you are seeking sources published prior to the twentieth century. In some cases the only way to search for older books and journal articles is through indexes, as the information in them may not be available in electronic format or your library may not have access to the online version of the index.

INTERNET

The Internet's massive network of shared data has made it possible for historians to access unprecedented amounts of information. Ever-increasing quantities of historical material previously accessible only by traveling to the document's physical location can now be read on one's personal computer, smart phone, or tablet computer.

As a historical researcher, you assume a great deal of responsibility when relying on websites to provide evidence for a history project. Although the Internet is filled with important, credible, and valuable information, you must be particularly critical in evaluating information that comes from free websites. Nonscholarly websites can be difficult to distinguish from scholarly websites. As noted earlier, anyone with a little programming knowledge can create a website that looks credible, and nonprofessional historians may unknowingly or mistakenly provide misinformation or incomplete information online.

Free websites usually do not require the researcher to provide payment or proof of membership in a particular organization in order to use the material as most electronic scholarly databases and journals do. However, many scholarly websites that are free for anyone to use are in reality funded by gifts of monetary support by individual donors or grants from charitable and government organizations that fund academic research projects. Authors who have their websites funded by such gifts must complete lengthy applications, usually requiring information about a well-defined project plan, proof of knowledge in the subject area, professionalism, and adherence to strict publishing standards. Scholars whose websites are funded by gifts or grants usually place a link to their sponsor on the website. Regardless of how the project is funded, the authors of reputable websites spend many hours of hard work researching, writing, editing, scanning photographs, and designing a page that is easy to navigate and aesthetically pleasant so that it is as useful as possible for many people. Material that is posted by a hobby historian without backing from a reputable institution may not have been created with such professional standards in mind. For more information about evaluating websites and sources, see chapter 2.

That said, there is quite a bit of valuable historical information on the Internet that should not be ignored, and in fact, sometimes using a website is the only reasonable way to access information that is owned in physical format by other libraries. Some reputable and free websites provide access to historical evidence that was once difficult or nearly impossible to get without waiting weeks for copies to be made, often for a fee, or by traveling to libraries in other states or countries. Table 3.1 provides a few examples of some well-known, reliable websites that provide access to unique historical information.

Table 3.1.   Websites with Historical Information

Site	Time Period	Description
AfricaBib http://www.africabib.org/default.htm	1800s to present	Bibliographic databases of secondary source social science materials in Africana studies.
American Memory: Historical Collections for the National Digital Library http://memory.loc.gov/ammem/index.html	1400s to present	The Library of Congress's digitized collections including war records, presidential papers, cultural history, African-American history, and Native American history.
Ancient History Sourcebook http://www.fordham.edu/halsall/ancient/asbook.html	30,000 B.C. to 500s	A collection of primary source texts from thousands of years ago, such as the code of Hammurabi. Edited by Paul Halsall at Fordham University.
Avalon Project http://avalon.law.yale.edu/	4,000 B.C. to present	Primary documents in law, history, and diplomacy from Yale University's Law School.
Documenting the American South http://docsouth.unc.edu/	1500s to 1900s	Primary sources including audio and images related to the history and culture of the American South, from the University of North Carolina at Chapel Hill.

Site	Time Period	Description
Eyewitness to History http://www. eyewitnesstohistory.com/	500 B.C. to present	Primary sources from ancient history to the 21st century. Includes documents, paintings and photographs, video and sound files, with background information and bibliographies.
Famous Trials http://www.law.umkc.edu/ faculty/projects/ftrails/ ftrials.htm	1500s to present	Background material and primary sources about famous criminal trials such as those of Galileo, the Boston Massacre instigators, John Brown, Sacco and Vanzetti, the Rosenbergs, Bill Clinton and more.
House Divided http://housedivided. dickinson.edu/	1840 to 1880	Stories of the U.S. Civil War from the perspective of Dickinson College with maps, images, original letters with transcriptions, and newspaper articles. Coproduced by Matthew Pinsker and John Osborne of Dickinson College.
Labyrinth http://labyrinth.georgetown. edu/	Prehistory to present	Resources for Medieval Studies from Georgetown University.
Perseus Digital Library http://www.perseus.tufts. edu/hopper/	4000 B.C. to 1800s	A digital collection of primary sources in history, literature and culture of the Greco-Roman world from Tufts University.

ARCHIVES, MUSEUMS, NATIONAL LIBRARIES, HISTORICAL SOCIETIES, AND OTHER PRIMARY SOURCE REPOSITORIES

Archives, museums, national libraries, and historical societies are institutions devoted to keeping and preserving original and unique pieces of historical evidence. These organizations collect historical information relevant to a specific place, such as a college, university, hospital, business, county, or state. Some focus on a specific person, such as a United States president or other political leader, while others focus on a specific event, such as the United

States Civil War or the Nazi Holocaust. Primary source institutions are important because they preserve memory so that future generations can examine the historical, social, and cultural progress of past generations.

Documents in archives and other primary source repositories are carefully protected and maintained in controlled environments by a staff of professionals known as *archivists*. Archivists protect historical material from extreme temperature changes, misuse, and theft while keeping it available for researchers to find and examine. Like librarians, archivists are research experts who have specialized knowledge of the material they collect and preserve. Archivists can help you figure out where helpful primary research material on your topic is likely to be found and how to search for it. They can also help you review documents that are difficult to read and provide historical context for the material you are examining.

Often funded by taxpayer money or public or private grant awards, many archival institutions are open the public or to researchers who can provide a demonstrated need or interest in viewing the archival material. However, you do need to prepare yourself in advance of a visit to an archival institution if you want to conduct research and handle the material. First, you should have a good idea of what material you want to use by searching the archives' catalog or website. When you enter an archive well informed about what you need, the staff will be able to more quickly gather material for you. Prior preparation also will allow you to spend most of your visit examining the material that is useful to you, as archival material is almost never allowed to leave the building in which it is kept.

Archivist: A research professional who collects, maintains, and preserves valuable documents and artifacts and helps researchers use them.

Additionally, you should keep in mind that archival material is valuable and often delicate. Therefore, you will probably have to agree to observe special rules before being allowed to handle the material. In order to ensure that the documents remain legible and undamaged, researchers usually are not permitted to bring their own writing implements or scanning equipment. Some institutions allow personal laptops or tablet computers for note taking and may permit the use of digital cameras (without a flash) to take pictures of documents and artifacts. Otherwise, the archives will provide nonpermanent pencils and acid-free paper for note taking. In rare cases, the documents held in an archive may be so fragile and valuable that only highly trained professionals are permitted to handle the material at all, such as would be the case with an original copy of the United States Constitution.

If you simply want to browse interesting historical material but do not need to examine it in depth for a research project, you may be able to take a tour of the premises. Sometimes you will find a museum attached to the archive that highlights the most interesting pieces in the collection.

Because of potential use restrictions, you should check the institution's website to find out about its rules and hours, and also take some time to speak with an archivist prior to your visit. Be sure to describe your project in detail and verify that the institution has relevant material. You might also ask if the archive contains additional material that is not noted on the website. Find out if you need to provide photo identification, fill out an application, or present a letter of introduction or a recommendation to use the material, and if you are required to meet with an archivist or trainer prior to handling the research material. If you cannot travel to the location of an institution that contains primary source documents you want to use, the archivists may be able to provide you with some information by phone or email. Some may be willing to provide scanned copies of documents for a small fee. In short, prior planning will help to make your research experience efficient, productive, and interesting.

Preparation for a trip to a primary source repository may sound time consuming, but the opportunity to touch the documents and artifacts that changed history is an exciting and rewarding experience that will help you connect with your project in a way that usually is not possible by reading black-and-white reproductions in books or online. Researching in an archive gives you the opportunity to view and read history as it was originally made and to see not only the words that were produced, but also the materials that were used to produce them. You will see, and possibly handle, unique artifacts that have been produced by people who are important to you, and who have had a profound effect on the course of historic events. Additionally, reproductions of documents may not include the context that the original does. For example, in a handwritten document, you might find misspellings or crossed-out phrases, which could indicate that the author was angry, indecisive, in a hurry, or a poor speller. You might also find marginal notes or doodles that could add additional perspective to the document. In addition, an intervening editor who is reproducing the document can make mistakes or unintentionally distort the meaning of the document during the process of editing.

Handling an original historic document has an intangible but definite coolness factor involved. You will be touching a piece of history; perhaps holding in your hand the same piece of paper that a president once signed and handed to his secretary for posting. In that moment, you can truly make your connection with history and sense it come alive as you read it.

Archives

An archive is a building or office within an institution that collects and preserves official records pertaining to individuals and events that shaped or affected that institution's history in some way. An archive often is maintained as a special office in an institution's library.

Archives exist within federal, state, and local governments, churches, hospitals, companies, colleges and universities, and other organizations. Historical figures are likely to have information about them kept in the places where they were born, lived, worked, married, had children, and died, as well as at any schools they attended. Items typically found in archives include primary sources such as letters, reports, notes, memos, photographs, maps, reports, ledgers, architectural plans, artifacts, and other original materials. Colleges and universities in the United States maintain physical archives to store important documents relating to the history of the college or university, as well as information about its students, alumni, faculty members, administration, and others who had some influence on the history of the institution.

Researching in archives tends to be time intensive. Although some archival material may be found in the online catalog of the library to which the archives belongs, many archives do not have databases or other automated search options for all of their sources available on the Internet. Sometimes, the holdings of archives must be searched using special books called *finding aids*. Finding aids are lists of the materials held by the archive that provide brief descriptions of the items and their specific locations. If you suspect that an archive may have material on a person or event you are researching, check its website for verification and speak with an archivist for additional information.

Table 3.2. International State Archives

Country	Archive	Description
Australia	**National Archives of Australia** http://www.naa.gov.au/	Established in 1961, the Archives of Australia contains records of the government's activities. It includes military records and papers of prime ministers.
Brazil	**Imperial Public Archives** http://www. arquivonacional.gov. br	Brazil's national archives was established in 1838. The website currently is available only in Portuguese.
Canada	**Library and Archives Canada** http://www. collectionscanada. gc.ca/	Documentary history of Canada in French and English.

Country	Archive	Description
Denmark	**Danish National Archives** http://www.sa.dk	Denmark's national archives, established in 1889, includes public records, parish registers, census lists, and genealogical information.
Egypt	**National Library and Archives of Egypt (Dar el-Kotob)** http://www.nationalarchives.gov.eg	Keeps documents pertinent to the Egyptian history since the Fatimid Era to the present day. It also keeps documents about the history of various Middle Eastern countries.
France	**Archives Nationales** http://www.archivesnationales.culture.gouv.fr/an/en/Index.html	Administered by the French government since the French Revolution. Most of the information on this site is available only in French.
Germany	**Bundesarchiv** http://www.bundesarchiv.de/	Germany's national archives, currently available only in German.
Russia	**State Archive of the Russian Federation** http://garf.ru/ Information in English: http://www.iisg.nl/abb/rep/B-1.tab1.php?b=B.php%23B-1	Contains history about the Russian Empire, the Soviet Union, and the current Russian Federation. Includes the papers of well-known politicians, state functionaries, and Russian royalty.
United Kingdom	**National Archives of the United Kingdom** http://www.nationalarchives.gov.uk/	The National Archives of the United Kingdom contains 900 years of history with records ranging from parchment and paper scrolls to digital files. It contains records of births, marriages, divorce, wills, deaths, real estate, census, passenger lists, and citizenship and naturalization.
United States	**National Archives and Records Administration (NARA)** http://www.archives.gov/	NARA preserves billions of documents related to American history, including maps, charts, architectural drawings photographs, and films. Includes some of the most important documents in American history, such as the Declaration of Independence, the United States Constitution, and the Bill of Rights.

Like many libraries, archives increasingly are taking advantage of the Internet and making their materials available online by providing scanned images of their documents and photographs of their artifacts. Some archives that make their material available via the Internet are listed in table 3.2.

Historical Societies

Historical societies are nonprofit organizations devoted to preserving the historical records of a place, institution, person or group of people, or event. Historical societies also may be devoted to special interests such as transportation, religion, racial and ethnic groups, and genealogy. In the United States, most cities have historical societies, as do some small towns and counties. They are crucial to the research of local and state history as their content often is devoted to a particular geographic region or local personality.

> **Historical Society:** A not-for-profit organization that preserves the historical documents and artifacts associated with a specific place, person, group, or event.

Researching history often requires you to consider local events within a larger context in order to find causes for events and draw conclusions about them. Some of the best historical studies rely on storytelling to powerfully illustrate the causes or impacts of larger events, and historians often rely on the stories of ordinary people to create such illustrations. Doing research in a historical society is a good way to learn the stories of individuals that may have never been told. You then have the opportunity not only to bring those stories to light, but also to place them within a national or global context. Experienced historians know that it takes the stories of many hundreds or even thousands of people to form a narrative for the events that end up in our collective historical consciousness. Local historical societies can provide that body of evidence needed to construct those narratives and to test broad interpretations of global or national events against local events. For instance, what was seen as a contentious state or national election overall may have passed quietly and without dispute in a particular locality. In examining these local differences and the reasons for them, we develop understanding about an event that may not have been previously noted.

Historical societies tend to be smaller than most libraries, and performing research in one can be a great introduction to the process of finding and using primary materials. However, historical societies may not have many employees or the money necessary to post a lot of their material on the Internet. The staff, though, will be quite willing to answer research questions by phone or by email. Some may charge a fee for research time if you cannot visit the historical society yourself.

The Directory of Affiliated Societies is a comprehensive list of historical societies based in the United States. It is published by the American Historical Association and can be found at http://www.historians.org/affiliates/index.cfm. This list can help you find the names and locations of historical societies that may contain information relevant to your research.

Museums

A museum is an institution that acquires, preserves, displays, and exhibits artifacts of historical, scientific, cultural, or artistic value. Museums often serve as teaching and training centers, and many have libraries or archives

Table 3.3. Museum Libraries

Museum	Description
American Museum of Natural History *New York, NY* http://www.amnh.org/	History of the natural sciences, with a library established in 1869.
Ellis Island *New York, NY* http://www.ellisisland.org	Passenger records and ship manifestos of immigrants who came to the United States via Ellis Island.
National Constitution Center *Philadelphia, PA* http://constitutioncenter.org/ncc_home_ Landing.aspx	Digital exhibits pertaining to the U.S. Constitution.
Royal Ontario Museum *Toronto, ON, Canada* http://www.rom.on.ca	Themed galleries on world cultures and natural history.
Smithsonian Institution Libraries *Washington, DC* http://www.sil.si.edu/	Collects and preserves information on American history, including natural history, the history of science and technology, Native American history, African American history, and cultural history.
UNESCO World Heritage List http://whc.unesco.org/	Provides lists of sites, monuments, or buildings worldwide deemed culturally and historically significant. Organized alphabetically by country.
United States Holocaust Memorial Museum Library *Washington, DC* http://www.ushmm.org/research/library/	Documents and images from the Holocaust, including the perspectives of survivors and Nazi officers.

in which researchers can find primary sources. Like other institutions, museums are using the Internet to display images of some of their most famous collections. Table 3.3 lists examples of historical museums with libraries. Additional links to museums in the United States can be found online at the Museum Directory at http://www.museumsusa.org/museums/.

National and State Libraries

National and state libraries contain information about the history and culture of the state or country they represent. They preserve documents and other evidence related to the creation, maintenance, and history of a government. National and state libraries may include documents such as deliberations of a congress or parliament, the texts of enacted laws, speeches and writings of important individuals, and genealogical and statistical information about the population, among many other sources. Often, they collect information about the scientific, geographic, and cultural information of the region, including photographs and works of literature and art. National and state libraries usually are funded by their states or countries through taxes. National libraries are not traditional libraries in the sense that you can walk in, browse around, and take books home to read. Rather, they are more like archives, as much of the material they contain is valuable and rare. Researchers usually can visit the libraries and use materials on the premises, but like archives, it is wise to call ahead of the visit to learn the library's policies.

A list of all United States state libraries, with links, can be found on the website PublicLibraries.com at http://www.publiclibraries.com/state_library.htm. A list of national libraries and websites for more than fifty countries around the world can be found on the same site at http://www.publiclibraries.com/world.htm. Some well-known state libraries are listed in table 3.4.

Manuscript Libraries

Manuscript libraries collect and preserve rare original drafts of compositions that are often unpublished. These may be political documents, art sketches, musical scores, illustrated tomes, letters and many other documents produced by hand rather than mechanically. Though sometimes original manuscripts cannot be reproduced because of their age and fragility, many manuscript libraries are making digital copies of selected documents available online. Some well-known manuscript libraries that offer some parts of their collections freely on the Internet are listed in table 3.5.

Public Libraries

Public libraries are institutions crucial to the preservation of a free society and have existed in some format since the Roman Empire. They allow any patron free access to information of all types, including scholarly sources and forms of entertainment in the way of books, magazines, music, and video. For historical research, public libraries are particularly useful for those who do not have access to a college or university library, and librarians in public libraries often can help patrons access or borrow material from colleges and university libraries as well as other public libraries. Public libraries may also contain historical information about their local societies and governments that cannot be found in college or university libraries. The collections of most public libraries can be searched online, though you often need to visit the library in person to access the material you want to read. Public libraries range in size from the small community library to large city, state, or national libraries. Some public libraries have special collections of valuable or fragile material that require registration or permission to view, but many of their collections are available for browsing and easy access. Some well-known public libraries in the United States are listed in table 3.6.

United States Presidential Libraries

Presidential libraries in the United States usually are established after a president has left office. Their function is to preserve and make available historic materials related to a president's administration, as well as his political career prior to his presidency. They are maintained by the National Archives and Records Administration (NARA), whose website includes interactive exhibits with photographs, video, and audio clips of presidential material. Most presidential libraries are located in the former president's home state and may be affiliated with a college or university.

Presidential libraries house thousands or even millions of pages of official records, personal papers, correspondence, photographs, speeches, briefings, and audio and video broadcasts. Some of these sources may be reproduced on the libraries' websites. Some also include information about vice presidents, cabinet members, first ladies, family members, important visitors to the White House, and friends. To date there have been twelve Presidential Libraries established in the United States, as listed in table 3.7, and there are plans to build a library to house documents from George W. Bush's administration, which lasted from 2001 to 2009. More information about presidential libraries can be found at http://www.archives.gov/presidential-libraries/. Information released by the current presidential administration can be found at whitehouse.gov.

Table 3.4. International Libraries

Country	National Library	Description
Argentina	**Biblioteca Nacional de la República** *Buenos Aires, Argentina* http://www.bn.gov.ar/	Cultural, scientific, and literary history of Argentina. The website is Spanish only.
Canada	**National Library of Canada** *Ottawa, Ontario, Canada* http://www.nlc-bnc.ca	Established by the Canadian Parliament in 1953, the National Library of Canada acquires, preserves, and promotes material related to the history and culture of Canada.
Columbia	**La Biblioteca Nacional de Colombia** *Bogotá, Colombia* http://www.bibliotecanacional.gov.co/	Contains documents pertaining to the history of Colombia. The site is Spanish only.
Egypt	**Bibliotheca Alexandrina** *Alexandria, Egypt* http://www.bibalex.org/English/index.aspx	The modern revival of the most famous library of antiquity. It contains information regarding the cultural and natural heritage of Egypt.
France	**Bibliothèque Nationale de France (BNF)** *Paris, France* http://www.bnf.fr/	The collection includes materials donated and seized since Charles V, the French Revolution, and the Third Republic. The collections include books, periodicals, audiovisual and digital documents, manuscripts, photographs, maps, and materials relating to the history of France.
Germany	**Bayerische Staatsbibliothek** *Munich, Germany* http://www.bsb-muenchen.de/	The Bavarian State Library holds nearly 10 million books and an extensive collection of historical manuscripts from prehistory to present.
Germany	**Die Deutsche Bibliothek** *Frankfurt am Main, Germany* http://www.ddb.de/	Founded in 1990 after unification, it preserves German and German-language publications, foreign publications about Germany, and the works of German-speaking emigrants published abroad between 1933 and 1945.

Country	National Library	Description
Ireland	**National Library of Ireland** *Dublin, Ireland* http://www.nli.ie	Established in 1877, the National Library of Ireland preserves documents and material related to the history of Ireland, excluding Northern Ireland.
Japan	**National Diet Library of Japan (NDL)** *Tokyo, Japan* http://www.ndl.go.jp/en/index.html	The main research library for members of the Japanese Diet. Copies of all new publications in Japan are collected by the NDL. Collections include Japanese politics and history, legal information, maps, music, and archival material.
Nigeria	**National Library of Nigeria** *Abuja, Nigeria* http://www.nlbn.org	The National Library of Nigeria was established in 1964 to preserve the cultural and intellectual history of Nigeria.
Spain	**La Biblioteca Nacional de Espana** *Madrid, Spain* http://www.bne.es	The library dates back to 1712, although most of its oldest holdings date to the 19th century. Most of the website is in Spanish.
United Kingdom	**British Library** *London, England* http://www.bl.uk/	Founded in 1753 through the private collections and libraries of King George II, King George III, and Thomas Grenville. Contains many important documents relating to the history of Great Britain, including historical, literary, political, etc.
United States	**Library of Congress** *Washington, DC, United States* http://www.loc.gov	Originally only a library for the U.S. Congress, the collection's growth eventually made it the national library of the United States. The collection houses rare books, legal materials, music collections, maps, and films. Many of these documents are available on the website.

Table 3.5. Manuscript Libraries

Manuscript Library	Description
Beinecke Rare Book & Manuscript Library *Yale University* http://www.library.yale.edu/beinecke/	A repository for literary papers, early manuscripts, and rare books in the fields of literature (mainly American and German), theology, history (Greek and Roman papyri, medieval and Renaissance manuscripts, Near-Eastern manuscripts, and historical archives of English and Italian families), and the natural sciences. Those who are interested in manuscripts or archival collections should present a letter of introduction from their academic advisor or college librarian.
Bodleian Library *Oxford, England* http://www.bodley.ox.ac.uk	The Bodleian Library at the University of Oxford is one of the oldest and largest libraries in Europe, with the second largest manuscript collection in Britain.
Burndy Library *Huntington Library in San Marino, CA* http://www.huntington.org/	One of the largest collections of science and technology books, including writings from Isaac Newton and Archimedes.
Folger Shakespeare Library *Washington, DC* http://www.folger.edu/	The world's largest collection of Shakespeare materials. Also includes major collections of other rare books, manuscripts, and works of art of the 16th and 17th centuries, as well as the second largest collection of English books printed prior to 1641.
Huntington Library *San Marino, CA* http://www.huntington.org/	Holds nearly 1 million rare books and 6.5 million manuscripts, as well as British, French, and American artwork dating back to the 1700s. Well-known materials are displayed for the public, though only professional researchers and graduate students pursuing a doctoral degree may handle the actual collections.
The Karpeles Library *Multiple locations in the US* http://www.rain.org/~karpeles/	The world's largest private holding of important original manuscripts and documents. There are nine Karpeles locations in the United States that are open to the public, and their collections rotate. The archives include literature, science, religion, history and art.
Vatican Library *Vatican City (Rome, Italy)* http://www.vatican.va/phome_en.htm	The Vatican Library collects specialized research material in the fields of philology and history, theology, law and science; notably, relations between the Holy See and Germany in the period between 1922 and 1939. Normally only professional researchers and graduate students pursuing a doctoral degree are admitted to the library. Few documents are available online.

Table 3.6.   Public Libraries

Library	Description
Boston Public Library http://www.bpl.org	The second largest public library in the United States, including more than 1.5 million rare books, as well as photograph, print, artwork, and map collections.
New York Public Library http://nypl.org/	Includes more than 83 branch libraries with more than 10 million books. NYPL has substantial special collections including rare books and manuscripts from the 15th to the 20th century and the papers of American authors in the Manuscripts and Archives Division. Its extensive digital library also offers thousands of images from its collections.
Free Library of Philadelphia http://www.freelibrary.org/	Opened in 1894, the Free Library of Philadelphia contains medieval manuscripts, a collection of books printed before 1500, the history Pennsylvania Germans, and the history of Philadelphia and the surrounding area represented by maps, transportation, photographs, and drawings.

Official presidential libraries may not exist for presidents in office prior to the twentieth century; however, a wealth of presidential information can be found on the website of the Library of Congress at www.loc.gov. Official collections of presidents without presidential libraries can be found on the sites listed in table 3.8. Additional documents relating to most presidents and their administrations can be found at the American President website (http://millercenter.org/academic/americanpresident), which is maintained by the University of Virginia's Miller Center for Public Affairs.

GOVERNMENT INFORMATION

The governments of most countries, states, cities, and towns collect and disseminate information about their populations, environments, political and cultural activity, and relations with other government entities. In countries where the government is run on taxpayer money, transparency of information may be a requirement of law. Government agencies provide reports and statistical data on many factors that influence the course of history, including weather, terrain, immigration, health, wealth, trade, armed forces, and the law. Documents and government releases may come in the form of architectural drawings, certificates, charts, drawings, forms, legal documents, letters, maps, memos, films, photographs, plans, posters, and many other types of materials.

Table 3.7. Presidential Libraries

President	Presidential Libraries
George W. Bush	**George W. Bush Presidential Library** *Lewisville, TX* http://www.georgewbushlibrary.gov/
William (Bill) Clinton	**William J. Clinton Presidential Library and Museum** *Little Rock, AR* http://www.clintonlibrary.gov/
George H. W. Bush	**George Bush Library** *Texas A&M University* http://bushlibrary.tamu.edu/
Ronald Reagan	**Ronald Reagan Presidential Library** *Simi Valley, CA* http://www.reagan.utexas.edu/
Jimmy Carter	**Jimmy Carter Library and Museum** *Atlanta, GA* http://www.jimmycarterlibrary.org/
Gerald Ford	**Gerald R. Ford Library at the University of Michigan** *Ann Arbor, MI* http://www.ford.utexas.edu/
Richard Nixon	**Richard Nixon Presidential Library and Museum** *Yorba Linda, CA* http://www.nixonlibraryfoundation.org/
Lyndon B. Johnson	**Lyndon Baines Johnson Presidential Library** *University of Texas, Austin* http://www.lbjlib.utexas.edu/
John F. Kennedy	**John F. Kennedy Presidential Library and Museum** *Boston, MA* http://www.jfklibrary.org/
Dwight D. Eisenhower	**Dwight D. Eisenhower Presidential Library and Museum** *Abilene, KS* http://www.eisenhower.archives.gov/
Harry S. Truman	**Harry S. Truman Library and Museum** *Independence, MO* http://www.trumanlibrary.org/
Franklin D. Roosevelt	**Franklin D. Roosevelt Presidential Library and Museum** *Hyde Park, NY* http://www.fdrlibrary.marist.edu/
Herbert Hoover	**Herbert Hoover Presidential Library and Museum** *West Branch, IA* http://hoover.archives.gov/

United States Government Information

In the United States, numerous departments and agencies are set up to run all of the programs and services mandated by law, such as the military, transportation, the census, border control, the environment, foreign relations, and the federal budget. A list of United States federal, state, and local agencies can be found at http://www.usa.gov/agencies.shtml. Most government agencies publish the information they collect as long as it does not compromise the country's national security, and much of that information can have historical significance. The depth, breadth, and scope of the information available varies by government agency, but most will provide at least the current year's information on their websites.

The Government Printing Office (GPO) is the official publisher and distributor of information regarding the three branches of the federal government in the United States: the White House, the House of Representatives and the Senate, and the Supreme Court. The GPO publishes the official documents not only of those branches of government, but also of the agencies that report to them. Important documents regularly released by the GPO include the Federal Register and the Congressional Record, which are the official records of the proceedings of the legislative branch of government. Material published by the GPO is available to the public for free via its website (http://www.gpo.gov/).

GPO information also is stored at certain libraries around the country designated as Federal Depositories, which are public and academic libraries officially authorized to collect material printed by the GPO. A list of libraries that serve as Federal Depositories can be found at http://www.gpoaccess.gov/libraries.html. GPO material stored in libraries can be found by searching the catalogs of depository libraries or WorldCat. For more information about searching library catalogs and WorldCat, see chapter 5. In addition to the GPO, examples of websites that publish information provided by United States government agencies are listed in table 3.9.

Worldwide Government Information

Most governments publish at least some information about their country's history and statistics online, though some are more restrictive than others about what they publish. Information about governments around the world often can be found with a simple Google search, or you can get started at one of the websites listed in table 3.10.

Table 3.8. Other U.S. Presidential Collections

President	Other Presidential Collections
George Washington	**Papers of George Washington** http://gwpapers.virginia.edu/
John Adams	**Adams Family Papers: An Electronic Archive** http://www.masshist.org/digitaladams/aea/
Thomas Jefferson	**Thomas Jefferson's Monticello** http://www.monticello.org/
James Madison	**James Madison Center** *James Madison University* http://www.jmu.edu/madison/center/index.html
James Monroe	**Papers of James Monroe** *University of Mary Washington in Fredericksburg, VA* http://www.umw.edu/monroepapers/
Andrew Jackson	**Papers of Andrew Jackson** *University of Tennessee, Knoxville* http://thepapersofandrewjackson.utk.edu/
Martin Van Buren	**Martin Van Buren National Historic Site** *Kinderhook, NY* http://www.nps.gov/mava
William Henry Harrison	**William Henry Harrison, Indiana Historical Society** *Indianapolis, IN* http://www.indianahistory.org/library/manuscripts/ collection_guides/m0364.html
John Tyler	**John Tyler Special Collections Research Center** *Swem Library, College of William and Mary, Williamsburg, VA* http://scrc.swem.wm.edu/?p=collections/ controlcard&id=7008
James K. Polk	**James K. Polk Ancestral Home** *Columbia, TN* http://www.jameskpolk.com
Zachary Taylor	**Zachary Taylor Papers 1812-1850 at the University of Kentucky** *Lexington, KY* http://www.uky.edu/Libraries/record.php?lir_id=1680
Millard Fillmore	**Millard Fillmore Letters from SUNY Oswego and Erie Country Historical Society** *Buffalo, NY* http://www.oswego.edu/library2/archives/digitized_ collections/fillmore1/ and http://www.bechs.org/library/ index.htm
Franklin Pierce	**Franklin Pierce Collection** *Bowdoin College, Brunswick, ME, and New Hampshire Historical Society* http://library.bowdoin.edu/arch/mss/fpsd.shtml and http:// www.nhhistory.org/museumexhibits/pierce/pierce1.htm

President	Other Presidential Collections
Abraham Lincoln	**Abraham Lincoln Presidential Library and Museum** *Springfield, IL* http://www.alplm.org/
Andrew Johnson	**Andrew Johnson Collection of Papers from State of Tennessee Archives** *Nashville, TN* http://www.tennessee.gov/tsla/history/manuscripts/findingaids/131.pdf
Ulysses S. Grant	**Ulysses S. Grant Association Presidential Collection of Mississippi State University** *Mississippi State University, MS* http://library.msstate.edu/USGrant/
Rutherford B. Hayes	**Rutherford B. Hayes Presidential Center** *Fremont, OH* http://www.rbhayes.org/hayes/
James A. Garfield	**James A. Garfield Papers from Hiram College** *Hiram, OH* http://library.hiram.edu/Archives/Garfield%20Collection/Home.htm
Grover Cleveland	**Grover Cleveland Library** *Buffalo, NY* http://groverclevelandlibrary.org
William McKinley	**William McKinley Library and Museum** *Canton, OH* http://www.mckinleymuseum.org/
Theodore Roosevelt	**Theodore Roosevelt Collection of Harvard University** *Cambridge, MA* http://hcl.harvard.edu/libraries/houghton/collections/roosevelt.html
William Howard Taft	**William Howard Taft National Historic Site** *Cincinnati, OH* http://www.nps.gov/wiho/index.htm
Woodrow Wilson	**Woodrow Wilson Presidential Library** *Staunton, VA* http://www.woodrowwilson.org/
Warren G. Harding	**Warren G. Harding Home** *Marion, OH* http://ohsweb.ohiohistory.org/places/c03/index.shtml
Calvin Coolidge	**Calvin Coolidge Presidential Library and Museum** *Northampton, MA* http://www.forbeslibrary.org/coolidge/coolidge.shtml

Table 3.9. Websites with U.S. Government Information

Site	Description
Centers for Disease Control and Prevention http://www.cdc.gov	Information and statistics on health topics.
Cyber Cemetery http://govinfo.library.unt.edu/browse_ expiration.htm	Archives all government websites since 1995 that have gone offline due to the agency being terminated or final reports being issued.
Government Printing Office http://www.gpoaccess.gov/	Congressional Record, Federal Register, U.S. Code, Federal Law, and other official publications of the U.S. government.
National Oceanic and Atmospheric Administration's National Weather Service http://www.nws.noaa.gov/	Current forecasts and weather conditions as well as weather and climate history of the United States.
Supreme Court of the United States http://www.supremecourtus.gov/	Includes the texts of recent decisions, opinions, dockets, briefs, and oral arguments of recent cases, as well as a history of the Court.
United States Department of Justice http://www.justice.gov	Records and reports on American laws and legal initiatives.
United States Department of State http://www.state.gov	Information on foreign policy initiatives on countries in which the United States has a strong interest. Also has information on general policies such as food security and counterterrorism.
US Congress: Senate and House of Representatives http://www.senate.govhttp://www. house.gov	Information on members of congress, committees, laws, and current issues.

STATISTICS

Statistical information can be critically important to historical research. Statistical analysis refers to the collection, analysis, and interpretation of quantitative data, and it can help support an assertion about historical events. Statistics may include numbers on economics, labor, income, industry, trade, human and animal populations, public opinion, ethnicity, age, birth and death rates, voting patterns, military, and much more.

You should find statistics to support quantifiable and comparative statements whenever possible. For example, you may state that a lot of people emigrated from Ireland to the United States in the nineteenth century. With statistics, you can strengthen that assertion to include a measureable compari-

Table 3.10. Websites with Worldwide Government Information

Site	Description
Association of Southeast Asian Nations http://www.asean.org/	Documents and statistics regarding the countries belonging to this union, which was established in 1967. Member countries include Cambodia, Indonesia, Malaysia, Myanmar, Philippines, Thailand, and Viet Nam.
Council of the European Union http://www.consilium.europa.eu/	Includes the Treaty of Lisbon and other documents produced by the European Union.
Embassy World http://www.embassyworld.com/	A directory of embassies and consulates worldwide.
Interparliamentary Union http://www.ipu.org/english/home.htm	Information about the political relations among countries with parliamentary systems of government.
North Atlantic Treaty Organization http://www.nato.int/	Current and historical documents about NATO's activities and its member countries.
Organization of American States http://www.oas.org/	News, speeches, reports, photographs, and other documents from this coalition of North, Central, and South American countries.
Political Resources on the Net http://www.politicalresources.net/	News, analyses, and Internet links regarding political parties and events around the world.
The Electronic Embassy Web http://www.embassy.org/	Information about foreign embassies in Washington, DC.
United Nations Headquarters http://www.un.org/index.html	Treaties, resolutions, maps, legal information, and other documents related to the member nations of the UN.

son and specific time frame by stating that approximately 1 million people immigrated to the United States from Ireland between 1850 and 1859 as compared to approximately 50,000 people between 1950 and 1959.[1]

Authors of books and journal and newspaper articles frequently use statistics to reinforce their arguments. If an author provides graphs or statistics that you would like to use, you should check the author's original source yourself if possible. Though it is technically not wrong to use the information as presented by the author, it is far better and safer to consult the original source of that information. This will ensure that no errors were accidentally reproduced in the book or article. More importantly, while fact checking, you should examine the statistics presented to determine if you agree with the author's use of the numbers and the conclusions he or she drew from them. Normally, you can trace back to the original source by consulting the author's bibliography or footnotes and looking up the cited sources in your own library. If you have difficulty finding the author's reference to the original source, consult a librarian for help.

Like all other pieces of evidence, statistics should be represented accurately and used to support and enhance valid arguments. Numbers should not be manipulated or changed in order to force them to support a statement. Statistics can have the effect of weakening your argument if they are used inappropriately. To make sure that your statistics will enhance and support your argument, adhere to the following guidelines.

- Only use statistics if you understand what they represent. Talk to a professor or librarian if you are unsure about the meaning of a set of statistics.
- Make sure your audience will understand the statistics and your use of them. Your reader should be able to recreate your logic and follow your conclusions. In addition to simply providing statistics, you must fully describe how you use the statistics to draw inferences.
- Make sure any statistics you use come from verifiable scholarly or government sources. Statistics can be biased and subject to error in reporting. Be sure to verify the source of your statistics and the methods used to collect them before quoting them in a research project.

Like any other type of source, statistical data must be cited, and your presentation of the data must be clearly presented to your readers so that, if they wish, they can find the original source themselves and draw independent conclusions from your numbers. More information about citing statistics can be found in appendixes A and B.

Statistics may be represented in graphs or charts, or even on maps. An example of statistical representation is illustrated in figure 3.9.

Subscription-Based Statistical Databases

Table 3.11 includes samples of subscription-based databases that offer historical statistics. Ask your librarian whether your library has access to these sources, or check your library's database list for access, as described in chapter 3.

Free Websites with Statistical Information

Table 3.12 provides a list of free websites that offer historical statistics.

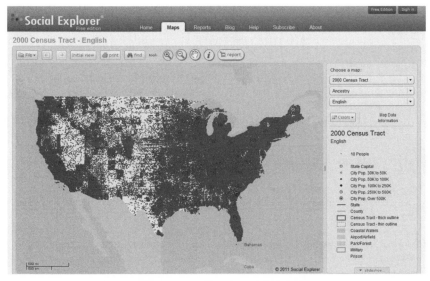

Figure 3.9. Historical Statistics from 2000 Census Data. Courtesy of Socialexplorer. com.

Books with Statistical Information

Statistical information may be found in annually or semiannually published books. Following are some well-known examples of statistical compilations:

Carter, Susan B., et al., eds. *The Historical Statistics of the United States*. 5 vols. Millenial ed. New York: Cambridge University Press, 2006. Includes information on population, work and welfare, economics, governance and international relations.

Mitchell, Brian R. *International Historical Statistics: 1750–2005*. New ed. 3 vols. Basingstoke: Palgrave MacMillan, 2007. Includes economic and social statistics for countries worldwide.

Maher, Joanne, ed. *Europa World Year Book*. 49th ed. London: Europa Publications Limited, 2008. Provides overviews of countries, including basic statistical information such as area, population, health, welfare, agriculture, forestry, fishing, industry, finance, trade, transport, tourism, the media, and education.

United States Bureau of the Census. *Statistical Abstract of the United States*. Washington, DC: U.S. Department of Commerce, 2009. A summary of the social, economic, and political organization of the United States. This source has been published yearly since 1878.

Table 3.11. Subscription-Based Databases with Historical Statistics

Site	Description
Ancestry.com http://www.ancestry.com/	Although Ancestry.com is primarily a website for genealogy, it also contains useful statistical information such as census information, military records, and vital statistics. It contains information from the United States, Canada, England, and other western European countries.
CQ Press Database: Voting and Elections Collection http://www.cqpress.com/product/ CQ-Voting-and-Elections-Collection. html	Data, graphs, and analysis grouped into six categories: presidential elections, congressional elections, gubernatorial elections, political parties, campaigns and elections, and voters and demographics.
Historical Statistics of the United States: Millennial Edition http://www.cambridge.org/us/ americanhistory/hsus/default.htm	Available online and in print, contains 1900 tables, 170 maps and graphs, over 100 essays, and one of the most comprehensive lists of quantitative facts on American history.
Statistical Universe *web.lexis-nexis.com/statuniv*	U.S. government statistical sources, state government and privately published statistical sources, and international intergovernmental statistical sources.
World Almanac http://www.worldalmanac.com/	Geographical, demographic, political, and brief biographical information and statistics for the United States and countries around the world.

Table 3.12. Free Websites with Historical Statistics

Site	Description
Bureau of Labor Statistics http://www.bls.gov/	Statistics on social and economic conditions of the United States, its workers, and their families.
CIA World Factbook https://www.cia.gov/library/publications/ the-world-factbook/	Provides economic, military, transportation, and historical statistics on countries around the world.
Country Studies/Area Handbooks http://memory.loc.gov/frd/cs/	Analyzes countries from a series of interrelated systems including historical, political, economic, science and technology, national security, cultural and social settings. Offers brief histories of the development of each system within the country.

Site	Description
County and City Data Books http://www2.lib.virginia.edu/ccdb/	From the University of Virginia library, contains county, city, and state datasets since 1944.
Federal Deposit Insurance Corporation: Historical Statistics on Banking http://www2.fdic.gov/hsob	Information on long-term trends in the banking industry and statistics on financial institutions.
Foreign Trade Statistics http://www.census.gov/foreign-trade/www/	Information about U.S. foreign trade, including historical statistics by country, state and commodity.
General Social Survey http://www.norc.org/GSS+Website/	An accumulation of statistics on Americans' attitudes toward elements of society and social change. Topics range from abortion to immigration.
Historical Census Browser http://fisher.lib.virginia.edu/collections/stats/histcensus/	Covers the United States census from 1790 to 1960. Allows comparisons and generates maps online down to the county level. Provided by the University of Virginia.
Inter-University Consortium for Political and Social Research (ICPSR) http://www.icpsr.umich.edu/icpsrweb/ICPSR/	Catalog and index to ICPSR's holdings of demographic, economic, and political data. Includes data on health, education, terrorism and other crime, and race and ethnicity. Some sets and codebooks are available online.
National Archive of Criminal Justice Data (NACJD) http://www.nationmaster.com/index.php	Preserves and distributes computerized crime and justice data from federal agencies, state agencies, and investigator initiated research projects to users for secondary statistical analysis.
NationMaster.com http://www.nationmaster.com	This website generates comparisons of countries via maps and graphs, using statistics of all kinds.
Social Explorer http://www.socialexplorer.com/pub/home/home.aspx	One of the most user friendly websites for viewing census data. Also allows saving and printing custom census data maps.
United Nations Statistics Division http://unstats.un.org/unsd/default.htm	Statistical information from countries that are members of the United Nations.
United States Census Bureau http://www.census.gov/	Decades of historical data, including numbers on income, immigration and migration, births and deaths, ancestry, education, voting, employment, and more.

United States Bureau of the Census. *County and City Data Book.* Washington, DC: U.S. Department of Commerce, 2007. Provides information about the individual counties and cities in the United States. It includes data for all U.S. states, counties, and cities with a population of 25,000 or more.

World Bank. *The Complete World Development Report, 1978-2009*: 30th anniversary ed. Washington, DC: World Bank, 2009. A guide to the economic, social, and environmental state of the world.

This chapter has provided examples of the many different types of material you might have occasion to use in a research paper for a history project. In chapters 4, 5, and 6, you will learn specifically how to find individual tertiary, secondary, and primary sources.

NOTE

1. Robert Barde, Susan B. Carter, and Richard Sutch, "Immigrants by Country of Last Residence: 1820-1997," *Historical Statistics of the United States*, Millennial Edition, vol. 1, ed. Susan B. Carter et al. (New York: Cambridge University Press, 2006), 561, 563.

Chapter Four

Tertiary Sources

A *tertiary source* is a collection of facts, figures, and dates that briefly describe biographies, events, places, and eras regarding a particular field of
knowledge.

Tertiary Source: Reference material that summarizes and condenses
the information found in primary and secondary sources.

Tertiary sources may cover general knowledge or may be specific to one
topic. Usually appearing in the form of books or websites, tertiary sources
are most often consulted for fact checking and background reading. General
examples of tertiary sources include encyclopedias, dictionaries, biographies,
fact books, almanacs, atlases, and classroom textbooks. Specific examples are
familiar sources such as the *Merriam-Webster Dictionary* and *Encyclopedia
Britannica*, and some are more specialized, such as the *New Encyclopedia
of the American West* or the *Historical Dictionary of Syria*. Many of these
sources are rather expensive to purchase because of the enormous production
costs associated with creating them, and therefore they usually are available
only at libraries. Many tertiary sources are produced in book form but they
are increasingly being produced online and made available through subscription.

Information found in tertiary sources is collected, condensed, and combined from primary and secondary sources. The purpose of a tertiary source
is to provide basic facts without analysis or criticism. Tertiary sources in
book form usually are arranged in alphabetical order by subject, topic, person,
place, or event. An online tertiary source may be searched by any relevant
keyword and also may have a browse function that lists all topics covered in
alphabetical order.

In addition to listing facts, tertiary sources may provide a few paragraphs or pages summarizing the most important details about the topic or person as well as a bibliography of citations that will lead you to additional important sources of information about each topic. The bibliographies can help you to start building a list of sources that have potential usefulness to your own project. Because bibliographies can give you a head start on identifying potentially useful research material, it is always a good idea to consult a tertiary source when beginning a project, even if you know quite a bit about the subject.

Writers of research papers at the college and university level should use tertiary sources as a launching point for a project, but these sources should never be used exclusively as source material for any history project. Tertiary sources should not be included in a bibliography or works cited list since they typically contain information that is considered to be common knowledge, even if that knowledge is new to an individual researcher. Additionally, tertiary sources need not be cited in footnotes unless there is some compelling reason to do so, such as when a fact is in dispute or reported differently by different sources. More information about properly citing tertiary sources can be found in appendixes A and B.

REFERENCE BOOKS

A reference book is the quintessential tertiary source. It is a book-form compilation of facts and figures on general knowledge or a specific topic. Reference books are generally easy to locate physically in libraries. They usually are separated from the main collection of books in a section called "Reference." Because they are the type of books typically not read cover to cover, but rather consulted by many researchers for small bits of information, they usually cannot be taken out of the library.

General examples of reference books are encyclopedias, dictionaries, bibliographies, map, atlases, book reviews, and other sources that provide facts. Specific examples of reference books are listed below.

Stearns, Peter N., ed. *The Oxford Encyclopedia of the Modern World*. 8 Vols. New York: Oxford University Press, 2008.
Wieczynski, Joseph L., ed. *The Modern Encyclopedia of Russian and Soviet History*. Gulf Breeze, FL: Academic International Press, 1976.

Although reference books often are kept in a special section of most libraries, there will probably be too many of them for you simply to browse and serendipitously discover the reference book you need. Many library catalogs provide a search feature that allows you to limit your search only to reference books.

Finding Reference Books

Before following these steps, access your local library's online book catalog and be sure that you are using the Advanced Search or More Options screen. See chapter 5 for detailed information about accessing a catalog's advanced search screen.

- In the Keyword search box, type a term that broadly describes the topic you are researching. For example, you might use "Korean War" or "Cambodia."
- Look for a search box that allows you to narrow your search to a physical location in the library and use that field to select "Reference." Your search should look similar to the one illustrated in figure 4.1.

Your results should look similar to those in figure 4.2, in which the catalog lists an encyclopedia on Korea available in the library's reference section.

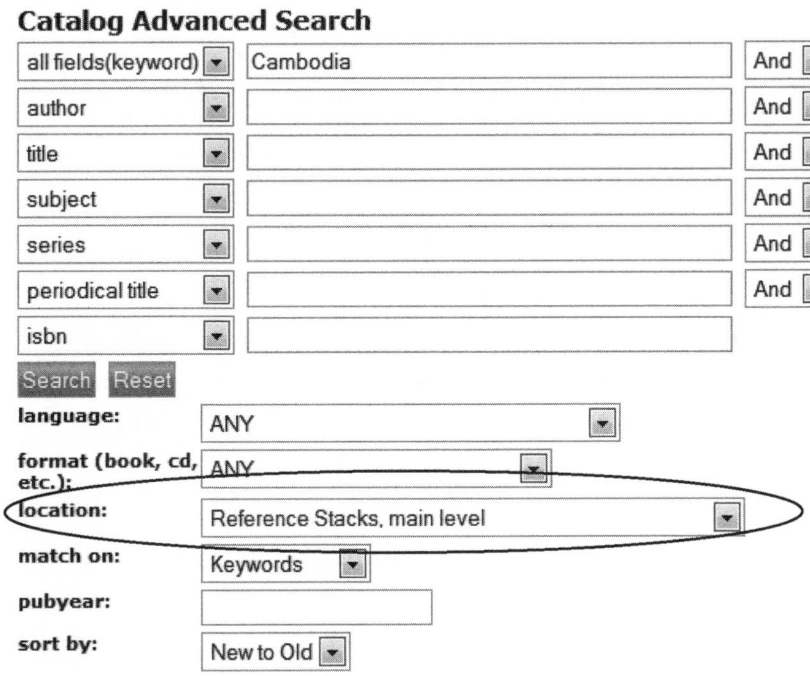

Figure 4.1. Library Catalog with Reference Location Selected. Courtesy of Dickinson College and SirsiDynix.

all fields(keyword) "Korean War" search found 5 titles.

Conflict in Korea : an encyclopedia
Hoare, James.
DS916 .H62 1999
1999
1 Item available in Reference Stacks, main level

Historical dictionary of the Korean War
Matray, James Irving, 1948-
DS918 .H536 1991
1991
1 Item available in Reference Stacks, main level

Korean War almanac
Summers, Harry G.
DS918 .S86 1990
1990
1 Item available in Reference Stacks, main level
▶ CLCD Review

Figure 4.2.   Results of Catalog Search for Reference Materials. Courtesy of Dickinson College and SirsiDynix.

Online Reference Sources

Tertiary sources increasingly are being converted to online editions or produced directly in electronic format. The disadvantages of printed tertiary sources are that only one person can use each volume at a time, one must be physically present in the library to use them, and individual volumes are subject to theft and damage. Many people can use online reference works at once, and their hyperlinks lead researchers to additional helpful primary and secondary source information. Most importantly, many online reference materials are updated frequently, thus eliminating the need for libraries to wait for print updates to be published, purchased, and delivered to the library.

To find online reference sources in your library, check the library's website for a *virtual reference shelf* or *online encyclopedias*. Many are being collected into big package services that allow you to search the full text of many popular reference works at once. Examples of tertiary sources available online are listed in table 4.1. Your library will probably have many more options available than just the commonly known sources listed here.

BIOGRAPHY

A biography is an account of a person's life. A biography can be quite detailed and appear in book-length form, or it can be in short form, appearing in an encyclopedia along with biographies of other people who are

Table 4.1. Free and Subscription Online Tertiary Sources

Source	Free/Subscription	Description
African-American Studies Center Online (AASC) http://www.oxfordaasc.com/	Subscription	Scholarly articles, images, maps, and other primary sources dedicated to African and African-American culture and history.
Canadian Encyclopedia http://www. thecanadianencyclopedia. com/	Free	Information on all aspects of Canada, ranging from politics to sports to music.
Credo Reference http://www.credoreference.com	Subscription	A combination of several hundred multidisciplinary reference works combined into one searchable database.
Dictionary of Greek and Roman Biography and Mythology http://www.ancientlibrary.com/ smith-bio/	Free	Descriptions of Greek and Roman mythological, historical, and literary figures.
Encyclopedia Britannica Online http://www.britannica.com/	Subscription	The classic encyclopedia is now constantly updated online. It includes bibliographies with links to primary sources and scholarly articles.
Encyclopedia of African-American Culture and History http://www.gale.cengage.com/	Subscription	Information on social movements, culture, history, and issues pertaining to African Americans.
Gale Virtual Reference Library www.gale.cengage.com/gvrl/	Subscription	A database of encyclopedias, almanacs and ebooks on interdisciplinary subjects.
Holocaust Encyclopedia http://www.ushmm.org/wlc/en/	Free	Contains articles and biographies published by the Holocaust Memorial Museum in Washington, DC.
Oxford Islamic Studies Online http://www. oxfordislamicstudies.com/	Subscription	Covers Islamic and Middle East topics including biographies, primary sources, and images.
Oxford Reference Online http://www.oxfordreference. com/	Subscription	Contains multidisciplinary subject and language reference works, including subjects ranging from accounting to zoology.
World Book Online Resource Center http://www.worldbookonline. com/training/pl_ref_center/ index.htm	Subscription	Multidisciplinary reference site that is built to be user friendly for high school students and public libraries. Contains tutorials and instructive videos.

from the same country or who engage in a similar profession. Biographies often are written by people somewhat removed from a direct relationship with the subject of the biography. When writing years after the death of the subject, the biography should rely predominantly on primary sources from the person's life. Historical biographies may be an overview of the person's life or set their focus to a specific event or action for which the person is known to have been involved. As with any other type of source, biographies may be scholarly or nonscholarly works; see chapter 2 for help in determining this.

Finding Biographies in Printed Reference Works

Table 4.2 lists some of the more commonly known biographical directories available in most U.S. libraries. Check your library's catalog to see if you own any of these titles, or ask a librarian for assistance.

Finding Biographies in Databases

There are many subscription databases available that offer short, overview-style biographies of historical figures. Table 4.3 lists a number of these sources that may be available in your library. If these particular sources are not available at your library, ask a librarian if alternative options are available.

Table 4.2. Print Biographical Directories

Source	Description
Biography Index	A guide to finding biographies that have appeared in books and magazines.
Dictionary of American Biography	Biographies from all periods of American history, including expanded entries on women and minorities.
Dictionary of National Biography	Profiles of nonliving people who shaped the history and culture of the British Isles.
Notable American Women 1607–1950: A Biographical Dictionary	Biographies of American women who made a significant impact on American history.
Who's Who (Marquis)	Biographies of living influential people in all professions, starting in the 20th century.

Table 4.3.   Subscription-Based Online Biography Sources

Source	Description
American National Biography http://www.anb.org/	Brief biographies of nonliving individuals who have influenced American history and culture.
Ancestry http://www.ancestry.com/	A genealogical resource that allows searching through census, military, immigration, and vital records and obituaries for the United States. Some records are included from Canada, England, Germany, and Australia.
Biography and Genealogy Master Index http://www.gale.cengage.com/servlet/Bro wseSeriesServlet?region=9&imprint=00 0&titleCode=BDMI&edition	Over 13 million biographical entries of living and deceased individuals. This source does not provide the complete biographical sketch, but helps you locate biographies published in other sources.
Biography Reference Bank http://www.ebscohost.com/academic/ biography-reference-bank	Biographies of living authors worldwide.
Dictionary of National Biography http://www.oxforddnb.com/l	Biographies of noteworthy nonliving individuals who shaped the British isles.
Dictionary of Scientific Biography http://www.gale.cengage.com/ndsb/	Provides information on the history of science through articles on the professional lives of scientists.
Marquis Who's Who http://www.marquiswhoswho.com/online- database	Biographical entries on people from around the world and across multiple subjects.

Finding Biographies in a Library Catalog

You should search for biographies in your library catalog when you are seeking book-length accounts of a person's life. Before following these steps, access your local library's online book catalog and be sure that you are using the Advanced Search or More Options screen. See chapter 5 for more information about accessing a catalog's advanced search screen.

- In the Keyword search box, type the name of the person for whom you want to find a biography. For example, you might use "Indira Gandhi" or "Boris Yeltsin."
- In the Subject box, type the word "biography." Your search should look similar to the one illustrated in figure 4.3.
- Optionally, if the person you are searching for is a native of a country whose language you cannot read, it is a good idea to limit your search to

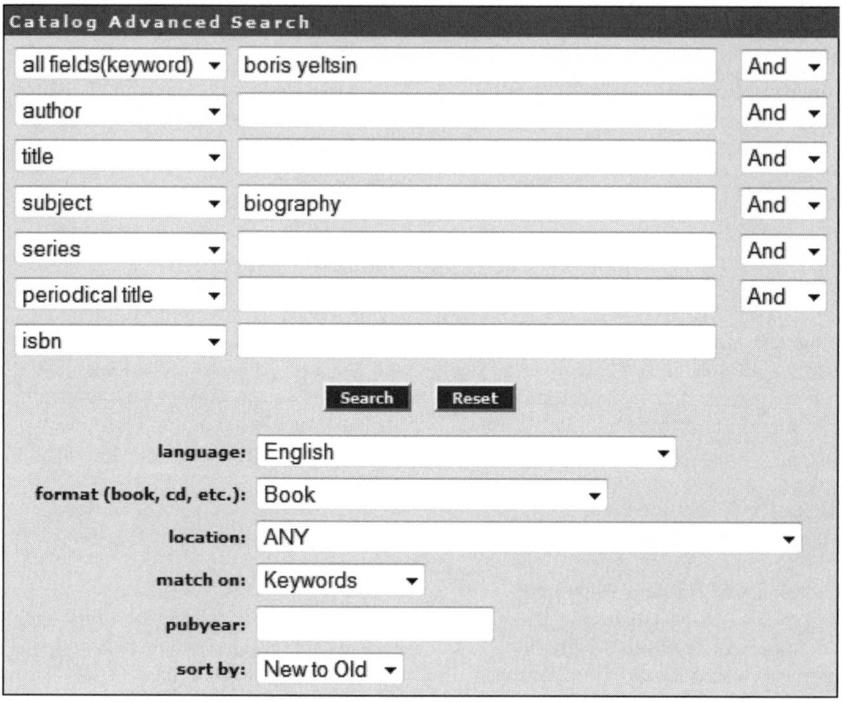

Catalog Advanced Search		
all fields(keyword) ▾	boris yeltsin	And ▾
author ▾		And ▾
title ▾		And ▾
subject ▾	biography	And ▾
series ▾		And ▾
periodical title ▾		And ▾
isbn ▾		

Search   Reset

language:	English ▾
format (book, cd, etc.):	Book ▾
location:	ANY ▾
match on:	Keywords ▾
pubyear:	
sort by:	New to Old ▾

Figure 4.3.   Catalog Search for Biographies. Courtesy of Dickinson College and Sirsi-Dynix.

languages you can read since your search may produce results that have not been translated.

When you complete your search, your results list should contain biographies of the person whose name you entered.

ENCYCLOPEDIAS AND DICTIONARIES

Encyclopedias and dictionaries provide short overviews of general knowledge or specific information on topics relating to one time period, subject, or event. Often, they will provide bibliographies that may be valuable in helping you find evidence to support your research project. Entries in encyclopedias and dictionaries are good, quick introductions to a topic and serve as a point from which to begin building your own bibliography for your project. It is a good idea to consult several encyclopedias or dictionaries for any topic as each one will address it in a different way and will provide different sources for additional reading. Note that the editors of encyclopedias and dictionaries have to make deliberate choices about what topics to include; therefore, not all of them address every aspect of every subject; or they may not address your subject at all.

Specific examples of historical encyclopedias and dictionaries are the *Oxford Dictionary of World History* and Richard B. Morris's *Encyclopedia of American History*. Your library will probably have many more options available, so be sure to search your library's catalog for additional titles.

Wikipedia is considered to be an encyclopedia, and although it is widely used, even by academic professionals, you should always verify its information against reliable scholarly sources, just as you would with any other source. Wikipedia is a social knowledge site that allows any registered user to change the information on its pages, and there is no assurance that Wikipedia pages are regularly edited by experts on the topic, as there is with scholarly encyclopedias. Even the presence of citations on Wikipedia pages does not guarantee the validity of its information, as all of the knowledge is submitted by users, and the site has even been subjected to hoaxes. That said, Wikipedia is a good source for refreshing your memory about facts that you have forgotten, and reading its broad overviews of historical topics can provide you with ideas for interesting directions in which to take your topic. Most useful are Wikipedia's reference lists, which provide you with citations and links to credible scholarly sources that you can use to pursue your topic in depth.

Finding Encyclopedias and Dictionaries in a Library Catalog

When you search for encyclopedias and dictionaries in your library's catalog, you are likely to find both printed as well as online or eBook sources. Before following these steps, access your local library's online book catalog and be sure that you are using the Advanced Search or More Options screen. See chapter 5 for detailed information about accessing a catalog's advanced search screen.

- On the Keyword line, type the most general descriptive term that relates to your topic. "African Americans" is an example of a search phrase you might use.
- Change the next line to read "keyword," and type the word "history." (This will prevent nonhistorical sources from appearing in your search.)
- On the Subject line, type the phrase "encyclopedia or encyclopedias." Your search should look similar to the one illustrated in figure 4.4.

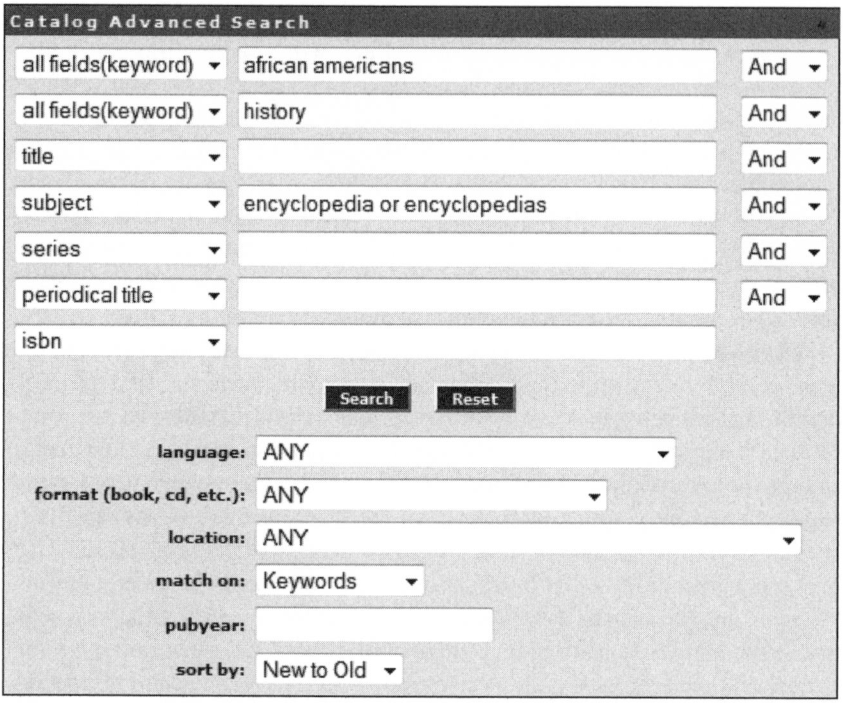

Catalog Advanced Search

all fields(keyword) ▾	african americans	And ▾
all fields(keyword) ▾	history	And ▾
title ▾		And ▾
subject ▾	encyclopedia or encyclopedias	And ▾
series ▾		And ▾
periodical title ▾		And ▾
isbn ▾		

Search   Reset

language: ANY ▾
format (book, cd, etc.): ANY ▾
location: ANY ▾
match on: Keywords ▾
pubyear:
sort by: New to Old ▾

Figure 4.4. Catalog Search for Encyclopedias. Courtesy of Dickinson College and SirsiDynix.

all fields(keyword) "african americans" AND all fields(keyword) "history" AND subject "encyclopedia or encyclopedias" search found 15 titles.

Encyclopedia of the Jazz Age : from the end of World War I to the great crash
Ciment, James.
E784 .E53 2008 v.1
2008
2 Items available
▸ URL

Class in America : an encyclopedia
Weir, Robert E., 1952-
HN90 .S6 C564 2007 v.1
2007
3 Items available
▸ URL

Encyclopedia of African American history, 1619-1895 : from the colonial period to the age of Frederick Douglass
Finkelman, Paul, 1949-
E185 .E545 2006 v.1
2006
3 Items available
▸ URL

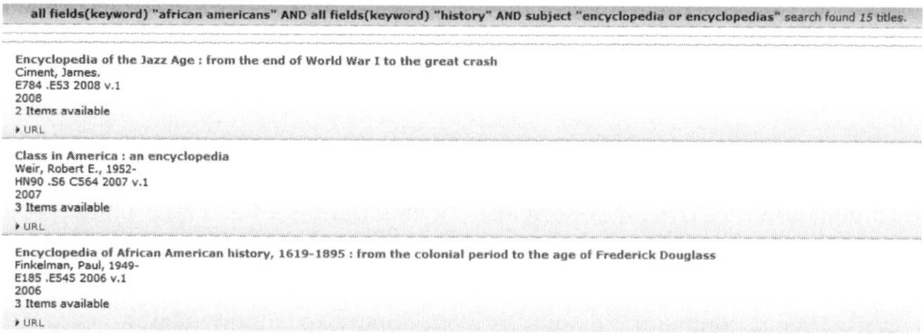

Figure 4.5. Results of Catalog Search for Encyclopedias and Dictionaries. Courtesy of Dickinson College and SirsiDynix.

Your completed search should produce a list of reference books. Your results list should look similar to that in figure 4.5.

Finding Encyclopedias and Dictionaries on the Internet

Free encyclopedias and dictionaries are available in abundance on the Internet. As with all other types of sources, print and online, some online encyclopedias and dictionaries are scholarly, and some are not. If you consult an encyclopedia or dictionary online to double check a simple fact or the spelling of a word, you probably do not need to worry about evaluating the source. However if you need an encyclopedia or dictionary for background reading as preparation for a research project, you should subject the source to the same evaluative process you would any other source, as described in chapter 2. For historical research, it is always best to use a recognized historical encyclopedia or dictionary that can be found on your library's shelves or provided online.

Many online encyclopedias and dictionaries may be accessed only by individuals or institutions that have a paid subscription to the source. Online tertiary sources such as *Encyclopedia Britannica* and *American National Biography* are examples of titles that are available only by subscription. If you encounter an encyclopedia or dictionary online that you are unable to access directly, check your library's website to see if it has a subscription to the source you need or if you can access a comparable source.

BIBLIOGRAPHIES

A *bibliography* can be one of two things. In one sense, a bibliography is a list of materials—largely primary and secondary—that a researcher consulted when preparing his or her book, article, paper, or presentation.

Bibliography: A list of research materials that an author consults when preparing a book or article.

When used in this way, a bibliography sometimes is known as a works cited list and is one of the main indicators that a secondary source is scholarly. The bibliographies that appear at the end of a secondary source book or article demonstrate to the reader that the author carefully researched the paper while writing it. The bibliography should include all the sources that influenced the author's opinions and all sources that the author consulted, even if the source is not directly quoted in the body of the paper. Bibliographies also may include items that the author thinks would benefit the reader who wants more information or additional viewpoints about the topic. The other definition of a bibliography is a book-length list of sources on a particular topic. Book-length bibliographies can be used to help a researcher easily find some of the most important books and articles that have been written about a topic.

Bibliographies are useful because they provide ready-made lists of valuable sources on a topic. They are particularly useful when they are *annotated*, meaning that the compiler of the bibliography will offer a short critical review of each item listed.

Annotation: A brief critical review of a scholarly work.

A good annotation will summarize the author's thesis and conclusion, comment on the author's authority, describe the sources the author consulted, and make an evaluative statement about the scholarly value of the book.

Finding Bibliographies in a Library Catalog

Before following these steps, access your local library's online book catalog and be sure that you are using the Advanced Search or More Options screen. See chapter 5 for more information about accessing a catalog's advanced search screen.

- In the Keyword search box, type a term that broadly describes the topic you are researching. For example, you might use "Cultural Revolution of China" or "Congo Free State."
- Change the next search field to read "subject" and type the word "bibliography" in the search box. Your search should look similar to the one illustrated in figure 4.6.

When you complete your search, your results should look similar to those in figure 4.7.

Finding Bibliographies on the Internet

It can be somewhat difficult to find scholarly bibliographies on the Internet. Many reputable websites, historical and nonhistorical, include the word "bibliography" when referring to a list of sources included on their pages. If you enter the word "bibliography" as a keyword in a Google search, you are likely to see a list of sites that may include bibliographies but are not themselves bibliographies. Additionally, some search engines may confuse the words

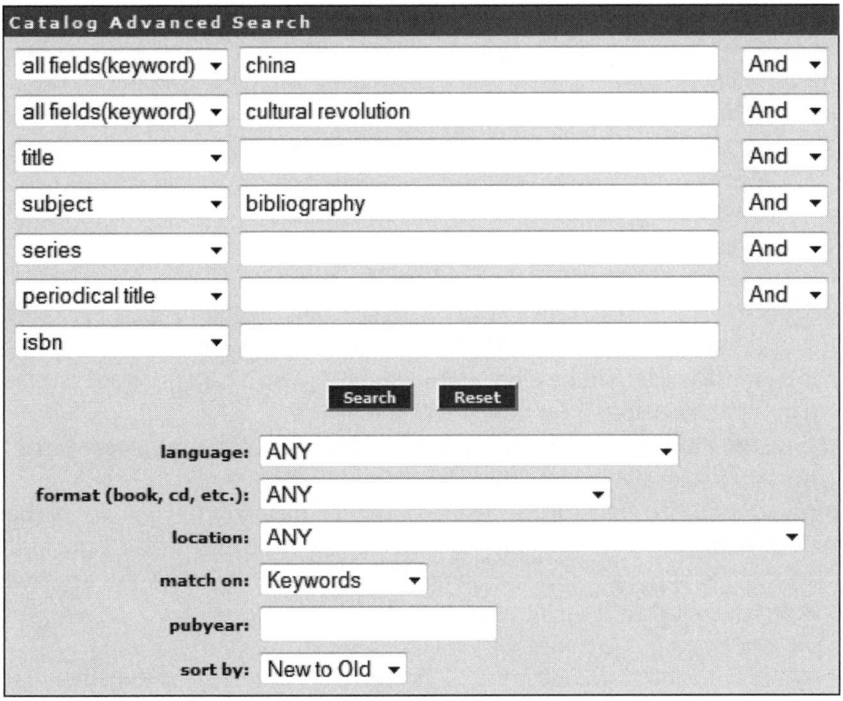

Catalog Advanced Search

all fields(keyword) ▼	china	And ▼
all fields(keyword) ▼	cultural revolution	And ▼
title ▼		And ▼
subject ▼	bibliography	And ▼
series ▼		And ▼
periodical title ▼		And ▼
isbn ▼		

[Search] [Reset]

language: ANY ▼
format (book, cd, etc.): ANY ▼
location: ANY ▼
match on: Keywords ▼
pubyear:
sort by: New to Old ▼

Figure 4.6.   Advanced Google Search for Bibliographies. Courtesy of Dickinson College SirsiDynix.

all fields(keyword) "china" AND all fields(keyword) "cultural revolution" AND subject "bibliography" search found 4 titles.

China during the cultural revolution, 1966-1976 : a selected bibliography of English language works
Chang, Tony H., 1951-
DS778.7 .C37 1999
1999
1 Item available in Reference Stacks, main level
▸ CLCD Review

The Cultural revolution : a bibliography, 1966-1996
Song, Yongyi.
DS778.7 .S66 1998
1998
2 Items available

The cultural revolution in China : an annotated bibliography
Wang, James C. F.
DS777.55 .W35 1976
1976
1 Item available in Book Stacks, main and upper level

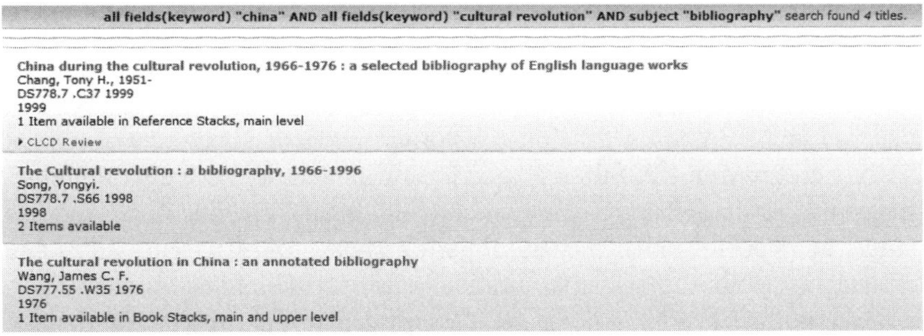

Figure 4.7.   Results of Google Search for Bibliographies. Courtesy of Dickinson College SirsiDynix.

"bibliography" and "biography," thus providing you with the wrong type of information. The easiest way to find bibliographies on the Internet is by taking advantage of your browser's advanced search option. For example, if you were looking for a bibliography on China's Boxer Rebellion using Google, you might construct a search using the following steps:

- Access Google's Advanced Search screen.
- Type the word "bibliography" in the box labeled "all these words."
- Type the words "Boxer Rebellion" in the box labeled "this exact wording or phrase." This will exclude any pages that mention either the words "boxer" or "rebellion" without the other word, pages that include both of those words separated by other words, and pages on which the word "rebellion" appears before the word "boxer."
- Type the word "biography" in the box labeled "any of the unwanted words" in order to exclude biographical pages from the results.
- A search for the Boxer Rebellion may include materials in Chinese. If you cannot read Chinese, you may want change the language option to include only a language you can read. For this example, English is the selected language option.

Figure 4.8 illustrates a search for a bibliography of the Boxer Rebellion using Google's advanced search feature. When you complete your search, the results should be similar to those shown in figure 4.9. As with all sources, be sure to subject any website you find to an evaluation of its credibility, as described in chapter 2.

MAPS AND ATLASES

Maps have been used throughout history to help people gain a sense of their location on the globe and to figure out how to get from one place to another. For the historian, though, history is about both time and space, and maps used in historical studies can reveal much more than location or distance. They are important tools in helping historians understand patterns of human location and movement, the influence of human activity on the surrounding geography, or the influence of geography on human behavior. Maps are important components in the successful performance of military operations and political campaigns. They are required in order to build reliable transportation systems, trade routes, and businesses. Maps can reveal growth and decline in population and wealth and can show patterns of weather and climate or

Google **Advanced Search**   Advanced Search Tips | About Google

bibliography "boxer rebellion" –biography

Find web pages that have...

all these words:	bibliography	
this exact wording or phrase:	boxer rebellion	tip
one or more of these words:		tip

But don't show pages that have...

| any of these unwanted words: | biography | tip |

Need more tools?

Reading level:	no reading level displayed ▾
Results per page:	10 results ▾
Language:	English ▾
File type:	any format ▾
Search within a site or domain:	
	(e.g. youtube.com, .edu)

⊞ Date, usage rights, region, and more

Advanced Search

Figure 4.8.   Catalog Search for a Bibliography. Courtesy of Google.

Google

bibliography "boxer rebellion" -biography   🔍

About 84,200 results (0.22 seconds)   Go to Google.com Advanced search

🔍 Everything
📷 Images
📹 Videos
📰 News
🛒 Shopping
More

The web
Pages from Australia
Custom

The **Boxer Rebellion**: bibliography 🔍
www.history.navy.mil/faqs/faq86-2.htm - Cached
22 Nov 2000 – **Boxer Rebellion**: A Select **Bibliography**. Related Resources: **Boxer
Rebellion** and the U.S. Navy, 1900-1901. Anderson, Johan Gunnar. ...

Boxer Rebellion: The Chinese React to Imperialism 🔍
www.u-s-history.com/pages/h902.html - Cached
Related Resources: Selected Documents of the **Boxer Rebellion Bibliography** on the
Boxer Rebellion Battle Streamer: China Relief Expedition 1900-1901 Medal: ...

VoS: The **Boxer Rebellion** 🔍
vos.ucsb.edu/browse.asp?id=4162 - Cached
Fei Ch'i-hao The **Boxer Rebellion**, 1900 (English translation of Chinese historical ... **Boxer
Rebellion** (Third China War) 1900 (articles, maps, **bibliography**, ...

Figure 4.9.   Results of Catalog Search for a Bibliography. Courtesy of Google.

health and disease. Historians frequently use maps to explain where people settled and what parts of an area's landscape made it a desirable place to live and work. In short, maps are indispensible tools for helping us visualize and understand the connections among the many factors that influence the course of history. There are many different types of maps, a few of which are described in table 4.4.

Maps may be available as single documents in print or online, or they may be gathered into sets collected in books known as *atlases*. The maps included in atlases are usually related in some way, by region, era, or event. The advantage of consulting an atlas over an isolated printed map is that atlases can depict changes in landscape and geography over time, whereas a single print map can represent only a single moment and only a few selected features. Examples of atlases include the following:

Archer, J. Clark, et al. *Historical Atlas of U.S. Presidential Elections, 1788-2004*. Washington, DC: CQ Press, 2006.
Curtis, Adrian. *Oxford Bible Atlas*. 4th ed. New York: Oxford University Press, 2009.

Atlas: A collection of maps, usually in book form.

Table 4.4.   Types of Maps

Type of Map	Description
Climate	Shows weather patterns and climate change.
Demographic	Displays population distribution and settlement patterns.
Directional	Tells you how to get from one place to another and what lies in between locations.
Economic	Shows economic indicators, such as per capita income, gross domestic product, income of industrial and service sectors, inflation, and unemployment.
Physical	Displays major geographic features such a land formations, borders, bodies of water, countries and major cities.
Political	Displays the borders between countries and states, as well as the results of voting patterns, party affiliations, and other political events.
Topographical	Shows the physical features and relief of an area, including elevation, land formations, and the depth of bodies of water.
Transportation	Shows land and water routes as well as industrial and urban growth and development.

Before using a map as evidence for a research project, you must make sure that you understand what information the creator of the map is trying to convey and for what reason. Misinterpreting a map could distort your understanding of history and cause you to draw incorrect conclusions. Clues to the purpose of the map usually are available in its accompanying captions and legend. The caption will explain the purpose of the map, and the legend will explain the meanings of colors and patterns, orient the map directionally, and provide a scale to help measure distances. For example, the map illustrated in figure 4.10 shows the positions of the Union and Confederate armies at the Battle of Ball's Bluff, Virginia, on October 21, 1861, during the United States Civil War. On this map, the dashed lines indicate the positions of units of the Union army, while the solid lines indicate the positions of the Confederate army. Mapmaking convention usually assumes that North is up if there is no directional symbol stating otherwise.

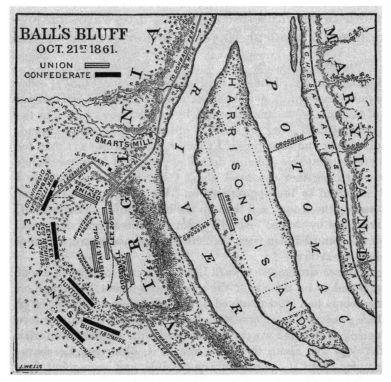

Figure 4.10. Map showing the positions of the Union and Confederate armies at the Battle of Ball's Bluff, VA, October 21, 1861. Courtesy of House Divided: The Civil War Research Engine at Dickinson College.

GIS Maps

In addition to two-dimensional maps appearing online, you may also find in databases or on the Internet examples of multilayer or interactive maps that are built with Geographic Information Systems (GIS) technology. GIS is a mapmaking technology that allows geographical areas to be studied with greater accuracy by combining traditional maps with new advances in database systems and digital mapmaking tools. Some GIS maps provide three-dimensional views of a region, while others provide interactive features that allow you to examine a space at ground level as well as from an elevated point of view. Most include metadata that provide statistics or additional historical context presented in the form of text blocks or audio or video files. The advantage of GIS for historians is that it allows many facets of information to be incorporated on to one map and then displayed or hidden depending on what specific elements you want to focus upon; it also allows different views of one geographic area to be compared. In short, GIS technology allows historians to see factors of historical significance that would otherwise have to be examined separately and to draw connections between incidents that initially may seem disparate.

Figures 4.11 and 4.12 are examples of maps showing drastically different views of the same geographic area, Pine Grove Furnace in Cooke, PA. In the seventeenth century, Pine Grove Furnace was the location of Pine Grove Iron Works, a company that produced cast-iron products for the home and railways. The region is now a state park where visitors can engage in outdoor recreational activities such as fishing and hiking.

The traditional topographical map in figure 4.11 shows the broad features of the Pine Grove Furnace area: the region's approximate land elevation, major roads and trails, mountain formations, and bodies of water including Fuller Lake, which was the source of the company's iron ore. This map alone, however, does not reveal the whole story of the Pine Grove Iron Works' effect on the area's environment. In contrast, figure 4.12 shows a recent and different view of the same region of Pine Grove Furnace. This map was created with Light Detection and Ranging (LiDAR) technology, a system that precisely measures distance and elevation with pulses of light.

In figure 4.12 we can more clearly see the remains of the Pine Grove Iron Works, including the location of the furnace itself, the mines from which quartz was taken to insulate the furnace stack, the pits from which sandstone was taken to make molds for iron products, and the piles of waste produced by the ironmaking process. These features of the landscape are not so obvious in the traditional map shown in figure 4.11. By studying the two maps together, we start to gain a comprehensive understanding of the Pine Grove Iron Works: why the business grew where it did, how the area was used, how

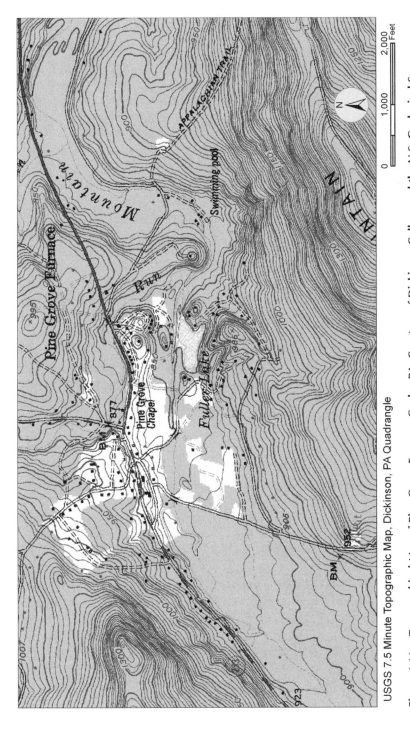

USGS 7.5 Minute Topographic Map, Dickinson, PA Quadrangle

Figure 4.11.   Topographical Map of Pine Grove Furnace, Cooke, PA. Courtesy of Dickinson College and the U.S. Geological Survey.

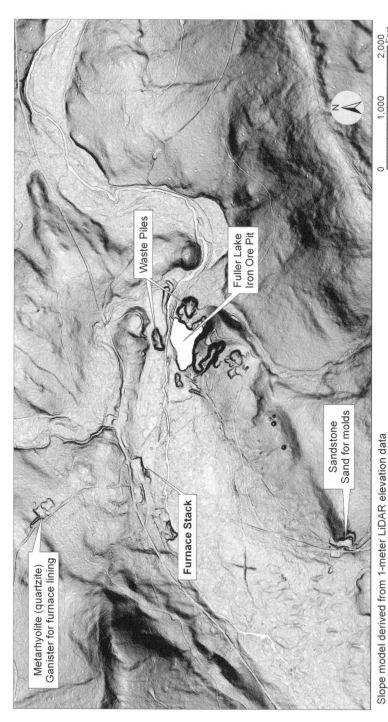

Slope model derived from 1-meter LiDAR elevation data

Figure 4.12.   Slope Map of Pine Grove Furnace, Cooke, PA. Courtesy of Dickinson College and the PAMAP Program of the Pennsylvania Department of Conservation and Natural Resources, Bureau of Topographic and Geologic Survey.

the business operated, how material and products moved around the region, and, ultimately, the business's lasting effects on the land.

Whether created by hand or with technology, maps graphically reveal causes and effects in history that may not otherwise be immediately obvious. Their visual representation of history provides unique context that is not possible to observe when considering a topic by way of text alone. The following sections will help you locate maps of all kinds.

Finding Maps and Atlases in a Library Catalog

Before following these steps, access your local library's online book catalog and be sure that you are using the Advanced Search or More Options screen. See chapter 5 for more information about accessing a catalog's advanced search screen.

- In the Keyword search box, type a term that broadly describes the continent, country, state, city, community, or other type of area you are researching. For example, you might use "Europe" or "Africa."
- Optionally, to make your search more precise, you can change the next search field to read "keyword" and type a term that more closely describes the era you are researching. For example, you might add "Medieval" to Europe or "Colonial" to Africa.
- In the Title search box, type either "map" or "atlas." Alternatively, you can type "geography" in a Subject search box. Your search should look similar to the one illustrated in figure 4.13.

When you complete your search, your results should look similar to those in figure 4.14.

Finding Maps and Atlases on the Internet

Maps are available in abundance on the Internet. To find them, you need only know the region and historical time period you want to examine and enter that information into your browser's search screen. Many of the secondary source websites mentioned in chapter 5 also include maps. Table 4.5 lists some websites that provide free current and historical maps and atlases.

BOOK REVIEWS

When a history book is newly published, other scholars who are experts in the same area of study may review it. A *book review* is a brief evaluation

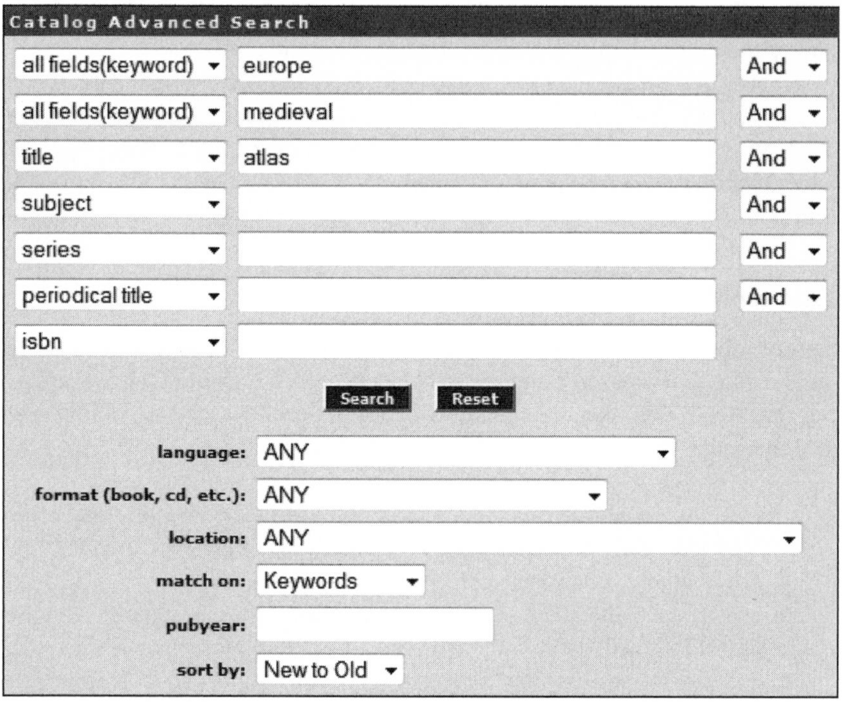

Catalog Advanced Search

all fields(keyword) ▼	europe	And ▼
all fields(keyword) ▼	medieval	And ▼
title ▼	atlas	And ▼
subject ▼		And ▼
series ▼		And ▼
periodical title ▼		And ▼
isbn ▼		

Search   Reset

language: ANY ▼
format (book, cd, etc.): ANY ▼
location: ANY ▼
match on: Keywords ▼
pubyear:
sort by: New to Old ▼

Figure 4.13.   Catalog Search for Atlases on Medieval Europe. Courtesy of Dickinson College and SirsiDynix.

all fields(keyword) "europe" AND all fields(keyword) "medieval" AND title "atlas" search found 7 titles.

The medieval world : an illustrated atlas
National Geographic Society (U.S.)
G1791 .N2 2009
2009
1 Item available in Oversized Book Section, upper level

Atlas of medieval Europe 2nd ed. / edited by David Ditchburn, Simon MacLean and Angus Mackay.
Ditchburn, David, 1961-
G1791 .M2 2007
2007
1 Item available in Reference Stacks, main level

Atlas of medieval Europe
MacKay, Angus, 1939-
G1791 .M2 1997
1997
1 Item available in Book Stacks, main and upper level
▶ CLCD Review

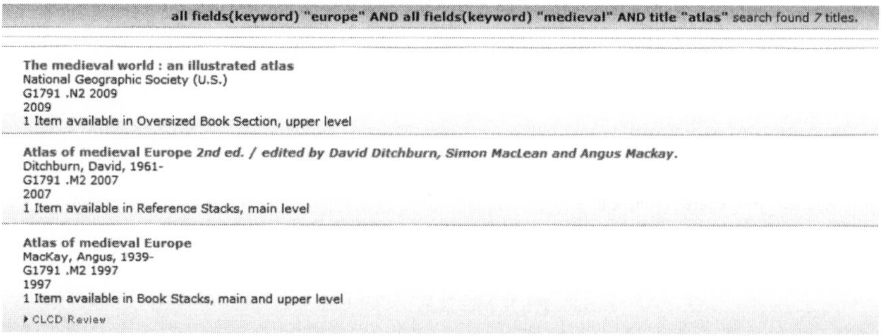

Figure 4.14.   Results of Catalog Search for Atlases on Medieval Europe. Courtesy of Dickinson College and SirsiDynix.

Table 4.5. Free Online Maps and Atlas Collections

Title	Time Period	Description
Ancient World Mapping Center http://www.unc.edu/awmc/	Ancient times	Displays ancient maps from a variety of online collections and atlases.
Atlapedia Online http://www.atlapedia.com	Present	Maps and brief historical background and information on every country in the world.
Atlas Obscura http://www.atlasobscura.com	Present	Maps of every country and various towns and cities within those countries.
David Rumsey Map Collection http://www.davidrumsey.com	1700s to 1800s	Rare maps of North and South America.
Google Maps http://maps.google.com/maps	Present	Directional, latitude and longitude, mass transit, and walking maps, including satellite views.
Library of Congress, Geography & Map Division http://www.loc.gov/rr/geogmap/ gmpage.html	14th century to present	Housing more than 5 million maps, this collection includes cartographic and geographic information for all parts of the world, dating back to the 14th century.
Map History/History of Cartography http://www.maphistory.info/ index.html	1500 to present	Hundreds of links to sites that provide maps, organized by time period, topic, collection, and country.
National Atlas http://www.nationalatlas.gov	Present	Various maps of the United States that focus on different areas such as agriculture, geology, and environmental science.
National Geographic http://www.maps. nationalgeographic.com/maps	Present	Different kinds of world and regional maps, including interactive maps and some that are available for purchase.
Perry-Casteneda Library Map Collection: Historical Maps of the United States http://www.lib.utexas.edu/maps/	1600s to present	Historical U.S. maps representing early inhabitants, explorations, settlement, military, territory growth, and state maps. Also includes maps from around the world.
UN Atlas of the Oceans http://www.oceansatlas.org	Present	Extensive information and maps on all of the oceans in the world.

of a book's content, organization, merit, originality, value to the historical profession, style, and quality of research. It is one type of tertiary source that includes analysis and professional opinion. Although book reviews focus on the quality of the book's scholarship and new contribution to the body of scholarly knowledge, the reviewer usually will summarize a book's content as well. Not every published book is reviewed, but many are.

> **Book Review:** An evaluation of a book's content, organization, merit, originality, and contribution to scholarly literature.

Book reviews can help save you time as you try to determine whether a book has scholarly value and is relevant to your research project. The review may help you figure out if the book's information will be helpful, particularly if the book is not available at your own library. Before you request a book from another library or buy a copy, you can use a book review to find the thesis, scope, and summary of the book and to determine whether the book is respected by other historians. Book reviews for monographs about history can be found as a regular feature in print and online historical journals, in journals that publish book reviews exclusively, in databases, and in printed indexes.

Many history journals include a section devoted to the review of new books related to the journal's theme. An example of the table of contents of a journal that includes book reviews is illustrated in figure 4.15. In addition, there are some journals published for the exclusive purpose of reviewing books in history as well as other subjects. Examples of such publications, which may be available in your library in either print or online versions, are listed in table 4.6.

Finding Book Reviews in Databases

Book reviews usually are not printed in books, and therefore cannot be located through library catalogs or WorldCat. There are, however, many databases that can help you locate book reviews for modern books published between approximately the mid-1880s to the present. You can often find a Book Review search option somewhere on the advanced search option screen of many databases. Historical Abstracts does not offer a book review option, but you can find them using many other databases such as ProQuest, Ebsco-Host, or America: History and Life. To find book reviews using America: History and Life:

- Select the database's Advanced Search option.
- Type the title of the book for which you would like to read a review in the Keyword field. In America: History and Life, the Keyword field is labeled

CONTENTS OF VOLUME 49 ■ 925

Containment: Managing Street Prostitution in London, 1918–1959 332
Stefan Anthony Slater

Scottish Nationalism and Stuart Unionism: The Edinburgh Council, 1745 47
Jeffrey Stephen

Home and Politics: Women and Conservative Activism in Early Twentieth-Century Britain 826
David Thackeray

Winston Churchill's "Crazy Broadcast": Party, Nation, and the 1945 Gestapo Speech 655
Richard Toye

Scotland, Northern Ireland, and Devolution, 1945–1979 117
Graham Walker

Algernon Sidney's Calvinist Republicanism 753
Michael P. Winship

BOOKS REVIEWED

MICHAEL ALEXANDER. Medievalism: The Middle Ages in Modern England. (Julie Pridmore) 681

DANIEL ANLEZARK. Water and Fire: The Myth of the Flood in Anglo-Saxon England. (Catherine Cubitt) 143

TONY BALLANTYNE and ANTOINETTE BURTON, eds. Moving Subjects: Gender, Mobility, and Intimacy in an Age of Global Empire. (T. Whitlock) 206

LUKE BARBER and GREG PRIESTLEY-BELL. Medieval Adaptation, Settlement and Economy of a Coastal Wetland: The Evidence from around Lydd, Romney Marsh, Kent. (Linda E. Mitchell) 147

REID BARBOUR and CLAIRE PRESTON, eds. Sir Thomas Browne: The World Proposed. (Colleen E. Kennedy) 171

DAVID G. BARRIE. Police in the Age of Improvement: Police Development and the Civic Tradition in Scotland, 1775–1865. (Isabella Boyce) 460

Figure 4.15. Table of Contents in the *Journal of British Studies* including book reviews. Courtesy of University of Chicago Press.

Table 4.6. Book Review Sources

Review Source	Description
Booklist http://www.booklistonline.com	Published by the American Library Association, Booklist has over 8,000 multidisciplinary reviews each year available online and in print.
Choice http://www.cro2.org/	Provides around 7,000 book reviews each year across multiple disciplines. Reviews are concise, and each ends with a recommendation and a recommended audience. Reviewers are college and university faculty members.
Kirkus Reviews http://www.kirkusreviews.com/	Kirkus editors review about 6,000 books per year, including scholarly publications. Highly recommended books are marked with a star.
London Review of Books http://www.lrb.co.uk/	Long essays and scholarly reviews that address literature within its social, political, scientific, and historical contexts.
New York Review of Books http://www.nybooks.com/	Scholarly reviews and discussions on literature and culture from the *New York Times*.
Publisher's Weekly http://www.publishersweekly.com/ pw/reviews/	Publishes around 7,000 multidisciplinary book reviews each year. These concise reviews are written by published authors and scholars.

Select a Field (Optional). For example, you might use Doris Kearns Goodwin's *Team of Rivals*.

- Optionally, you might add the author of the book on a second Keyword line.
- Look for a field marked Type or Document Type and change the option to Book Review or Review. This will ensure that your results display only book reviews, and excludes all other types of documents.

Your search should look similar to that in figure 4.16. Your results should include citations similar to that illustrated in figure 4.17. Notice that the citation is marked with the term "Reviews," indicating that the source is a book review.

Many other databases for history and other subjects have an option similar to America: History and Life's document type, which can be used to narrow a search to specific types of documents, such as conference papers and doctoral dissertations, in addition to book reviews.

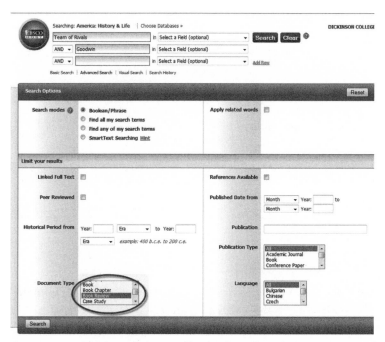

Figure 4.16.   America: History & Life's Book Review Limiter. Courtesy of EBSCOhost.

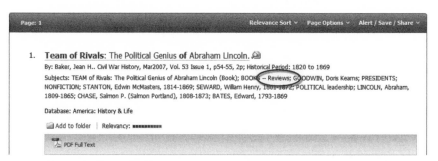

Figure 4.17.   Result of Book Review Search in America: History & Life. Courtesy of EBSCOhost.

Table 4.7. Book Review Indexes

Title	Publisher	Start of Publication
An Index to Book Reviews in the Humanities	Phillip Thompson	1960
Book Review Digest	H. W. Wilson	1905
Book Review Index	Gale	1965
Combined Retrospective Index to Book Reviews in Humanities Journals	Research Publications	1982
Combined Retrospective Index to Book Reviews in Scholarly Journals	Carrollton Press	1979
History: Reviews of New Books	Heldref Publications	1972
National Library Service Cumulative Book Review Index	National Library Service	1905
New York Times Book Review Index	New York Times	1896

Finding Book Reviews in Indexes

If you are looking for reviews of books published prior to the mid-1980s, you may not be able to find them by searching a database. Your library may not have databases that cover as far back as the book's publication year or the book might be too old to have been covered in a database. If you cannot locate reviews for an older book in a database, you might instead have to use printed indexes to find them. Indexes are described in more detail in chapter 5. Some indexes you might consult for book reviews are listed in table 4.7.

Consulting tertiary sources is the crucial first step in the research process. Using these sources will not only inform your knowledge of the topic you are researching but will also provide you with many leads for further scholarly reading and bibliography building. When you consult a variety of tertiary sources, you will start to consider your topic from angles you had not previously considered. Additionally, consulting tertiary sources as a first step in your research will leave you better prepared to gather, understand, and analyze secondary sources, your next step in the research process.

Chapter Five

Secondary Sources

Secondary sources provide summaries, analyses, commentary, and criticism of events in history based on the study and interpretation of primary sources. Although secondary sources can take various forms such as essays, films, and websites, your project likely will be made up mostly of articles, which are short treatments of a subject published in magazines or journals, and monographs, which are nonfiction books that explore a single subject in great detail.

> **Secondary Source:** A summary, analysis, commentary, or criticism of events in history based on the study of primary sources relating to those events.

Secondary sources are vitally important to the historical research process. They offer far more detail about any given topic than tertiary sources are designed to provide. Secondary sources show historians at work analyzing the arguments and controversies of history. By interpreting history, they powerfully influence the way we understand the evidence of past events. The authors of secondary sources put events in context, raise questions about why and how things occurred, link people and events to one another, reveal similarities between seemingly dissimilar events, and draw conclusions about how and why things happened. Secondary sources also help you place your primary sources within their historical context and thereby help you understand them better.

Examples of Secondary Source Books

Darnton, Robert. *The Great Cat Massacre and Other Episodes in French Cultural History.* New York: Basic Books, 1984.
Mitchell, Richard P. *The Society of Muslim Brothers.* New York: Oxford University Press, 1993.
Womack, Jr., John. *Zapata and the Mexican Revolution.* New York: Vintage Books, 1968.

Examples of Secondary Source Journal Articles

Brown, Elizabeth. "The Tyranny of a Construct: Feudalism and Historians of Medieval Europe." *American Historical Review* 79, no. 4 (1974): 1063–1088.
Thompson, E.P. "Time, Work-Discipline, and Industrial Capitalism." *Past & Present* 38 (1967): 56–97.

Classroom textbooks are not considered to be secondary sources and usually are not acceptable sources to cite as evidence in college and university level research papers.

SCHOLARLY VS. POPULAR SECONDARY SOURCES

Every source you ultimately include in your research project's footnotes and bibliography must in some way support your thesis. With any type of secondary source, particularly journals, some individual sources are more appropriate to use than others for scholarly historical research. Secondary sources usually are divided into two categories: *popular sources* and *scholarly sources*. Although there are circumstances under which a project might call for the use of popular sources, such as when one conducts a cultural study or seeks opinions about current events, most of the evidence for historical research should come from scholarly sources.

Popular Secondary Sources

Popular sources are produced mainly to entertain and inform the general public. They concern such broad subject matter as current events, news topics, controversy, entertainment, fashion, beauty, health, and sports.

Popular Source: A source of information that is produced mainly to entertain and appeal to the general public.

Popular books and articles usually are written in a casual tone by professional writers or journalists rather than scholars who study an academic subject for a living and write more formally. Popular secondary sources can be found on the shelves of newsstands, major book retailers, grocery stores, and convenience stores.

Popular journals or magazines are relatively easy to identify. Publications such as *Time* and *Newsweek* are examples of popular magazines. Though they do often address historical figures and events, the articles are almost always written by professional journalists who are employed by the magazines and may not have advanced degrees in history. Popular magazines usually are riddled with consumer advertisements for such things as household goods, pharmaceuticals, automobiles, and personal care products.

Scholarly sources, on the other hand, can be identified by the presence of a thesis, which is a statement laying out a scholarly argument and telling the reader how that thesis will be supported with evidence. Popular sources may lack a thesis. However, the most obvious clue that an item is a popular source is a lack of footnotes or a bibliography. Footnotes and bibliographies list the sources that the author used when conducting research in preparation for writing the book or article. More information about bibliographies and footnotes can be found in appendixes A and B.

Though popular magazines are relatively easy to distinguish from scholarly journals, popular history books may be somewhat more difficult to distinguish from scholarly history books. For example, the books *A Short History of Nearly Everything* by Bill Bryson, and *The Wordy Shipmates* by Sarah Vowell are examples of popular history books that have elements characteristic of scholarly sources, such as theses and bibliographies. In these cases, it is important to consider the book's intended audience and purpose for publication. Popular histories certainly are written to inform and even stimulate thinking, but usually in an entertaining way and always with the intent of making a profit for the author and publisher. Popular works are not expected to be reviewed by other scholars for their advancement of historical knowledge as scholarly sources are. The success of a popular work is generally measured by its sales revenue, whereas the success of a scholarly work is judged by how much it is cited and by what it contributes to the existing body historical knowledge. One good way to determine whether a book is scholarly is to read any reviews that have been published about it. For a popular book, a review will generally focus on its entertainment value and popular appeal. For scholarly works, the review will address the book's thesis, content, style, quality of research, and originality. Chapter 4 provides information about finding book reviews.

If you are in doubt about whether an item is scholarly or popular, ask an expert such as a professor or librarian. Although most books in the history section of a college or university library are scholarly, some are not, and you should examine all potential sources carefully to make sure that they are appropriate for your project.

Scholarly Secondary Sources

Secondary sources of the high academic quality needed for college research papers are referred to as scholarly sources. Scholarly secondary sources examine historical subjects from a serious, academic perspective, often in great detail. They may appear as full-length books, journal articles, or websites.

Scholarly secondary sources are easily discernable once you know what they should look like. As already noted, they are distinctly different from popular magazines or books produced for entertainment. Scholarly works contain a thesis and a bibliography, and will have an appearance that, in contrast to popular materials, is simple but serious. The language style of scholarly works is precise and formal. Authors who submit manuscripts of articles or books for publication have their work subject to strict review by an editorial board made up of other scholars who evaluate the submission for the quality of the scholarship. Scholarly works are published by well-respected academic presses often associated with a college or university, such as Oxford University Press and Harvard University Press. All images or illustrations, such as portraits, photographs, maps, architectural plans, or graphs are included to enhance the reader's understanding of the topic.

The reader of a scholarly secondary source usually can pick out a sentence or a paragraph that clearly identifies a work's goals and historical focus. As previously noted, this statement is called the thesis and it is often found within the preface, introduction, or first chapter of a book, or within the first few paragraphs of an article. The thesis tells you exactly what points will be addressed in the book or article. As it guides the flow of the book or article, you should find that every section of an article or chapter of a book in some way relates to the thesis statement. By skimming an article or book for the thesis statement, you will be able to determine quickly if that source is likely to be helpful for any given research project. Students of history should note that any projects completed for upper-level undergraduate courses or graduate courses should also be guided by original, well-developed thesis statements.

Finally, and most importantly, the author of a scholarly work is obligated to acknowledge when he or she has borrowed ideas and quotations from primary or secondary sources by including a bibliography and notes, usually footnotes or endnotes, in the body of the writing. Bibliographies are addressed in more detail in appendix A. Notes are used to indicate that the author has borrowed a direct quote or idea from another author and to provide the citations that lead the reader to the original source that the author quoted or paraphrased. You may be required to create citations using footnotes or endnotes. The rules for proper presentation are presented in the work according to the rules of the *Chicago Manual of Style*, published in print and online by the University of Chicago Press (see http://www.chicagomanualofstyle.org/home.html). More information about creating notes is in appendix B.

All serious secondary historical research works, including anything published on a website and any paper written for any class, should include notes and a bibliography. For a researcher beginning to look for the evidence needed to write his or her own paper, the bibliographies and notes other scholars provide can be indispensable because they offer the readers a ready-made list of sources to use to begin investigating the historical topic. A good researcher will carefully examine the bibliographies of secondary sources for ideas on where to look for additional evidence and will use library resources to track down copies of those cited sources. Figure 5.1 illustrates a Chicago-style bibliography on a website.

Figure 5.1. Bibliography of Secondary Sources. Courtesy of House Divided: The Civil War Research Engine at Dickinson College.

Scholarly secondary sources are almost always written by authors with academic credentials, such as a Ph.D. (doctor of philosophy, usually the highest degree conferred upon professors in the United States), many of whom also teach their subjects in colleges and universities. The author's credentials should be clearly listed somewhere within the work, such as at the bottom of the first page of an article, at the beginning or end of a book, or on a book's cover or jacket. If a hardcover book has had the book jacket removed, you may be able to find an image of it in the library's catalog record for the book or on the website of an online bookseller. Author credentials might look like the example in figure 5.2, in which multiple scholars contributed chapters to the book.

Scholarly journals, which are periodical publications containing individual articles written by academic experts, are highly specialized in subject matter and provide short but detailed studies of specific historical topics. Scholarly journals usually are available only at the libraries of colleges and universities that teach those specialized subjects, though a few are available by individual subscription. Scholarly journal articles are easily recognizable by certain characteristic elements that make them acceptable for use in an academic paper. As previously noted, they are written by college or university professors, are published by an academic press, and contain footnotes and bibliographies. Additional content will be limited to notices of job openings in the history profession, announcements of conferences and special events, or advertisements for databases and newly published books in the field of history. Most scholarly journals include a mission statement in the front cover of the journal or on the journal's website to explain the journal's purpose and scope. When deciding to use a journal article, you should look for these characteristics, regardless of whether the journal is published in print or online.

Figure 5.3 is the informational page from the online version of the *Journal of British Studies* showing the elements necessary to determine if the journal is scholarly. If a journal is online, you can click the About Us or Journal Information button to find the journal's description; if the journal is in print, this information should appear within the first few pages of any issue.

Many scholarly journal articles are subject to a special evaluation process known as *peer review*. Articles submitted to a peer-reviewed journal are evaluated by a panel of academic specialists with expertise similar to the author's. Along with a chief editor, this panel of reviewers judges the academic significance and uniqueness of the article and whether or not the article fits within the journal's scope. To prevent personal bias in the publication decision, this process usually is done in a manner called double blind review, meaning that neither the reviewers nor the author know who the others are. Articles submitted for consideration may be rejected if they do not meet the journal's standards. Those that are accepted usually go through heavy revi-

CONTRIBUTORS

STEPHEN BELYEA is currently head of the Art Department at Boston's Cathedral High School, where he also teaches classes focusing on issues of racism in America. He has been involved in "living history" projects for more than twenty years.

MARTIN H. BLATT is the Chief of Cultural Resources/Historian at Boston National Historical Park. Among his books are *Free Love and Anarchism: The Biography of Ezra Heywood* (1989) and (co-editor) *The Meaning of Slavery in the North* (1998). A leader in the field of public history for two decades, he has developed museum exhibits, popular publications, audiovisual productions, and a variety of special programs.

DAVID W. BLIGHT, Professor of History and Black Studies at Amherst College, has written widely on abolitionism, American historical memory, and African American intellectual and cultural history. Among his many works is *Frederick Douglass's Civil War: Keeping Faith in Jubilee* (1989). His most recent book is *Race and Reunion: The Civil War in American Memory* (2001).

THOMAS J. BROWN, Assistant Professor of History at the University of South Carolina, is the author of *Dorothea Dix, New England Reformer* (1998).

THOMAS CRIPPS, University Distinguished Professor retired at Morgan State University, has written five books, among them *Slow Fade to Black: The Negro in American Film, 1900–1942* (1997). He also has authored many articles and television scripts, including *Black Shadows on a Silver Screen* (1976), which won gold medals at several international film festivals. He has been a fellow of the Rockfeller, Guggenheim, and Daedalus Foundations, the Woodrow Wilson International Center, and the National Humanities Center.

KATHRYN GREENTHAL, former Assistant Curator in the Department of American Paintings and Sculpture at the Metropolitan Museum of Art, is a Trustee of the Augustus Saint-Gaudens Memorial in Cornish, New Hampshire. She also was a member of the committee formed in 1980 to restore the Shaw Memorial. Among her publications are *Augustus Saint-Gaudens: Master Sculptor* (1985); *American Figurative Sculpture in the Museum of Fine Arts, Boston* (1986) (coauthor); and "Augustus Saint-Gaudens et la sculpture américaine," in *Augustus Saint-Gaudens 1848–1907: Un maître de la sculpture américaine* (1999).

321

Figure 5.2. Authors' Credentials in a Secondary Source. Courtesy of University of Massachusetts Press.

sion based on the panel's evaluation before the final version is published. Many databases allow you to limit your search only to journals that are peer reviewed. More information about limiting your searches in databases can be found in chapter 7. For a list of some well-known scholarly academic publishers and journal titles, see appendix C.

Figure 5.3. "About" Page for the Journal of British Studies. Courtesy of University of Chicago Press.

Peer Review: A process by which books and articles are reviewed by a group of experts to determine if the item is fit for publication in a scholarly journal.

FINDING SECONDARY SOURCE BOOKS

Secondary sources are most easily found in library catalogs and databases. These sources not only provide all of the citation information required to retrieve helpful research material, such as title and author, but they also provide additional descriptive information that will help you determine whether or not that material is relevant to your topic. Titles alone often are not descriptive enough to reveal whether an item will be relevant and specific enough to address a particular research project. Tables of contents, summaries, and critical reviews are examples of the added value that many library catalogs and databases provide about the sources they contain.

Secondary sources often will make up the bulk of your bibliography, especially for shorter research projects. It is critical to examine a variety of secondary sources before deciding which ones to include in your bibliography. Some secondary sources initially may appear to be relevant but ultimately prove less useful after closer investigation. Taking the time to examine a variety of sources and consider various perspectives about your topic not only demonstrates that you did your research carefully and thoughtfully, but also provides you with a solid knowledge of your topic and allows you to form your own opinions about it. For more information about how to examine secondary sources efficiently, see appendix E.

There are thousands of secondary sources available on any historical topic and many sources in which to find them. Most of them should come from your institution's library and some may have to be obtained from other libraries through sharing services. Most researchers should start the search for secondary source books in a library catalog or WorldCat for books; for articles, use either of the databases—America: History and Life or Historical Abstracts—depending on which is appropriate for the topic. Many good secondary sources also can be found on the Internet. The following sections describe some of the search techniques you can use to locate secondary sources.

Finding Secondary Source Books in Library Catalogs Using Basic and Advanced Search Screens

A library's catalog is the first source to consult when seeking books for a history research project. An online catalog is a database of materials owned by and stored in that particular library. Most college, university, and public libraries make their catalogs accessible on their websites at no cost, and they are often accessible by the general public.

Once you access a library catalog by clicking on its link, which should be featured prominently on the library's website, you will be able to perform a simple search for books and other materials in that library by typing words that describe your topic in the search boxes provided. Although different library catalogs vary in appearance, they all work in more or less the same way.

The initial search screen of many library catalogs display what is known as a basic search, meaning that your search options are limited. As shown in figure 5.4, a basic search screen usually provides only one line on which to type general terms relating your search. If you need multiple words or phrases to describe what you are looking for, it is best to separate each distinct word or phrase by the word "and."

Alternatively, a library catalog may present you with an advanced search screen. The difference between a basic search and an advanced search is the number of search options available to you. While a basic search screen usually provides you with only one textbox in which to type your keywords, an advanced search screen provides multiple search boxes that allow you to make the search quite specific. If the first screen the library provides is a

Figure 5.4.   Library Catalog Basic Search Screen. Courtesy of Lehigh University.

basic search screen, you may be able to access additional search options by clicking a More Options or Advanced Search link, similar to the link visible in figure 5.4. An advanced search screen will look similar to the one shown in figure 5.5.

Advanced search screens are useful and efficient if you know exactly what you need, such as when you are seeking a specific item by its title or author. If you have that information, simply type it on the appropriate line and click Search or press the Enter key. You will find the desired item more quickly

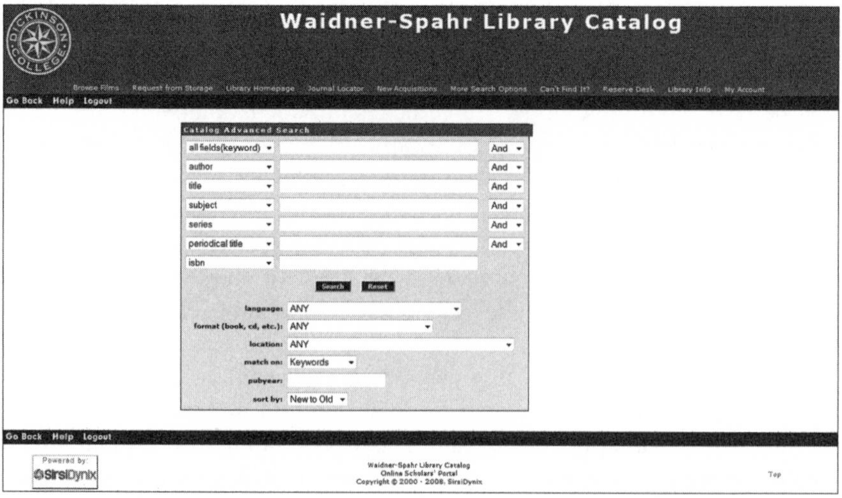

Figure 5.5.   Library Catalog Advanced Search Screen. Courtesy of Dickinson College and SirsiDynix.

that way. Usually, a catalog's options will allow you to search by some or all of the following elements:

- Author or editor of item.
- Title of item.
- Language of book. This feature is particularly useful if your search produces many results in a language or languages you cannot read.
- Series title. This refers to a sequence of books published under a special topic or theme, tied together with an overarching title. For example, the *Bedford Series of History and Culture* is a series of books that combine critical analysis with primary source documents. Books in this series include *Napoleonic Foot Soldiers and Civilians: A Brief History with Documents* by Rafe Blaufarband and *Religious Transformations in the Early Modern World : A Brief History with Documents* by Merry E. Wiesner.
- Location of item in the library.

Other advanced search fields and techniques are discussed throughout this book. Many library catalogs provide more information about the library's materials besides just the title, author, and location. Often, titles alone are not descriptive enough to reveal whether the book will be relevant and specific enough to address a particular research project. Therefore, you should pay attention to the additional information that many library catalogs provide about the books, such as a table of contents, a summary, or a critical review. Figure 5.6 shows an example of a book's catalog record with added value provided. Note that these features may not be available for older books, particularly those published before the 1990s.

If you are a student searching the library catalog of your own college or university library, you should be able to check out most of the books you find and take them home with you for a specified period of time. If you are a not a student or a registered borrower at the library in which you are searching and you wish to check out a book, ask a librarian for that library's specific rules for borrowing books and using other resources.

Call Numbers

Printed books in most U.S. libraries are arranged on shelves according to their *call numbers*. A call number is a code devised of letters and numbers that libraries use to arrange books on the shelves. These can be found in the catalog record for the book and on a sticker on the book's spine. Call number systems divide books into categories by general subject area. Every book in a library has a unique call number.

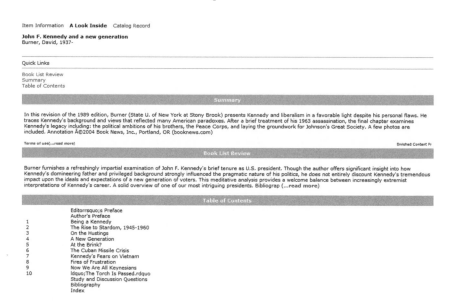

Item Information   **A Look Inside**   Catalog Record

John F. Kennedy and a new generation
Burner, David, 1937-

Quick Links

Book List Review
Summary
Table of Contents

Summary

In this revision of the 1989 edition, Burner (State U. of New York at Stony Brook) presents Kennedy and liberalism in a favorable light despite his personal flaws. He traces Kennedy's background and views that reflected many American paradoxes. After a brief treatment of his 1963 assassination, the final chapter examines Kennedy's legacy including: the political ambitions of his brothers, the Peace Corps, and laying the groundwork for Johnson's Great Society. A few photos are included. Annotation Â©2004 Book News, Inc., Portland, OR (booknews.com)

Terms of use(...read more)   Enriched Content Pr

Book List Review

Burner furnishes a refreshingly impartial examination of John F. Kennedy's brief tenure as U.S. president. Though the author offers significant insight into how Kennedy's domineering father and privileged background strongly influenced the pragmatic nature of his politics, he does not entirely discount Kennedy's tremendous impact upon the ideals and expectations of a new generation of voters. This meditative analysis provides a welcome balance between increasingly extremist interpretations of Kennedy's career. A solid overview of one of our most intriguing presidents. Bibliograp (...read more)

Table of Contents

	Editorrsquo;s Preface
	Author's Preface
1	Being a Kennedy
2	The Rise to Stardom, 1945-1960
3	On the Hustings
4	A New Generation
5	At the Brink?
6	The Cuban Missile Crisis
7	Kennedy's Fears on Vietnam
8	Fires of Frustration
9	Now We Are All Keynesians
10	ldquo;The Torch Is Passed.rdquo
	Study and Discussion Questions
	Bibliography
	Index

Figure 5.6.   Catalog Record with Added Value. Courtesy of Dickinson College and SirsiDynix.

Call Number: A code used by libraries to indicate a book's location in the building. It is usually found on the spine of the book and is matched in the library's catalog.

Call numbers are numbering systems composed of letters, ordinal numbers, and decimal numbers. Though they might seem complicated at first glance, call numbers are logically designed to keep books of a similar topic in close proximity to each other on the bookshelves. In general, the easiest way to use a call number to locate a book is to break it down by its natural divisions of spaces, dots, and transitions from numbers to letters or vice versa. Each part of the call number represents some element of the book—the subject area, author or editor, and publication year. Most libraries use either the Library of Congress system, which always begins with a letter, or the Dewey Decimal system, which always begins with a number.

Library of Congress Classification System

Many colleges and universities use the Library of Congress system, in which book subjects are divided into twenty-one categories, including general knowledge, science and technology, social sciences, the arts and humanities, and military science. Each subject category begins with a letter. In libraries that use the Library of Congress classification system, most books that pertain to history will begin with one of the following letters:

C: Auxiliary Sciences of History
D: World History and History of Europe, Asia, Africa, Australia, New Zealand, etc.
E: History of the Americas (United States)
F: History of the Americas (Local United States history, Canada, and South America)

Call numbers in the Library of Congress system look like these examples:

The History of the Decline and Fall of the Roman Empire by Edward Gibbon. Library of Congress Call Number: DG311 .G5 1994b.
A Thousand Days: John F. Kennedy in the White House by Arthur M. Schlesinger, Jr. Library of Congress Call Number: E841 .S3 2002.
A Nation of Enemies: Chile Under Pinochet by Pamela Constable. Library of Congress Call Number: F3100 .C64 1993.

The entire Library of Congress system breakdown can be found on the Library of Congress website at http://www.loc.gov/catdir/cpso/lcco/. In order to illustrate the use of Library of Congress call numbers to locate a book, let us examine a book entitled *The Influence of Sea Power upon History* by Alfred Thayer Mahan. Mahan's book was found in the catalog of the Library of Congress with the following call number: D215 .M342 2004. In the Library of Congress Classification System, the call number for *The Influence of Sea Power upon History* breaks down as follows:

D	D denotes World History. In some cases, a Library of Congress call number will start with two letters, the second of which represents a subdivision of the first broad category. DT, for example, denotes the history of Africa.
215	The first set of numbers denotes a more specific historical era. D215 represents general modern world history from 1450 to the twentieth century.
M342	This section represents the author. The letter represents the first letter of the author's last name. The number immediately following the letter further subdivides the section so that the author is situated more or less in alphabetical order within the entire list of authors who have written about naval tactics in world history and whose last names begins with M.

2004   The last four digits represent the year in which the book was published. The year represents specific editions of the book. Therefore, as in this case, the book may be a newer reprint, not a version from its original publication year, which for Mahan's book was 1890.

We would use the following steps to locate this book:

- Write down the entire call number of the book you need, along with its title, author, and publication year.
- Locate a map of your library's building. If not prominently displayed, a library's help desk or website can direct you to one. Your library's stacks should follow an alphabetical organizational scheme by call number. Use the first letter of your call number to find the section in which your book is located. For our example, look for the section containing books beginning with the letter D. If your call number starts with two letters, such as DT, you would first locate the range of books beginning with D alone, then move along the stacks toward DA, then DB, then DC, and so forth until you reach DT.
- Continue to read the call number by its naturally occurring divisions where letters change to numbers and vice versa. For example, our call number is D215 .M342 2004, so after finding section D, look down the shelf from call numbers beginning with D1, then move along the shelves to D10, then D100 and so on until you reach those beginning with D215.
- After finding the range of books beginning with D215, scan the books on the shelf for next subdivision. Mahan's book will follow D215 A, D215 B, and so on through D215 M. Once there, look for D215 M1, D215 M10, D215 M100 and so on through D215 M342.
- If there are additional subdivisions in the call number, continue following the method of scanning the shelves at the subdivisions of letters and numbers.
- As the final set of numbers represents the book's publication year, simply select the correct edition of the book if there is more than one available.
- After selecting the book from the shelf, take a moment to make sure it is the one you wanted and that it is the correct edition and publication year.

Dewey Decimal Classification System

The Dewey Decimal system organizes books by breaking down knowledge into ten broad subject categories, including philosophy, religion, social sciences, technology, literature, and history. Each subject category begins with an ordinal number and continues with a series of decimal and whole numbers. In libraries that use the Dewey Decimal Classification System, most books that pertain to history begin with numbers from 900 to 999, as follows:

900: Geography & History
910: Geography & Travel
920: Biography, Genealogy, Insignia
930: History of Ancient World
940: General History of Europe
950: General History of Asia; Far East
960: General History of Africa
970: General History of North America
980: General History of South America
990: General History of Other Areas

Call numbers in the Dewey Decimal system look like these examples:

The History of the Decline and Fall of the Roman Empire by Edward Gibbon. Dewey Decimal Call Number: 937.09 G351d 1845.
A Thousand Days: John F. Kennedy in the White House by Arthur M. Schlesinger, Jr. Dewey Decimal Call Number: 973.922 K38WSC.
A Nation of Enemies: Chile under Pinochet by Pamela Constable. Dewey Decimal Call Number: 983.065 C765N.

A breakdown of the Dewey Decimal Classification System can be found at http://en.wikipedia.org/wiki/Dewey_Decimal_Classification. In order to illustrate the use of Dewey call numbers to locate a book, let us consider another book written by Alfred Thayer Mahan, entitled *The Influence of Sea Power upon the French Revolution and Empire, 1793–1812*, which has the following Dewey Decimal call number: 944.04 M27I 1892. In the Dewey Decimal Classification System, the call number for *The Influence of Sea Power upon the French Revolution and Empire, 1793–1812* breaks down as follows:

944   Books starting with 944 concern the general history of France & Monaco.
.04   The second part of the Dewey call number is a subdivision of the main topic area. This part of the call number is considered to be a decimal, hence the system's name.

M27I   This section represents the author and title of the book. The letter
         represents the first letter of the author's last name. The numbers
         following the letter further subdivide the section so that the author
         is situated more or less in alphabetical order within the entire list
         of authors who have written about naval tactics in French history
         and whose last names begins with M. If the author has several
         works in a subject area, the additional letter represents the first
         distinctive word in the title. In this case, the I stands for influence.
1892   The last four digits represent the year in which the book was
         published. The year represents specific editions of the book. In
         this case, the book is a version from its original publication year,
         which was 1892.

We would use the following steps to locate this book:

- Write down the entire call number of the book you need, along with its title,
  author, and publication year.
- Locate a map of your library's building. If not prominently displayed, a
  library's help desk or website can direct you to one. Your library's book
  stacks should follow a numerical organizational scheme by call number.
  Use the first part of your call number to find the section in which your book
  is located. For our example, look for the section containing books whose
  call numbers begin with 900.
- After you locate the section beginning with 900, scan the shelves for call
  numbers beginning with 901, 910, 940, 941, and so forth until you reach 944.
- The books in the 944 range will be subdivided by the decimal numbers
  following the decimal point. To find *The Influence of Sea Power upon
  the French Revolution and Empire, 1793–1812*, look for 944.01, 944.02,
  944.03, then 944.04.
- Continue to read the call number by its naturally occurring divisions of
  dots and changes from letters to numbers and vice versa. After finding the
  range of books beginning with 944.04, scan the books on the shelf for next
  subdivision. Mahan's book will follow 944.04 A, 944.04 B, and so forth
  until 944.04 M. Once there, look for until 944.04 M1, 944.04 M10, 944.04
  M20 and so on until you reach 944.04 M27.
- As Alfred Thayer Mahan was a rather prolific author, you will at this point
  probably see several of his books on the shelf. To get to *The Influence of
  Sea Power upon the French Revolution and Empire, 1793–1812*, look for
  944.04 M27A, 944.04 M27B, and so forth until you reach 944.04 M27I.
- If there are additional subdivisions in the call number, continue following
  the method of scanning the shelves at the subdivisions of decimals, letters,
  and numbers.

- As the final set of numbers represents the book's publication year, simply select the correct edition of the book if there is more than one available.
- After selecting the book from the shelf, take a moment to make sure it is the one you wanted and that it is the correct edition and publication year.

Browsing for Books

When you find a useful book on the library's shelf, take a few moments to browse the titles of the other books on the same shelf, as well as those before and after it. As previously noted, a call number is assigned to a book according to its topic; therefore, you can often find additional relevant, useful, and interesting books in close proximity to the one you were originally seeking. Browsing can be a critical part of the research process because you may discover important sources for your project that you may not have found while searching the library's catalog. In addition to physically browsing a shelf, some library catalogs allow you to take a virtual walk through the book stacks by way of a *virtual browse*. A virtual browse feature allows you to examine online, via the library catalog, the titles of books shelved near the one that originally interested you. A virtual browse can be quite useful if you are not in the library building while conducting your catalog search. In addition to browsing by call number, some catalogs allow you to browse by author, title, or subject as well. Figure 5.7 illustrates a virtual browse option.

WorldCat

WorldCat is a free network that connects the catalogs of thousands of libraries around the world and allows you to search all of those catalogs at the same time. WorldCat can be accessed at http://www.worldcat.org. Its search screen is illustrated in figure 5.8.

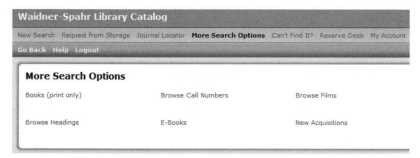

Figure 5.7. Virtual Browsing Search. Courtesy of Lehigh University.

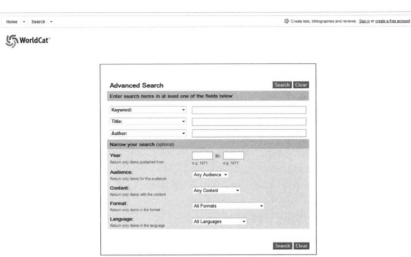

Figure 5.8. WorldCat Advanced Search Screen. Copyright 2011 OCLC Online Computer Library Center, Inc. Used with Permission. FirstSearch, OCLC, WorldCat, and the WorldCat logo are registered trademarks/service marks of OCLC.

Your library may have an enhanced subscription version of WorldCat, usually available on the library's database section of its website, which offers many advanced search features. More information about advanced search features in databases can be found in chapter 7. One of those features of WorldCat is an indicator telling you whether or not the item is available in your own library. If the item is available at your library, you should check your library's catalog for the call number, as described in the previous section. If the item is not available at your own library, you can ask a librarian to help you borrow the material through interlibrary loan services. Some public libraries have similar services.

In addition to books, WorldCat allows you to search for films, sound recordings, archival material, maps, musical scores, and journal titles, as shown in figure 5.9. To narrow your results in WorldCat by source type, simply click the corresponding check boxes before completing your search.

FINDING SECONDARY SOURCE JOURNAL ARTICLES

There are many databases available to help history researchers find secondary source articles on any topic in history. Although there are a few standard "go-to" databases for history research, you will never find the entire range of available information by relying solely on only one or two databases. Some-

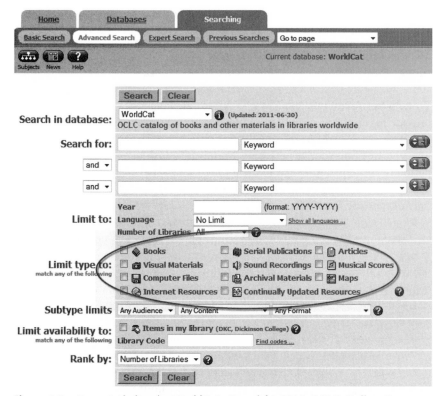

Figure 5.9. Format Limiter in WorldCat. Copyright 2011 OCLC Online Computer Library Center, Inc. Used with Permission. FirstSearch, OCLC, WorldCat, and the WorldCat logo are registered trademarks/service marks of OCLC.

times you will even have to search in sources that are technically outside the scope of history. You can almost always supplement your research by consulting databases that focus on your topic from different positions or that address it from a multidisciplinary point of view. Different databases may vary in appearance, but they all work in more or less the same way. Like library catalogs and Google, when you enter a search in a database, it will present you with a list of sources that relate to your search, which you can then further examine for validity to your research. Databases often first present you with a basic search screen that allows you to find sources by entering a few key words related to your topic. They also provide advanced screens that allow you to construct a search that is more focused and limited than the type of search you can create with a basic search screen.

Finding Secondary Source Articles in Databases
Using Basic and Advanced Search Screens

Most databases are easy to use and their initial search screens resemble the simple search box you find on Google. However, valuable research material sometimes may be missed when a database is not used to its fullest potential. To help improve your chances of finding relevant material, most databases provide a variety of advanced search features and options designed to help you improve the results of your search. For example, the database might allow you to limit your results only to items published within a certain time period or to items published in a particular language. Listed below are some advanced search features available in many databases.

Linked Full Text. When you check this option, the database will provide you only with items that are available in full text through the database you are searching. Checking this option will suppress items that your library owns in print and items that are supplied by other database companies. You should use this option only when you have a pressing need for full text material and cannot wait to obtain materials in print or through an interlibrary loan service.

Document Type. This option allows you to search by specific source type. You can use this feature to limit your results to articles, book chapters, complete monographs, book reviews, or dissertations.

Peer Reviewed. When you click on this option, the database will return only material that is published after being subjected to the peer review process.

Year Published. This feature allows you to limit your material by publication year. It is particularly useful when you want to view a snapshot of historical literature from specific time periods.

Language. If your search is likely to return material written in languages you cannot read, you can use this option to limit your results to materials written in a language you can read.

Some of the search features listed above, and other limiters not mentioned here, may use terminology that is unfamiliar to you, leaving you confused about what exactly the feature will do to improve your search. Because using advanced search features can have such a positive impact on your search by helping you to quickly identify only the items that are most relevant to your topic, it is a good idea to read the database's Help page before searching. If online help is not available for a particular database or if you still have questions about the database after reading the help section, see your librarian for assistance.

America: History and Life and Historical Abstracts

Although there are many possible databases to search for secondary source articles in history, most researchers should begin the search in one of two databases: America: History and Life or Historical Abstracts. America: History and Life and Historical Abstracts are the most important secondary source databases for history scholars. America: History and Life contains the citations of secondary articles, scholarly books, book reviews, and Ph.D. dissertations regarding the history and culture of North America from prehistory to the present. Historical Abstracts contains the citations of secondary scholarly articles, scholarly books, and Ph.D. dissertations about all of world history from 1450 to the present except for North America. These databases contain information from more than 1,700 academic historical journals published since the mid-twentieth century and cover materials published in more than forty languages. America: History and Life and Historical Abstracts are the authoritative databases for articles in history, and no research project on any historical topic that falls within their coverage range can be considered complete without them.

America: History and Life and Historical Abstracts not only contain the standard material needed for historical research, but they also provide ways of making your search more efficient via their advanced search options. It is a good idea to explore the Advanced Search screen and use as many of these options as possible, especially if your initial attempt at searching produces too many or too few results. America: History and Life and Historical Abstracts contain advanced search features that cannot be found on other databases.

One of the most notable features of America: History and Life and Historical Abstracts is the option to search a specific historical period by a range of years on the Advanced Search screen. The Historical Period option is particularly useful because it allows you to narrow the search if your topic covers a large span of time but you are interested only in certain years relating to a particular event. For example, a researcher might be interested in the Hundred Years War, but needs only to investigate the period known as the Lancastrian War, which lasted from 1415 to 1429. To research only this span, simply type "Hundred Years War" in the Select A Field box and narrow the search down to 1415 to 1429 in the Historical Period From and To boxes. Figure 5.10 illustrates the use of this feature. Another search feature unique to America: History and Life and Historical Abstracts is the References Available limiter. Checking this option will return only items that allow you to view their bibliographies in their descriptions.

America: History and Life and Historical Abstracts are two of the most important sources for secondary materials in history; however, it is not possible for them to contain all the relevant material ever published about history. Neither of these databases covers ancient or medieval history, for example. In addition, many history researchers study topics with elements that are technically outside the scope of what might be collected in a history database,

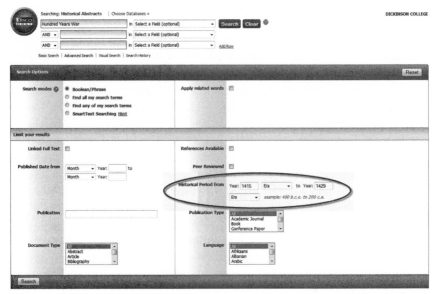

Figure 5.10.   Historical Abstracts Advanced Search Options. Courtesy of EBSCOhost.

but are nonetheless critical to a comprehensive understanding of a historical topic. Some of these subject areas might be cultural studies, literature, religion, political science, education, science, and the arts.

Other Secondary Source Databases

Researchers needing material outside the scope of America: History and Life and Historical Abstracts have numerous options with which to supplement their research. In fact, even subjects that America: History and Life and Historical Abstracts cover well must be supplemented with material from other databases in order to obtain a well-rounded account of the topic. Table 5.1 provides a list of some databases that are quite helpful for researching historical topics. All of the databases in the following list are available only by subscription, usually through academic libraries.

If your library subscribes to any of the databases listed in table 5.1, you should access them directly from the library's website in order to authenticate yourself as an authorized user of the product. Otherwise, you may be blocked from the database or asked to pay a fee to use it. If your library does not have access to these particular databases, there may be a comparable source that you can use instead. Be sure to ask your librarian for help if you are not sure whether your library subscribes to a database you want to use, if you cannot locate a database on the library's website, or if you are asked to provide payment to use a database.

FINDING SECONDARY SOURCE NEWSPAPERS

Many newspapers around the world have transformed the way they disseminate information. Since they have started publishing online, it is now quite easy to obtain up-to-the-minute news as well as past issues of articles that have been digitized and made available on the Internet. Many newspapers provide access to their articles in both the traditional print format as well as online editions that are updated at least once daily or even more frequently.

Most newspapers are not entirely freely accessible, even online. Many will offer limited free access to the most current news releases or headlines but charge for access to complete articles or older articles. If you try to access a newspaper article directly from its website and are asked to pay for it, check to see if your library has subscription access to it or to a comparable title. If your library subscribes to an online newspaper you want to read, be sure to access it directly from the library's website in order confirm that you are an authorized user of the newspaper and thus gain complete access to all current and past issues.

Some examples of newspapers from around the world that you can find online are listed in table 5.2. Most of these newspapers offer at least limited access to the news for free, and many include bonus features such as audio and video files, slide shows, and links to additional information. Unlimited access to many of the titles listed in table 5.2 are available through academic libraries. In addition to these direct newspaper links, the website Onlinenewspapers.com (http://www.onlinenewspapers.com) will help you find newspapers in countries around the world. If you are searching for the website of a specific newspaper, the easiest way to find it is to enter the title into your Internet browser's search box. If the title of the newspaper is common or vague, such as the *Daily News* or the *Times*, it helps to add the city of publication to your search.

Various databases collect articles from many different newspapers, historical and current, and make the articles easily searchable by subject, title, author, and date. Newspaper databases will help you find newspaper articles when you do not know which particular newspapers might provide useful articles. Table 5.3 lists some of the fee-based newspaper databases that may be available in your library. If your library subscribes to any of these sources, access them directly from the library's website in order to authenticate yourself as an authorized user of the product. Otherwise, you may be blocked

Table 5.1.   Subscription Databases for Historical Research

Title of Database	Publication Years	Description
American Bibliography of Slavic and Eastern European Studies (ABSEES) http://www.ebscohost.com/academic/american-bibliography-of-slavic-eastern-european-studies	1939 to present	Citations of journals, books, and select government publications from the United States and Canada regarding Central Europe and the former USSR.
Annee Philologique http://www.annee-philologique.com/aph/	1924 to present	All aspects of Greco-Roman history and culture.
Arts and Humanities Search http://thomsonreuters.com/products_services/science/science_products/a-z/arts_humanities_citation_index/	1980 to present	Citations to books and journal articles, and reviews in the humanities, including history.
ATLA Religion Database http://www.atla.com/products/catalog/Pages/rdb-db.aspx	1949 to present	Essays, book reviews, and journal articles that concern history of religion and its role in culture and society.
Bibliography of Asian Studies http://www.asian-studies.org/bassub.htm	1779 to present	Mostly western-language articles and book chapters on Asia.
British Humanities Index http://www.proquest.com/en-US/catalogs/databases/detail/bhi-set-c.shtml	1962 to present	A collection of scholarly journals and magazines on the humanities, including history. All materials cited originated in English-speaking countries.
Dissertation Abstracts http://www.proquest.com/en-US/catalogs/databases/detail/dai.shtml	1861 to present	Doctoral dissertations and master's theses from accredited colleges and universities in the United States and abroad. Covers all academic disciplines including history.
EBSCO Host http://www.ebscohost.com/	Prehistory to present	Specific subject coverage depends on your library's subscription level. Usually includes multidisciplinary subject areas in the humanities, sciences, and social sciences, including history.
Expanded Academic ASAP http://www.gale.cengage.com/PeriodicalSolutions/academicAsap.htm?grid=ExpandedAcademicASAPRedirect	1980 to present	Multidisciplinary subject areas in the humanities, natural sciences, and social sciences, including history.

Title of Database	Publication Years	Description
Handbook of Latin American Studies http://lcweb2.loc.gov/ hlas/mdbquery.html	1935 to present	English and non-English materials regarding Latin American history and culture.
Humanities Abstract and Humanities and Social Sciences Retrospective	1907 to present	Citations of articles and reviews covering topics in the humanities and social sciences, including history. Some versions of this database are known as Humanities Full Text and provide full-text copies of the articles in the database.
IMBO (International Medieval Bibliography Online) http://www.brepolis.net/	1967 to present	Interdisciplinary bibliography of the European Middle Ages, covering Europe, the Middle East, and North Africa in the period 400 to 1500.
Index Islamicus http://www.brill.nl/ indexislamicus	1906 to present	Citations to monographs, journal articles, and book reviews on Islam, the Middle East, and the Muslim world.
Iter: Gateway to the Middle Ages and Renaissance http://www.itergateway. org/	1784 to present	Citations of articles, essays, books, encyclopedia entries, reviews, and primary sources on the history and culture of the Middle Ages and Renaissance (400 to 1700).
JSTOR http://www.jstor.org	Prehistory to present	Full-text articles on multidisciplinary subject areas in the humanities, natural sciences, and social sciences, including history. Titles have "moving walls," meaning there is a time lag of 1 to 5 years between the last available issue and the most current issue.
Project Muse http://muse.jhu.edu/	Prehistory to present	Full-text articles from academic presses on multidisciplinary subject areas in the humanities and social sciences, including history. Coverage varies by subscription.
ProQuest http://www.proquest.com/	Prehistory to present	Citations and full-text of articles on multidisciplinary subject areas including the humanities, sciences, and social sciences, including history. Coverage varies by subscription.
Social Sciences Abstracts http://www.ebscohost. com/academic/social- sciences-abstracts	1983 to present	Citations of articles and reviews in the social sciences related to history, including political science and gender studies.
World History Collection http://www.ebscohost. com/academic/world- history-collection	1964 to present	Citations and full-text of articles on world history including Asia, North and South America, Europe, and the Middle East.

Table 5.2. World Newspapers

Newspaper	City	Description
Al-Ahram Weekly http://weekly.ahram.org. eg/	Cairo, Egypt	One of the largest newspapers in the world, primarily owned by the Egyptian government.
al-Hayat http://www.daralhayat. com	London, UK	Popular world-circulated newspaper covering Middle-Eastern issues. The website is entirely in Arabic.
Arab News http://www.arabnews. com/	Saudi Arabia	The first English-language newspaper established in Saudi Arabia, started in 1975.
Asharq Al-Awsat http://www.asharq-e.com/	London, UK	English-language Arab international newspaper.
Ballymena Times http://www. ballymenatimes.com/	Ballymena, Northern Ireland	A weekly newspaper sold around central County Antrim.
Corriere della Sera http://www.corriere.it/	Milan, Italy	Italian daily newspaper that started in 1876.
Daily Telegraph http://www.telegraph. co.uk/	London, UK	Major daily newspaper in Britain that is often conservative leaning.
Der Spiegel http://www.spiegel.de/ international/	Hamburg, Germany	Weekly magazine of German, European, and world news.
El Tiempo http://www.eltiempo.com	Bogotá, Colombia	Daily newspaper with the largest circulation in Colombia. Website in Spanish only.
El Universal http://english.eluniversal. com/	Caracas, Venezuela	Daily conservative newspaper, in both English and Spanish.
Frankfurter Allgemeine Zeitung http://www.faz.net/s/ homepage.html	Frankfurt, Germany	Germany's national daily newspaper.
Guardian http://www.guardian. co.uk/	Manchester, UK	Daily British newspaper founded in 1821, well known for its coverage of world news.
Gulf News http://gulfnews.com/	Dubai, United Arab Emirates	English-language international newspaper based in Dubai.
Haaretz http://www.haaretz.com/	Tel Aviv, Israel	An international source of news, available online in Hebrew and English.
Hindustan Times http://www. hindustantimes.com	New Delhi, India	A major English-language newspaper widely circulated in India.
Jerusalem Post http://www.jpost.com	Jerusalem, Israel	Daily English-language newspaper.

Newspaper	City	Description
Khaleej Times http://www.khaleejtimes. com/	Dubai, United Arab Emirates	Daily newspaper based in Dubai that focuses on the Gulf Region.
La Nación http://www.lanacion. com.ar/	Buenos Aires, Argentina	A major daily newspaper in Spanish only.
Le Figaro http://www.lefigaro.fr	Paris, France	The oldest daily newspaper in France. Website in French only.
Le Monde http://www.lemonde.fr/	Paris, France	An evening publication with the largest circulation in France. The website is in French only.
London Times http://www.thetimes. co.uk	London, UK	Daily British newspaper founded in 1785 with editions published around the world.
Moscow News http://www.mn.ru	Moscow, Russia	English-language newspaper with Moscow, Russian, and world news.
New York Times http://www.nytimes.com	New York, NY, United States	Founded in 1851, this newspaper covers U.S. and world news.
People's Daily of China http://english.peopledaily. com.cn/	Beijing, China	Official newspaper of China's Communist Party.
The Globe and Mail http://www.globeandmail. com	Toronto, Canada	Regarded as Canada's national newspaper, it covers a wide range of local, regional, national, and world news.

from the service or asked to pay a fee to use it. If your library does not have access to these particular sources, ask your librarian if there is a comparable source that you can use instead.

Many news services that require a subscription may be available only on the website of a college, university, or public library. There are, however, some free online newspaper sources, such as those listed in table 5.4, that may help you find newspapers from different countries and bygone time periods. You can find additional free newspaper sources on the Internet by searching the phrase "free newspaper archives."

Small town local newspapers, especially older issues, may not be covered in any online database or paper index. For historical newspapers, you should consult an archivist at the local historical society or archives associated with the person or event you are researching. Discussing your research project with an expert will help to ensure that you consult all possible sources of information. For more information about researching at historical societies,

Table 5.3.   Subscription-Based Newspaper Services

Source	Description
Alternative Press Index http://www.altpress.org	Covers leftist and radical publications newspapers and magazines dating back to the late 1960s.
Current Digest of the Post-Soviet Press http://www.eastview.com/cdpsp/	Russian language news sources translated into English. Includes sources from 2001; news prior to that is in Current Digest of the Soviet Press.
Ethnic News Watch http://www.proquest.com/en-US/catalogs/ databases/detail/ethnic_ newswatch.shtml	Archives of publications of ethnic and minority news dating back to 1990.
Factiva https://global.factiva.com/	Database provides full-text access to over 9,000 business and main news sources.
Historical Newspapers http://historynews.chadwyck.com/	Full-text access to the *London Times* from 1785 to 1870 and the *New York Times* from 1851 to 1923.
LexisNexis http://www.lexisnexis.com/	Covers United States and international newspapers going back to 1980. It also contains United States Congressional information, legal information, and statistical information.
Newsbank http://www.newsbank.com/	Contains more than 2,000 newspaper titles, as well as newswires, transcripts, and business journals, from the United States and international sources. Includes news video clips.
Newspaper Archive http://www.newspaperarchive.com/	Newspaper Archive contains millions of newspaper pages from 1759 to present. Includes newspapers from the United States as well as a few other countries including the United Kingdom and Canada.
Newspaper Source http://www.ebscohost.com/public/ newspaper-source	Full-text access to 70 U.S. and world newspapers, and select full-text articles from over 300 regional U.S. publications. Coverage starts in 1995.
Pennsylvania Gazette, 1728-1800 http://www.accessible.com/accessible/ aboutPG.jsp	Contains articles, editorials, and letters from this newspaper published in Philadelphia in the 18th century.
ProQuest http://www.proquest.com/en-US/	ProQuest provides current and historical newspaper products from the United States and countries all over the world. Coverage varies by subscription.
Regional Business News http://www.ebscohost.com/academic/ regional-business-news	Includes over 80 business journals and newspapers from around the United States.
SmallTownPapers http://www.smalltownpapers.com/	Covers local and small-town newspapers not usually included in national or international databases.

Source	Description
World History Collection http://www.ebscohost.com/public/world-history-collection	Full-text access to over 150 sources dating back to 1964. Coverage of Asia, North and South America, Europe, and the Middle East.
World News Connection http://wnc.fedworld.gov/	Produced for the United States Foreign Broadcast Service, a government agency that monitors and translates newspapers, radio and television broadcasts, and official statements of foreign governments. It covers from the mid-1990s to the present.

Table 5.4.   Free Online Newspaper Sources

Source	Description
British Library Online Newspapers http://www.uk.olivesoftware.com	Access to articles from the *Daily News, Manchester Guardian, News of the World,* and *Weekly Dispatch.* Mid-19th century to early 20th centuries.
Chronicling America: Historic American Newspapers http://chroniclingamerica.loc.gov/	Newspapers from 1860 to 1922, digitized by the Library of Congress.
Google News http://news.google.com/news/advanced_news_search?as_drrb=a	Though not entirely full text, Google's news archive is a good, free way to get started on newspaper research. Includes U.S. and international news sources.
Kenya Indexing Project http://www.indexkenya.org	Access to various Nairobi newspapers from 1986 to 2002.
Latin American Database http://ladb.unm.edu/	Full-text articles and journals on Latin American and Mexican topics. Collections back date to 1966.

see chapter 3. Some local papers are kept only by state archives or historical societies of the city or town in which they were published. If you do not know the name of a paper you need, you might be able to find out what newspapers have been published in the region you are researching by searching the website Online Newspapers.com at http://www.onlinenewspapers.com. Once you know the name of newspaper you need to consult, you may be able to find what libraries have the issues by searching WorldCat using the following steps.

- Access WorldCat at http://www.worldcat.org or use your library's sub-scription version.
- Choose the Advanced Search option. (See chapter 7 for information on us-ing advanced search features.)
- On the Keyword line, type the name of a town, county, city, state, or country in which newspapers likely related to your topic would have been published.
- In the format option, choose "newspaper." Your search should look similar to that in figure 5.11.

Your search should produce a set of results similar to those in figure 5.12. Once you get to a results list, you can find more detailed information about a newspaper by clicking on its title. This will reveal where the newspaper is preserved. For example, clicking on the *Cecil Democrat* in the list from figure

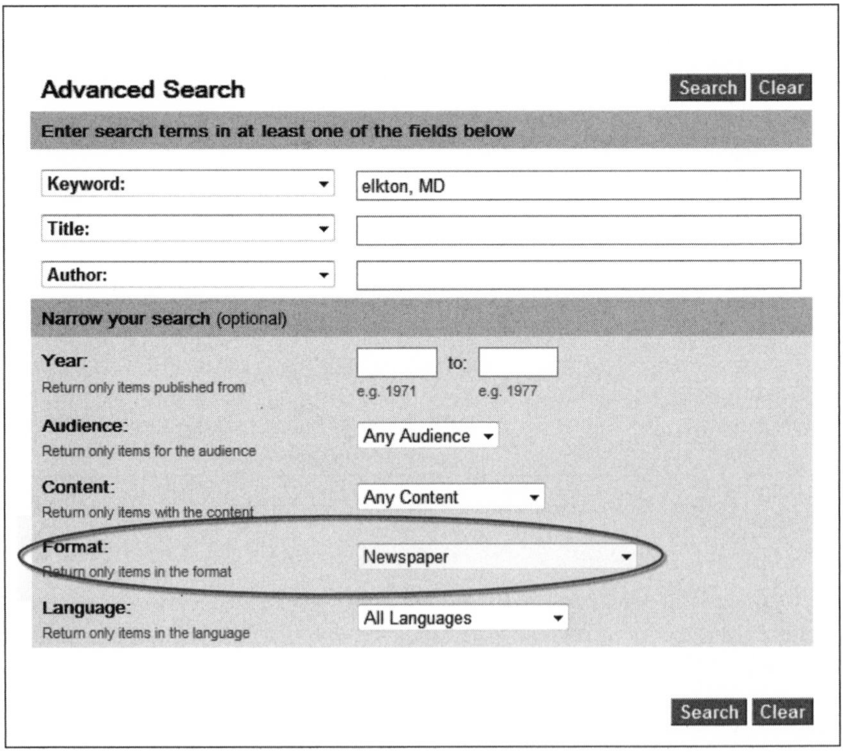

Figure 5.11.   Advanced Search for Newspapers in WorldCat. Copyright 2011 OCLC Online Computer Library Center, Inc. Used with Permission. FirstSearch, OCLC, World-Cat, and the WorldCat logo are registered trademarks/service marks of OCLC.

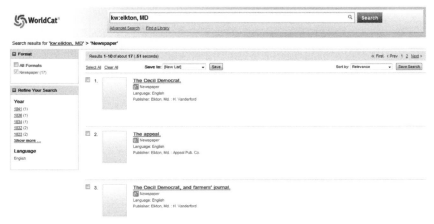

Figure 5.12. Results of Advanced Search for Newspapers in WorldCat. Copyright 2011 OCLC Online Computer Library Center, Inc. Used with Permission. FirstSearch, OCLC, WorldCat, and the WorldCat logo are registered trademarks/service marks of OCLC.

5.12 will display the locations that own copies of the newspaper, as shown in figure 5.13.

While searching in WorldCat is an effective way to find where materials may be held, it is not necessarily comprehensive. The accuracy of WorldCat relies on individual libraries uploading their holdings information to the database. The search above, for example, does not reveal that the *Cecil Democrat* is in fact held at the Historical Society of Cecil County. This is most likely because the historical society did not add records of its holdings to WorldCat, either because they are not connected to the service (which requires the payment of membership fees) or do not have a librarian on hand who can upload all of their holdings. It is important to keep in mind that it is your responsibility as a historian to check all possible sources of information on your topic.

Library	Held formats	Distance	
1. 🏛 **Enoch Pratt Free Library** Baltimore, MD 21201 United States	📄📰 Journal / Magazine / Newspaper	70 miles MAP IT	📖 Library info 🔖 Ask a librarian ♥ Add to favorites
2. 🏛 **Maryland Newsp Project, Cecil County** BALTIMORE, MD 20742 United States	📄📰 Journal / Magazine / Newspaper	85 miles MAP IT	📖 Library info ♥ Add to favorites
3. 🏛 **American Antiquarian Society** WORCESTER, MA 01609 United States	📄📰 Journal / Magazine / Newspaper	315 miles MAP IT	📖 Library info ♥ Add to favorites
4. 🏛 **American Antiquarian Society** WORCESTER, MA 01609 United States	📄📰 Journal / Magazine / Newspaper	315 miles MAP IT	📖 Library info ♥ Add to favorites
5. 🏛 **Brigham Young University** Harold B. Lee Library PROVO, UT 84602 United States	📄📰 Journal / Magazine / Newspaper	1800 miles MAP IT	📖 Library info ♥ Add to favorites

Figure 5.13. Holdings List for *The Cecil Democrat*. Copyright 2011 OCLC Online Computer Library Center, Inc. Used with Permission. FirstSearch, OCLC, WorldCat, and the WorldCat logo are registered trademarks/service marks of OCLC.

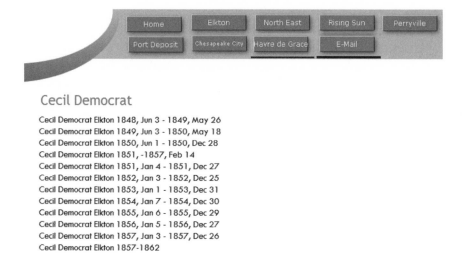

Cecil Democrat

Cecil Democrat Elkton 1848, Jun 3 - 1849, May 26
Cecil Democrat Elkton 1849, Jun 3 - 1850, May 18
Cecil Democrat Elkton 1850, Jun 1 - 1850, Dec 28
Cecil Democrat Elkton 1851, -1857, Feb 14
Cecil Democrat Elkton 1851, Jan 4 - 1851, Dec 27
Cecil Democrat Elkton 1852, Jan 3 - 1852, Dec 25
Cecil Democrat Elkton 1853, Jan 1 - 1853, Dec 31
Cecil Democrat Elkton 1854, Jan 7 - 1854, Dec 30
Cecil Democrat Elkton 1855, Jan 6 - 1855, Dec 29
Cecil Democrat Elkton 1856, Jan 5 - 1856, Dec 27
Cecil Democrat Elkton 1857, Jan 3 - 1857, Dec 26
Cecil Democrat Elkton 1857-1862
Cecil Democrat Elkton 1858, Jan 3 - 1858, Dec 25
Cecil Democrat Elkton 1859, Jan 1 - 1859, Dec 31
Cecil Democrat Elkton 1860, Jan 7 - 1860, Dec 29
Cecil Democrat Elkton 1861, Jan 5 - 1861, Dec 28
Cecil Democrat Elkton 1862, Jan 4 - 1862, Dec 27

Figure 5.14. Detail of Historical Society of Cecil County's Holdings of The Cecil Democrat. Courtesy of Historical Society of Cecil County.

Note also that the WorldCat record tells you only where the newspaper is held. It does not give you direct full-text access to the newspaper itself. Once you locate a source of information, you must take the necessary steps to access the material. This might involve borrowing material through your library's interlibrary loan service or taking a trip to a different library or historical society. Your librarian can help you identify the best method for obtaining research material.

In the case of the *Cecil Democrat*, it is possible to find more information about the newspaper on the website of the Historical Society of Cecil County. A list of their holdings for the newspaper, though not full-text copies, is available to the public via their website at http://www.cecilhistory.org/, as illustrated in figure 5.14. Anyone wishing to view copies of this newspaper would have to travel to the Historical Society of Cecil County or one of the other libraries listed in WorldCat.

FINDING SECONDARY SOURCE
JOURNAL ARTICLES IN PRINTED INDEXES

Printed indexes are the predecessors of online databases. Because databases can be quite expensive, some libraries may have indexes instead; they might also have older printed indexes to supplement early publication years not yet digitized. Indexes were the only way to search for journal articles before databases were available, and they still sometimes will be the only option you have, particularly when you are searching for journals published before the 1980s. Some examples of indexes you may have occasion to use are listed in table 5.5.

Indexes are searchable only by a limited set of keywords or subject terms. These terms are listed either on separate pages at the beginning of each volume or in a separate volume if many terms are used. It is important that you browse these lists for terms related to your topic. It is likely that several different terms apply to your topic or that it may be described using terms different from those that you might have guessed.

Printed indexes are relatively simple to use. They usually are arranged in alphabetical order by subject. Underneath each subject is a list of articles published about that topic for the time period that the index covers—usually six months to one year—as indicated on the cover and spine of the volume. Indexes tend to arrange topics in a hierarchical fashion, starting with a broad subject area that is then subdivided into more and more specific topics.

Imagine, for example, that you are looking for articles about volunteers in the English army during the late nineteenth century. You might consult *Poole's Index to Periodical Literature* to find articles published during the time period. Your first step should be to scan Poole's topic list for the terms that best match. There are several terms that come to mind—including "volunteers," "army," or "England"—and these might indeed produce some

Table 5.5. Indexes

Index	Description
British Humanities Index	Early 20th-century journals published in England. Covers the social sciences and humanities. An earlier version of this index was known as the *Subject Index to Periodicals*.
Poole's Index to Periodical Literature	Covers 19th-century periodicals dealing with literature, religion, politics, social sciences, and economics. Also includes some popular journals. Covers English and American journals.
Reader's Guide to Periodical Literature	Covers primarily popular journals from the early 20th century to the present.
Social Sciences Index	Covers topics such as political science, law, and country studies starting in 1974.

results; however, thinking about the topic more broadly, you might start with "Great Britain," as illustrated in figure 5.15.

You can see on this index page that "army" is a subdivision of "Great Britain" as a main topic and that "volunteers" is an even more specific subdivision of "army." Upon finding your subject in the index, you will see underneath it a list of citations to journal articles related to the topic; some indexes may even provide a summary of the article included with each citation. The citation will provide all the information necessary to locate the article, including the author, article title, journal title, year of publication, and the pages upon which the article appeared. Upon identifying articles that appear to be useful, you should write down their complete citation information and then use your library's journal subscription list to obtain a copy of the article, as described in chapter 3. If your library does not have a copy of the article you need, you can probably order it through your library's interlibrary loan service.

Indexes do not repeat citations from one volume to the next and each volume of an index covers only a relatively short publication period. Each citation is listed in an index only in the year the article was originally published. Therefore, you must repeat your search process in all available volumes or risk missing important articles or books about your topic.

Because there is so much information to print on the pages, indexes almost always use many abbreviations to save space, particularly for long journal and newspaper titles. These abbreviations usually are explained in the first volume of each year of the index, if not in every volume. If you need to use an index and you have trouble deciphering the information in it, see a librarian for help.

FINDING SECONDARY SOURCES ON THE INTERNET

Good quality academic sources increasingly are becoming available at no cost on the Internet. Generally, you will find two types of secondary sources on the Internet. The first are digital reproductions of sources such as books and articles that were originally found only in print. The second are websites that are themselves original secondary sources of information created exclusively for the Internet and that never existed elsewhere. Examples of such original sources include historical blogs such as Cardinal Wolsey's Today in History (http://www.this-day-in-history.blogspot.com/) or websites such as ConstitutionFacts.com. The website shown in figure 5.16 is itself a secondary source, and additionally, it provides links to other secondary sources and primary sources.

180 GREAT

Great Britain, Army; Volunteers. (C. B. Brackenbury) Contemp. **55**: 929. — (R. W. Routledge) 19th Cent. **21**: 742. — (Lord Wolmer) 19th Cent. **21**: 566.

— — — and Bisley Common. (Lord Wantage) Un. Serv. M. n. s. **1**: 50.

— — — Are they Fit for War? Un. Serv. M. '87, **1**: 289.

— — — Citizen-Soldiers of the First Class Army-Reserve. (Maj.-Gen. Chapman) Un. Serv. M. n. s. **2**: 566.

— — — Easter Manœuvres, 1890. Un. Serv. M. n. s. **1**: 153.

— — — Education of Officers. Un. Serv. M. n. s. **2**: 262.

— — — Increasing Dearth of Officers. Un. Serv. M. **2** ('88–89): 602.

— — — Position of. Sat. R. **71**: 407.

— — — Suggestions for the Improvement of. Un. Serv. M. n. s. **3**: 45–341.

— — Wimbledon Meeting. (S. F. Page) Murray, **6**: 32.

— — Yeomanry Cavalry. All the Year, **64**: 558. — (Viscount Melgund) 19th Cent. **23**: 555.

— — — Truth about. (W. A. B. Hamilton) Un. Serv. M. n. s. **3**: 433.

— Capital in, Accumulations of, in 1875–85. (R. Giffen) J. Statis. Soc. **53**: 1.

— Census of, Annual, Suggestions for. (Sir E. Chadwick) J. Statis. Soc. **52**: 468.

— — of 1891. (S. J. Low) Contemp. **60**: 545.

— — — Prelim. Report of. J. Statis. Soc. **54**: 457.

— — — Some Lessons of. (G. B. Longstaff) New R. **5**: 331.

— — — Suggestions for. (G. B. Longstaff) J. Statis. Soc. **52**: 436.

— The Civil Service. Un. Serv. M. '88, **1**: 111.

Figure 5.15. Poole's Index to Periodical Literature. Printed Index. Image scan courtesy of Dickinson College.

Figure 5.16.   Scholarly Secondary Source Website, WinstonChurchill.org. Courtesy of the Churchill Centre and Museum, London.

Finding Secondary Source Websites

Scholarly secondary sources can be found relatively easily on the Internet when you use appropriate search techniques. Finding secondary sources for history projects can be as simple as typing your topic in the search box in your browser of choice. More often than not though, performing a basic search like that on the Internet will produce thousands if not millions of results, many of which are irrelevant or nonscholarly and thus not appropriate for your history project. You might also find when conducting an Internet search that your browser arranges the results in such a way that the least relevant material appears first, pushing more relevant sources several pages into your list of results. For example, a Google search for "Genghis Khan" produces more than seven million results, the entire first page and a half of which are not produced by historians or hosted by colleges or universities. The challenge, then, is not whether you can find good secondary sources on the Internet, but how to construct your search to maximize your chances of locating sources that history professionals created and that other historians widely recognize as scholarly.

As with scholarly subscription databases, using the advanced search screen to perform research on the Internet can help you quickly focus your search so that scholarly, relevant sources are more likely to appear in your results. One good way to do this is to limit your search by domain type using the option Search Within a Site or Domain in Google. This will help you retrieve only sites that are maintained by nonprofit organizations (.org), colleges and universities (.edu), or by government agencies (.gov). Figure 5.17 illustrates a Google search limited by domain type. The search illustrated in figure 5.17 directs Google to return only web pages that end with a domain of .edu.

Finding Free Books on the Internet

Some historical texts, or significant excerpts from them, increasingly can be found at no charge on the Internet. The Internet Archive (http://www.archive.org/), Google Books (http://books.google.com/) and Project Gutenberg (http://www.gutenberg.org/wiki/Main_Page) are examples of websites that provide complete copies of selected books that are in the public domain or, in other words, not protected by copyright law. When a book is in the public domain, the rights to collect profits from the books are no longer held

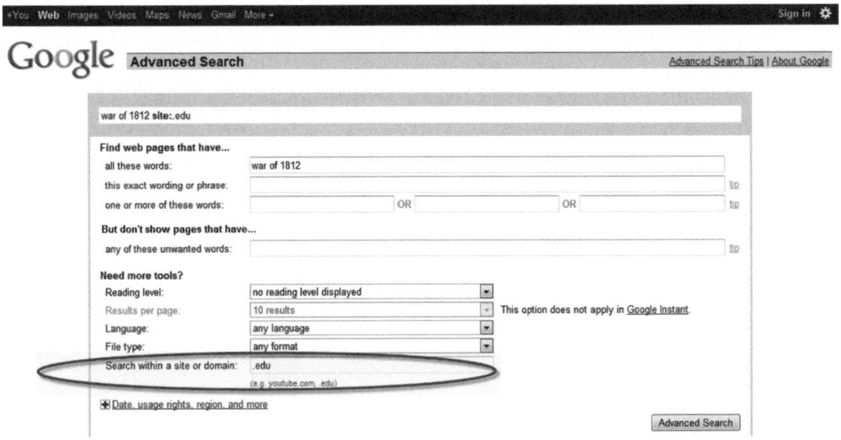

Figure 5.17. Google Advanced Search Page. Courtesy of Google.

by the author or the author's heirs and therefore can be reprinted, exchanged, and copied without gaining permission. Most modern books are protected by copyright law, but many older works published prior to the early part of the twentieth century are now in the public domain. Texts provided online by services like Internet Archive, Google Books, and Project Gutenberg usually are scanned copies of the books made available in formats that can be read on most desktop and laptop computers, tablet devices, eBook readers, and smart phones.

The Internet Archive (http://www.archive.org/) is an online collection of historical documents including texts, still and moving images, and audio files. It has many useful features, including the Wayback Machine, which is an application that allows you to view older versions of web pages. One of the Internet Archives' biggest attractions for historians is its collection of free digitized books. Examples of titles available on the Internet Archive include the following:

- *Philosophical Transactions* of the Royal Society of London
- Plutarch's *Lives of the Noble Greeks and Roman*s
- The writings of Benjamin Franklin and William Penn
- Many works of historical fiction and classic literature in the English language

Google Books (http://books.google.com/) is a remarkable source for selected historical books that are in the public domain. Google Books reproduces both classical works of history and literature and selected modern titles with the permission of the works' authors and publishers. In addition to the histories of many countries and U.S. states, some of the unabridged titles available on Google Books include the following:

- *The Wealth of Nations* (1776) by Adam Smith
- *The Federalist Papers* (1787–1788) by Alexander Hamilton, John Jay, and James Madison
- *My Bondage and Freedom* (1855) by Frederick Douglass
- *History of Julius Caesar* (1868) by Napoleon III
- *Personal Memoirs of Ulysses S. Grant* (1886) by Ulysses S. Grant
- *History of Woman Suffrage 1876–1885* (1886) by Elizabeth Cady Stanton, Susan Brownell Anthony, Matilda Joslyn Gage, and Ida Husted Harper
- *All Quiet on the Western Front* (1929), Erich Maria Remarque's novel about World War I

In addition to its free offerings, Google has made arrangements with some universities and publishers to make excerpts of modern copyright-protected books available. This allows you to read parts of the book and then decide if you want to borrow it from your library or purchase your own copy.

Novel: A book-length work of fiction.

Project Gutenberg (http://www.gutenberg.org/wiki/Main_Page) reproduces classic works of history and literature. Some of the titles available through Project Gutenberg are listed below:

- Sun Tzu's *The Art of War* (6th century BC)
- Dante Alighieri's *The Divine Comedy* (1308–1321)
- Niccolò Machiavelli's *The Prince* (1513)
- Thomas Paine's *Common Sense* (1776)
- Giacomo Casanova's *Histoire de Ma Vie* [*History of My Life*] (1797)

Also available from Project Gutenberg are the writings of international statesmen such as Woodrow Wilson, Winston Churchill, Adam Smith, Plato, and Friedrich Wilhelm Nietzsche.

CITATION SEARCHING IN BOOKS AND JOURNAL ARTICLES

Most history books and journal articles that scholarly presses publish are researched carefully by their authors. As mentioned earlier in this chapter, any scholarly secondary work should contain a bibliography and either footnotes or endnotes that reveal the original sources of all cited material. A bibliography is a list of citations containing the books, periodical articles, audiovisual materials, and other documents that an author read, quoted, and otherwise used to form opinions and conclusions while writing the book or article. Bibliographies usually are found near the end of most books, sometimes at the end of individual chapters in a book, or at the end of a journal article.

Your research will gain considerable momentum if you examine the bibliographies and footnotes of any books or articles you find helpful, as they will tell you what sources the author found useful. After perusing the bibliographies of several sources, you should be able to determine which sources are the most influential on your topic because they will be cited the most often by many scholars. Frequent citing is a clear indication of the sources with which you should be familiar. Your library may own many of the items you discover by scanning footnotes and bibliographies. As with other secondary sources, you should examine any source you identify in bibliographies and footnotes to ensure that they are scholarly. Tips for determining whether a source is scholarly can be found earlier in this chapter.

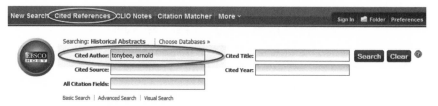

Figure 5.18.   Cited References Feature in America: History & Life and Historical Abstracts. Courtesy of EBSCOhost.

The databases America: History and Life and Historical Abstracts allow you to perform *citation searches* for authors, books, and articles. Citation searching shows how many times a particular author or work has been cited in other books and articles that are contained within the same database. Citation searching can help you determine who is most actively engaged in research on your topic and what authors have been cited most frequently, thus indicating who are the most prolific and/or respected authors on any particular topic. You can use the citations you find to see how historians have responded to an author's work. To access the citation search option in either America: History and Life or Historical Abstracts, follow the steps below.

• Access America: History and Life or Historical Abstracts from your library's databases page. More information can be found in chapter 3.
• At the top of the screen, click Cited References.
• In the Cited Author box, type the name of the author whose work you want to trace. For best results, you should type the author's last name, followed by a comma, followed by the author's first name or first initial. Alternatively, you can search by the title of a book or article by typing the title in the Cited Source box. Your search should look similar to that in figure 5.18.

For the example illustrated in figure 5.18, clicking the Search button will provide you with a list of books and articles in which Arnold Toynbee's work has been cited. Note though, that this list is not exhaustive; it will return only books and articles contained in America: History and Life and/or Historical Abstracts. There are other databases that can help you broaden a citation search, such as Humanities International Complete and Web of Science.

The majority of citations in your bibliography will likely be classified as secondary sources, and you will probably spend most of your research hours reading and analyzing secondary sources and using them to inform your own research. Secondary sources are crucial in helping you understand and contextualize the primary sources you also will examine.

Chapter Six

Primary Sources

Primary sources are documents, artifacts, images, and other evidence of an event created by firsthand witnesses. Primary sources help a researcher understand how people interpret and make sense of their own environment and may reveal a person's thoughts or reactions to an event or reasons for taking certain actions and not others. An effective research paper should incorporate as many relevant primary sources as possible in order to place the events under consideration in their appropriate historical context and to gain insight on historical issues from those who lived through them. Primary sources will give you a truer sense of a past event than any description by a secondary source could. The best professional secondary sources regularly make references to primary sources and draw arguments and conclusions directly from them. Using primary sources will help you develop your own opinions about historical questions and prevent you from simply restating the conclusions of other historians.

Primary Sources: Documents, artifacts, and other evidence of an event produced by firsthand witnesses.

Examples of primary sources are diaries, correspondence, professional papers, memoirs, manuscripts, photographs, original works of art and literature, artifacts, speeches, autobiographies, data, and newspaper articles reporting on an event as it unfolds. Primary sources also include constitutions, treaties, pacts, records of governmental debates and transactions, and other political documents. Interviews conducted during or shortly after an event or interviews in which a person is asked to recall an event through which he or she lived also may be considered primary sources.

Specific examples of primary sources are England's *Magna Carta*, Martin Luther's *Ninety-Five Theses*, the *Ottoman Constitution of 1876,* or Abraham Lincoln's *Gettysburg Address*. Figure 6.1 is an image of an excerpt of a copy the Gettysburg Address found on the Library of Congress website. This particular copy was handwritten by Abraham Lincoln's private secretary, John

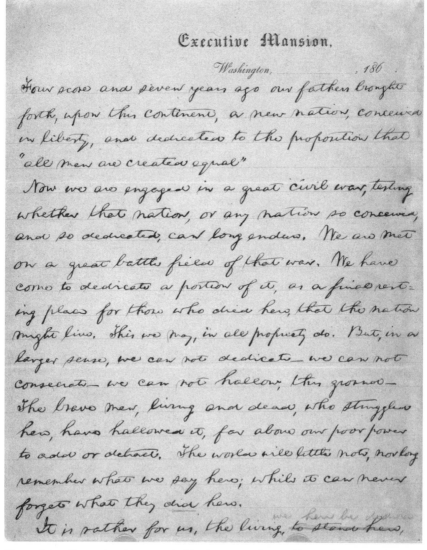

Figure 6.1. Copy of an Excerpt of Lincoln's Gettysburg Address. Courtesy of the Library of Congress.

Nicolay. According to the Library of Congress website, this copy "represents the earliest known of the five drafts of what may be the most famous American speech."[1] Photographs also may be considered primary sources. For example, the primary source photograph in figure 6.2 depicts a civil rights march on Washington, DC, in 1963.

You do not need to be in possession of an original copy of the document in order for a source to be considered primary. That is, when writing a paper on the United States Constitution, one does not need to go to Washington, DC, to view the actual document housed in the National Archives. Instead, you could use a copy of the text that has been reprinted on a website such as the National Constitution Center (http://constitutioncenter.org/) or in a book such as Henry Steele Commager's classic *Documents of American History.*

HOW TO USE PRIMARY SOURCES

Primary sources offer important insight about how and why historical events occurred. They can tell you who was present at an event, when it took place,

Figure 6.2.   Photograph of a Civil Rights March on Washington, 1963. Courtesy of the Library of Congress.

what the contemporary opinion was regarding it, and how it unfolded. Primary sources can be used to verify facts and resolve misconceptions about the past. As with any source, however, a primary source must be considered within its historical context and examined with the perspective and bias of the creator in mind. You should question why the document was created and what the author intended to do with it. The creator might be self-promoting or trying to influence the opinions or actions of others and may conflate opinion with fact. Though primary sources should be used to support historical arguments, researchers should make themselves familiar with the history surrounding sources and avoid using them to impose the opinions of the present upon the events of the past.

When using primary sources such as autobiographies and personal interviews that have been compiled many months or years after an event, you should bear in mind that human memory sometimes is unreliable. A person's memories of detail may fade with time or may be influenced by external factors, such as hearing another person recount the same story, misinterpreting something seen or heard, or simply not thinking about it often. A person writing an autobiography or memoir may misremember certain things or choose to present him or herself favorably by ignoring, downplaying, or justifying decisions that caused critical reaction at the time they occurred. As a researcher, it is your responsibility to make sure that everything reported in your final project is as accurate as possible. Dates, times, names, places, and other facts that firsthand witnesses provide always must be confirmed and verified against sources such as newspapers and encyclopedias.

Transcribe: To make a handwritten or typed copy of a document.

Professional historians frequently *transcribe* and reprint copies of primary sources in books or on websites for other researchers to read. Reprinted primary materials are particularly valuable because they provide access to old and rare materials that are fragile and would otherwise not be available to the public. If a person's handwriting is difficult to read or if the writer uses terminology that a modern researcher may not understand, viewing these reprints may even be preferable. Modern books and websites often will display a transcribed document next to the original document so that the researcher may examine both the original copy and the transcriber's interpretation. Some transcriptions include notes that explain unfamiliar terms or place the document in its historical context. Such reprints are perfectly acceptable to use as primary sources as long as they are accurate reproductions of the originals with no major alterations or omissions that could potentially change the document's meaning. A professionally transcribed document should include the transcriber's name and credentials, a physical description of the original item, notes about how the transcription was done, and an explanation about any differences between the original text and the transcription, why changes were made, and how you can tell what has been changed.

Figure 6.3 is an example of a transcribed document that can be found at the website The Complete Work of Charles Darwin Online (http://darwin-online.org.uk/). In this example, we see an image of Charles Darwin's original notebook in his own writing next to a transcription of the text. Note that in this example, the transcriber has included text that Darwin crossed out, as well as his marginal notes. Additionally, the transcriber included explanatory footnotes explaining in greater detail how Darwin's drawings appear in the notebooks.

It is also possible to find translated copies of primary sources that were originally written in languages you cannot read. Translations may be available in print or on the Internet. As with transcribed sources, you must be able to verify that a source has been translated by a trustworthy professional who has not altered the meaning of the document in the course of the translation.

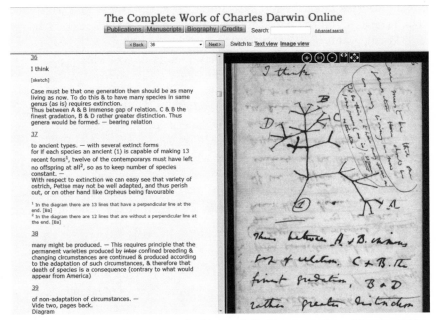

Figure 6.3. Page 36 of C. R. Darwin, Notebook B: [Transmutation of Species (1837–1838)]. Reproduced with permission from John van Wyhe ed., 2002, The Complete Work of Charles Darwin Online (http://darwin-online.org.uk/).

FINDING PRIMARY SOURCES

Primary sources are easier than ever to find. As stated earlier, copies of primary sources are available in books, databases, and on the Internet and are even available in translation from other languages. Yet they can be the most difficult type of source for a new researcher to locate when one is not familiar with the search techniques required to find them. This is because many primary sources existed originally as handwritten or typed sheets of paper that must be collected, categorized, organized, and digitized or printed before they can be made available to the public and easily searched. Even after they are published, primary sources may be difficult to locate because they may be scattered within the texts of secondary sources to help the author demonstrate his or her point. Though primary sources speckle the entire landscape of historical evidence, the other sources that surround them sometimes also have the effect of hiding them. Therefore, you must employ a variety of search techniques, look through an assortment of materials, and use a bit of creativity to dig primary sources out of their nooks.

Primary sources often are reprinted in books. For example, scholars might consolidate into a book a person's collection of letters or memoirs, or a collection of documents relating to a country's foreign or domestic policies. Or, primary sources might be reprinted in the appendix of a secondary source book in order to provide the reader easy access to the same sources the author used to support his or her assertions.

The most effective way to find primary sources in your library's catalogs and databases is to use specific terminology in your searches. Library and archival databases use specific words and phrases to identify every kind of source, and ironically, library catalogs and databases rarely refer to primary sources as "primary sources." Primary sources collected in books often are described in library catalogs as "documents" or, simply, "sources." Therefore, it is important to describe exactly what type of source you are seeking and include in your search as many synonyms as you can think of for the type of material you need. Following is a list of many of the words that are used in library catalogs and databases to describe materials that contain primary sources:

- autobiography
- correspondence
- diary
- document
- interview

- journal
- letter
- manuscript
- memoir
- papers

- personal narrative
- photograph
- reader
- report
- source

If you are looking for a person's letters, you might try to search for the person's name combined with "letters," "correspondence," "communication," or "messages." Or, for example, if you are writing a paper about Brazilian history, you probably do not want just any primary source relating to that country but something more specific, such as the Constitution of 1824 or a set of letters that mid-twentieth-century dictator Getulio Vargas wrote to his top advisor, Luis Vergara.

In addition, there are several more obscure subject terms used in library catalogs to describe individuals when they are the subjects of books and other works, as noted below. Although applied inconsistently, these terms often are indicators that primary source materials exist within an item.

Anecdotes. Used for collections of brief narratives of true incidents from an individual's life.

Discography. Used for lists of sound recordings created by an individual or musical group.

Friends and associates. Used for discussions of a person's close and immediate contacts, such as companions and coworkers.

Notebooks and sketchbooks. Materials in early stages of completion, in the author's own hand, either handwritten or typed.

Quotations. Used for collections or discussions of quotations by or about a person.

Written works. Used for the written words of musicians and artists.

Official copies of many primary sources are available for free on some websites. For example, sources such as the Library of Congress's American Memory Project provides digital copies of documents relating to the history of the United States (http://memory.loc.gov/ammem/index.html), and Brigham Young University's Eurodocs provides digital copies of documents relating to the history of Europe (http://eudocs.lib.byu.edu/index.php/Main_Page). Many primary sources available online cannot otherwise be found anywhere else except in the archive in which the original copy is stored. The following sections describe some specific search tips for finding primary materials in library catalogs, in scholarly historical databases, and on the Internet.

FINDING PRIMARY SOURCES COLLECTED IN BOOKS

Primary sources such as treaties, political correspondence, photographs, works of art, speeches, oral histories, and interviews are often reproduced in books. The documents may be combined with analysis or commentary written by the editor of the book, or the documents may simply be reproduced with no such remarks.

Finding Primary Sources in a Library Catalog or on WorldCat

Before following these steps, access your local library's online catalog or WorldCat (http://www.worldcat.org) and be sure that you are using the Advanced Search or More Options screen. See chapter 5 for more information about accessing a catalog's advanced search screen.

- In the first Keyword Search box, type the most general descriptive term that relates to your topic. Examples of general search terms might be "American history" or "Risorgimento" or "Bolivia."
- On the second Keyword line, type the phrase "documents or sources."
- Optionally, if the topic you are searching for is likely to produce primary sources in a language you cannot read, it is a good idea to limit your search to a language you can read. Your search should look similar to the one in figure 6.4.

When you complete your search results, your list should include materials that contain primary sources relating to the broad topic you used in your search strategy.

Catalog Advanced Search

all fields(keyword) ▾	American history	And ▾
all fields(keyword) ▾	documents or sources	And ▾
title ▾		And ▾
subject ▾		And ▾
series ▾		And ▾
periodical title ▾		And ▾
isbn ▾		

Search Reset

language:	ANY ▾
format (book, cd, etc.):	ANY ▾
location:	ANY ▾
match on:	Keywords ▾
pubyear:	
sort by:	New to Old ▾

Figure 6.4. Advanced Search for Primary Sources in a Library Catalog. Courtesy of Dickinson College and SirsiDynix.

Finding Primary Sources by Well-Known Individuals Collected in Books

Politicians, authors, artists, composers, activists, military personnel, and other individuals often have their correspondence, professional papers, diaries, memoirs, manuscripts, autobiographies, and other writings collected in books. When you already know the name of the person whose documents you are seeking, the easiest way to find them, presuming that they have been published, is to search your library catalog or OCLC's WorldCat for the person as an author. More information on searching library catalogs and WorldCat can be found in chapter 5.

Suppose, for example, that you were interesting in finding letters that Franklin Delano Roosevelt wrote during his presidential administration. You can use the following steps to locate books in which copies of his letters have been published.

- Access the Advanced Search screen of your local library's online book catalog, or WorldCat's catalog (http://www.worldcat.org). Refer to chapter 3, or ask a librarian if you need help accessing a catalog.
- On the Keyword line, type "letters or correspondence." (Using "or" between search words indicates to the database that you will accept any item that is described with either word. For more information about constructing search phrases, see chapter 7.)
- On the Author line, type the words "Franklin Roosevelt."

Your search screen should look similar to a search conducted on WorldCat, as reproduced in figure 6.5. Your completed search will most likely yield results similar to those in figure 6.6.

Finding Primary Sources by Ordinary Individuals Collected in Books

One way of studying history is to examine the way in which historical events impacted the lives of ordinary people. Much of what we know about history comes from the recollections, memoirs, artifacts, and other evidence from unknown members of society. Many books have been written about the lives of ordinary people, with the authors of those books using primary sources such as diaries, letters, and artifacts as evidence. Examples of such books include the following.

Dzengseo. *The Diary of a Manchu Soldier in Seventeenth-Century China: My Service in the Army*. Routledge Studies in the Early History of Asia.

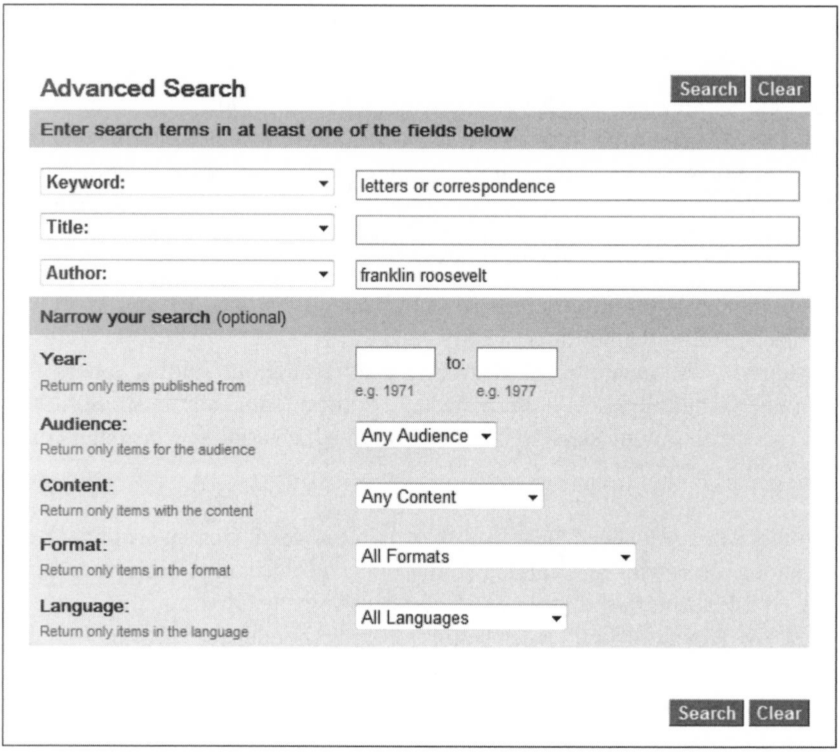

Figure 6.5. Advanced Search for Franklin Roosevelt's Correspondence in WorldCat. Copyright 2011 OCLC Online Computer Library Center, Inc. Used with Permission. FirstSearch, OCLC, WorldCat, and the WorldCat logo are registered trademarks/service marks of OCLC.

Introduction, translation, and notes by Nicola Di Cosmo. New York: Routledge, 2006.

Semyonova Tian-Shanskaia, Olga. *Village Life in Late Tsarist Russia*. Edited by David L. Ransel. Translated by David L. Ransel and Michael Levine. Bloomington: Indiana University Press, 1993.

Walter, Jakob. *Diary of a Napoleonic Foot Soldier*. Edited by Mark Raeff. New York: Penguin Books, 1991.

If you are looking for personal memoirs not necessarily written by a well-known person, or if you want to browse the relevant primary sources available at your library, you can perform a general search by time period, event, location, occupation, or group. For example, if you are looking for primary sources created by women during the Victorian era, a search for "Victorian" and "women" and "documents" might produce a book such as this one:

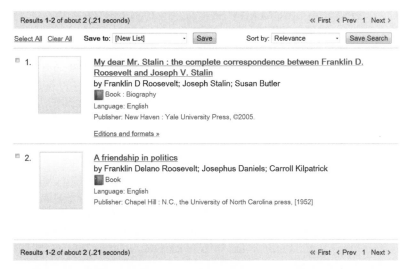

Hellerstein, Erna Olafson, et al., eds. *Victorian Women: A Documentary Account of Women's Lives in Nineteenth-Century England, France, and the United States*. Stanford: Stanford University Press, 1981.

Similarly, a search for "women" and "diaries" and "war" might produce a book such as this one:

Simmons, Cynthia, and Nina Perlina. *Writing the Siege of Leningrad: Women's Diaries, Memoirs, and Documentary Prose*. Pittsburgh: University of Pittsburgh Press, 2002.

Various combinations of search terms can and should be used for each topic you research. If you use only one set of search terms, you are likely to exclude from your search many relevant books and articles. Each search you initiate will likely provide you with different results, so it is imperative that you use as many synonyms for searching as possible. You can use a historical dictionary or encyclopedia for help in coming up with search terms, as explained in chapter 4. Also, chapter 7 provides tips and tricks on how to combine multiple search terms into one search.

FINDING PRIMARY SOURCES COLLECTED IN SUBSCRIPTION-BASED DATABASES

Increasingly, primary sources are being reproduced in digital format and made available online. Some primary source databases are available for free, but most are designed for use by the populations of colleges and universities and cannot be accessed for free on the Internet. Primary source databases often charge relatively high subscription fees, and many do not offer subscriptions to individuals. Therefore, often the only way you can access primary source databases is directly from your library's website.

There are many subscription-based primary source databases currently available, with new ones being released each year. Remember that not every library can subscribe to every available primary source database. If your library does not have access to a particular primary source database that interests you, ask your librarian for help identifying comparable alternatives. Table 6.1 contains examples of some well-known subscription-based primary source databases that you might find on your library's website.

FINDING PRIMARY SOURCES ON THE INTERNET

In addition to being printed in books, primary sources increasingly are becoming available via the Internet, often for free. A simple Google search on your topic will often lead to a site containing primary sources. For example, if you are looking for a copy of Martin Luther's *Ninety-Five Theses on the Power and Efficacy of Indulgences*, the search term "Luther's 95 Theses" might lead you to copies of the original Latin document or a translated copy reprinted at *Project Wittenburg* (http://www.ctsfw.edu/etext/luther/theses/) or at *Project Gutenberg* (http://www.gutenberg.org/etext/274). Any of these copies would be acceptable to use and quote in a research paper, when cited properly. (See appendixes A and B for more information about citing sources.) Table 6.2 provides some examples of the thousands of websites that make primary sources available to researchers. The number of primary source websites continues to increase as more scholars begin to carry out their work with Internet technology.

FINDING PRIMARY SOURCES IN ARCHIVES, MUSEUMS, AND HISTORICAL SOCIETIES

By definition, archives, museums, historical societies, and other institutions dedicated to the study and preservation of the past keep primary sources in their collections. If you know that a person lived in a particular area or attended a particular college or university, chances are some information about that person is available in an archive or historical society. These organizations increasingly are posting digital copies of their material online for free, though many organizations are able to post only a small percentage of their entire collections. What the websites of most archives and similar operations will do is describe the subject matter and scope of the material you are likely to find there, even if the material is not digitized and available online. Most well-known historical figures have collections of their documents kept somewhere, as do lesser-known figures who were influential in their local societies. Most colleges, universities, states, counties, and churches have an archive or historical society that keeps records of attendees and residents. If you are researching an individual and you know where the person was born, lived, married, was educated, or died, you can search the Internet to find the website of a local government records office, church, historical society, or college to search for useful information.

Most archival institutions have a search feature on their website that allows you to browse their collections. However, some provide descriptions of collections only and do not allow you to search online for specific documents. If you find an archive or historical society that you think might contain helpful information, but which has little information on its website, do not give up your search. Many of these organizations have limited budgets and must rely on government money or grants from private philanthropic organizations to begin special projects such as digitizing documents. Some organizations may not have enough staff members to complete large projects. If an organization you believe should be able to provide material about your research project does not have much information available on its website, call and speak with an archivist. Consultation with an archivist is a normal and important part of the primary research process, and archivists are quite used to handling telephone inquiries to help researchers find needed documentation, particularly when they are not able to travel to the archive's location.

Lists of websites of well-known archives, historical societies, and other organizations that preserve historical documents can be found in chapter 3. Additionally, there are some websites that keep track of the material likely to be found in archives around the world, such as those listed in table 6.3. You can use these aggregator sites to determine which archives might be the best to use when researching your topic. Most of the sites listed in table 6.3 are free unless so noted. Be sure to ask a librarian whether your library has a subscription to a fee-based site before you pay to use it.

Table 6.1. Subscription-Based Primary Source Databases

Database & Information Link	Time Period	Coverage
19th Century Masterfile http://www.paratext.com/19th_century.html	1800 to 1925	American and British periodicals and books. Includes some foreign language material from the time period.
Accessible Archives http://www.accessible.com/accessible/	1700s to 1800s	United States periodicals and newspapers.
American Civil War: Letters and Diaries http://solomon.cwld.alexanderstreet.com	1855 to 1875	Copies of personal documents from over 200 people who experienced the Civil War.
Ancestry http://www.ancestrylibrary.com/	1790 to present	Genealogy, military records, census data, immigration records. Individual subscriptions available in addition to library subscriptions.
ArtStor http://www.artstor.org/	Prehistory to present	Images of art works and architecture from all time periods and all parts of the world.
British and Irish Women's Letters and Diaries http://alexanderstreet.com/products/bwld.htm	1500s to 1900s	Primary source database offering women's diaries and letters.
CQ Historic Documents Online Library http://www.cqpress.com/product/CQ-Online-Editions-Historic-Documents.html	1972 to present	A full-text database of primary source documents relating to the United States.
Early American Newspapers http://www.newsbank.com/readex/product.cfm?product=10	1690 to 1876	Cover-to-cover reproductions of hundreds of U.S. historic newspapers.
Early Encounters in North America: Peoples, Cultures and the Environment http://alexanderstreet.com/products/eena.htm	1534 to 1850	Primary source collection of personal accounts of traders, slaves, missionaries, explorers, soldiers, and native peoples.
Early English Books Online (EEBO) http://www.gale.cengage.com/DigitalCollections/products/ecco/index.htm	1400s to 1600s	Books, pamphlets, and other documents.

Database & Information Link	Time Period	Coverage
Eighteenth Century Collection Online (ECCO) http://www.gale.cengage.com/ DigitalCollections/products/ ecco/index.htm	1700 to 1800	English-language and foreign-language titles printed in Great Britain and the Americas during the 18th century, along with thousands of important works from the Americas.
European History Primary Sources http://primary-sources.eui.eu/	1500 to present	European scholarly primary source websites and links from the European University Institute.
Historical Newspapers Online http://historynews.chadwyck. com/	1790 to 1980	Full-text articles from the *Times* of London and from the *New York Times*.
North American Immigrant Letters, Diaries, and Oral Histories http://solomon.imld. alexanderstreet.com	1800 to 1950	Primary sources written by North American immigrants.
PictureHistory http://www.picturehistory.com/	1700s to 1900s	Photographs, drawings, woodcuts, and other images from United States history. Thumbnail searches are free. High-quality images and reproductions available for a fee.
ProQuest Historical Newspapers http://www.proquest.com/ en-US/catalogs/databases/ detail/pq-hist-news.shtml	1764 to present	United States newspapers.

FINDING GENEALOGY

Genealogy is the study of a person's ancestry and family history. Though many people engage in genealogy as a hobby out of personal interest, it is also a useful exercise when studying a historical figure. A person's genealogy can give you a wealth of information about his or her life, including places and dates of birth, marriage, and death and the names of parents, siblings, spouses, children, and other relatives. Additionally, embarking on a genealogical study will lead you to a person's hometown, thus helping you uncover a person's friends, political contacts, coworkers, and other affiliations. A genealogy can fill in missing, interesting, and enlightening details of a person's

Table 6.2. Free Primary Source Websites

Site	Time Period	Description
Ad*Access http://scriptorium.lib.duke. edu:80/ adaccess/	1911 to 1955	Images from advertisements in U.S. and Canadian magazines. Subject areas include radio, television, and transportation.
American Civil War Homepage http://sunsite.utk.edu/civil-war	1840 to 1880	Images, documents, and photographs from the U.S. Civil War.
American Memory http://memory.loc.gov/	1500 to present	United States historical documents from the Library of Congress. Includes written and spoken words, sound recordings, still and moving images, prints, maps, and sheet music.
American Radicalism http://digital.lib.msu. edu/collections/index. cfm?CollectionID=1	1800s to 1900s	Texts and images from the American Radicalism collection at Michigan State University. Includes subjects such as Wounded Knee, Black Panthers, and Students for a Democratic Society.
Avalon Project http://avalon.law.yale.edu/	450 BC to 2003	Documents of world history from ancient times through the present. Covers law, history, and diplomacy.
British History Online http://www.british-history. ac.uk	1000s to 1800s	Core printed primary and secondary sources for the medieval and modern history of the British Isles.
EuroDocs http://eudocs.lib.byu.edu/	Prehistory to present	A wiki presenting sources in European history, with many political documents.
Europeana http://www.europeana.eu	1100 to present	Contains more than 2 million digital images including paintings, drawings, maps, texts, letters, diaries, photos and pictures of museum objects, some of which are world famous. Also includes video and sound recordings.
Famous Trials http://www.law.umkc.edu/ faculty/projects/ftrials/ ftrials.htm	400 BC to 2006	Contains documents from trials dating back to Socrates and up to Zacarias Moussaoui in 2006.
Gallica http://gallica.bnf.fr/	Prehistory to present	Primary sources relating to French history.

Site	Time Period	Description
House Divided http://housedivided. dickinson.edu/	1840 to 1880	The U.S. Civil War from the perspective of Dickinson College.
Internet Library of Early Journals http://www.bodley.ox.ac. uk/ilej/	1700s to 1800s	A project of 4 universities in England to digitize journals from the 18th and 19th centuries.
Jacob Leisler Project http://www.nyu.edu/leisler/ History.html	1650 to 1700	The papers of a famous 17th century New York merchant, provided by New York University.
Labyrinth http://labyrinth.georgetown. edu	Medieval period	Primary sources on Medieval studies from Georgetown University.
Making of America http://quod.lib.umich. edu/m/moagrp/ or http://cdl.library.cornell.edu/ moa/	1850 to 1900	A collection of documents on American history, sociology, and development of infrastructure before and after the Civil War.
Marxist Internet Archive http://www.marx.org/	1750 to 1980	Papers of Marx and Engels, as well as works of their ideological associates. Contains documents from different social movements such as the French Revolution and the struggles for independence in Africa.
The Online Medieval and Classical Library http://omacl.org/	Medieval period	An extensive collection of literary works from the Middle Ages.
Nuremberg Trials Project http://nuremberg.law. harvard.edu	1945 to 1946	One million pages of documents relating to the trial of military and political leaders of Nazi Germany before the International Military Tribunal (IMT) following World War II. From Harvard University.
Papers of Benjamin Franklin http://franklinpapers.org/ franklin	1706 to 1792	A digital archive of Franklin's papers held in print at Yale University.
Project Gutenberg http://www.gutenberg.org	1600 to 2000	A site that allows downloading of e-books in various formats. Books can be found in 59 languages.
Project Wittenberg http://www. projectwittenberg.org/	1400 to 1900	Works by and about Martin Luther and other Lutherans.

Table 6.2.   (Continued)

Site	Time Period	Description
Seventeen Moments in Soviet History http://soviethistory.org/index. php	1917 to 1991	Archive of texts, images, maps, and audio and video materials from the Soviet era, translated into English. Includes materials about Soviet propaganda, politics, economics, society, crime, literature, art, dissidents, and many other topics.
Slave Narratives http://xroads.virginia. edu/~hyper/wpa/index. html	1800s	Primary accounts of slavery from former slaves.
Slave Voyages http://Slavevoyages.org	1514 to 1866	A record of slave voyages that includes information on ships, routes, slaves, and slave owners.
Slavery and Abolition in the US: Select Publications of the 1800s http://deila.dickinson.edu/ slaveryandabolition/	1787 to 1911	First person narratives, legal proceedings and decisions, antislavery tracts, religious sermons, and early secondary works on both sides of the slavery issue. Materials are from the holdings of Millersville University and Dickinson College.
Thomas http://thomas.loc.gov/	1960s to present	United States legislative information from the Library of Congress. The site was named for Thomas Jefferson.
Valley of the Shadow: Living the Civil War in Pennsylvania and Virginia http://valley.lib.virginia. edu/	1859 to 1871	Narrative on histories of two towns during the Civil War. This site has an electronic archive with primary sources.
Victorian Web http://www.victorianweb.org	1800s	British literature, history, and culture including comparative materials from countries outside the United Kingdom.
World War II Resources http://www.ibiblio.org/pha/	1939 to 1945	Documents covering all aspects of World War II.

life and provide you with a rich and broad sense of who the person was and what motivated his or her actions. Genealogical information can be obtained from the following types of sources:

Vital Records. The term "vital records" refers to the information about individuals that is recorded by government agencies. This information includes

Table 6.3. Archive Aggregators

Site	Free/Subscription	Description
Africa Research Central http://www.africa-research.org/	Subscription	A directory for finding museums, libraries, and archives in African countries.
ArchiveGrid http://www.archivegrid.org/ web	Subscription	Contains descriptions of primary source collections from various countries.
Archives Made Easy http://www.archivesmadeeasy. org/	Free	A guide to archives around the world, hosted by the International History department at the London School of Economics and Political Science. Contains links to different archives by country.
Berkeley Digital Library – Other Collections http://sunsite.berkeley.edu/ siteindex.html	Free	From Cal-Berkeley, a list of links to other projects around the web with primary sources.
Library and Archival Exhibitions on the Web http://www.sil.si.edu/ SILPublications/Online- Exhibitions/	Free	Links to online exhibitions created by archives, historical societies, libraries, and museums.
Repositories of Primary Sources http://www.uiweb.uidaho.edu/ special-collections/Other. Repositories.html	Free	A listing of more than 5,000 websites describing holdings of manuscripts, archives, rare books, historical photographs, and other primary sources for the research scholar.
State Historic Preservation Offices http://www.nps.gov/history/nr/ shpolist.htm	Free	A compilation of every registered historic site in America, by state.
SunSITE Digital Collections http://sunsite.berkeley.edu/ Collections/	Free	Sources on U.S. history and culture and incunabula from Cal-Berkeley's Digital Library, with links to other projects.

birth and death certificates, marriage licenses, divorce decrees, and wills. Such records are kept by the local government offices in the district where the life event takes place.

Military records. Records about a person's military enlistment, places of service, and awards are kept by the federal government entities such as the National Archives and Records Administration (NARA) in the United States.

Birth records. Although record of births have been collected in some form or another throughout history, compulsory registration of documents with a government agency in the form of a birth certificate did not exist until the mid-nineteenth century. It is often possible, however, to find birth announcements in historical newspapers published in the nineteenth century and earlier. Other sources in which birth records are kept include hospitals and churches or other religious organizations in which records of a baptism or initiation into the congregation would be kept. Additionally, births were often recorded in family Bibles, which may be preserved by local historical societies.

Marriage announcements. Marriage announcements began to appear with regularity in major newspapers in the early twentieth century. With the exception of high-profile marriages, such as the union of royalty, they are most likely to have been recorded only in local newspapers or at houses of worship prior to then.

Obituaries. An obituary is a notice of a person's death, often accompanied by a brief biography, usually printed in a newspaper. Obituaries may list the person's relatives (both living and deceased) and may describe the person's interests and activities in the community. Local newspapers are likely to devote more space to individual obituaries of nonfamous people than a paper serving a large metropolitan area.

You should be aware that announcements may not appear in a newspaper for several days or even weeks following an event, particularly in historical newspapers when information did not travel quickly. Therefore, you should seek such information in issues of the newspapers for a few weeks following the day the event occurred.

Genealogy: The study of family history.

Often the best place to search for genealogical information is in the local newspapers of the town or city in which a person was born, lived, and died. Many national and international newspapers are available to search online, and many have archival copies available to search via subscription-based databases. Local newspapers, however, may be more difficult to access. You usually can find out which libraries hold older newspapers by searching WorldCat, as described in chapter 5, or you can consult a state library or local historical society, as described earlier in this chapter.

Cemeteries also can be great resources during your search for primary documentation. Information recorded on tombstones can help you gather information about obscure individuals. In addition to birth and death dates, you might be able to discover the names of a person's spouse and children, years of military service, and a woman's maiden name if she assumed her husband's last name upon getting married. Cemeteries may be private, public, or national; some are open to the public and some are not. To find out if a person you are researching is interred in a particular cemetery, you can call the cemetery's records office or the local historical society to get more information. Information about the graves of public figures and the family members who are interred with them can be found at the website Find a Grave (http://www.findagrave.com/).

There are many good websites that provide genealogical and other personal information, but often the best way to research a personal history is to go directly to its original source. You might, for example, research at a county courthouse where a marriage, divorce, or land transfer might have been recorded or where wills are registered. Historical societies also collect information about important local people and regional businesses and often preserve sources that cannot found anywhere else, such as small-town newspapers or minutes of local council meetings.

In the United States, federal agencies also are good sources of information about individuals. In addition to vital records, federal agencies keep track of census data, people's movements in and out of the United States, and personnel in all branches of the military. Much of this material is held in physical format at the National Archives in Washington, DC, but some now is also available online via free or subscription sources. Increasingly, federal agencies are no longer publishing data in print; rather, they are making information available exclusively online. Table 6.4 lists some sources that provide vital records and government information for citizens and immigrants to the United States.

FINDING IMAGES AND OTHER MEDIA

It almost goes without saying that images provide powerful visual context to the stories of history that often are told to us only in text. Sometimes images have more power over our emotions and thoughts than the written word. Like the famous image of the American flag being raised over Iwo Jima, images can instantly seize the imaginations and influence the thoughts of thousands or even millions of people. Images can show us what life was like at specific points in time, capture the intensity of a moment during an event, and help us visualize how people and places change over decades or centuries. In addition to showing us how people looked and dressed, images can provide us with clues as to a person's relative station in society, economic situation, and other people with whom they associated. Images may be still pictures or moving

Table 6.4. Genealogy Websites

Record Type	Free/Subscription	Description
Acquiring Land (United States) http://www.directlinesoftware.com/landacq.htm	Free	Provides information on land records and how to obtain copies of them. Also has links to state websites and a few on local history and geographies.
Ancestor Hunt http://www.ancestorhunt.com/mormon_church_records.htm	Free (portal to free sites, such as familysearch.org)	Extensive genealogy records collected by the Mormon Church (The Church of Jesus Christ of Latter-day Saints) that cover the 12th through the early 20th centuries.
Ancestry www.ancestry.com	Subscription	Primarily for genealogy, but also contains useful statistical information including census records. Allows personal subscriptions and institutional subscriptions. Contains information from the United States, Canada, England, and other western European countries.
Ellis Island www.ellisisland.org	Free	Passenger records and ship manifestos of immigrants who came to the United States via Ellis Island.
Immigration Records - Ships Passenger Arrival Records http://www.archives.gov/research/immigration/index.html	Free	Contains information on immigration records as well as links to other websites, such as Castle Garden (an online database that spans 1830 to 1902) and Ellis Island.
Naturalization Records http://www.archives.gov/genealogy/naturalization/	Free	From the National Archives and Records Administration of the United States. Describes what naturalization is and the process. Allows microfilm records searching and links to other places where additional information might be found.
Tips for Determining Your Ancestor's Probable Port of Arrival http://www.genealogybranches.com/arrivalports.html	Free	Covers the ports of New York, Philadelphia, Boston, Baltimore, and New Orleans with arrivals from Europe between the 1820s and the 1850s.

films, and during the course of your research, you may find original copies of the images or digital reproductions of them. In the context of historical research, images may include photographs, paintings, cartoons, and engravings.

Traditionally, images have not been included in library organizational schemes that are designed to describe and retrieve texts in library catalogs and databases. The sheer volume of images created throughout the centuries has made them quite difficult to catalog. However, advances in database technology now make images easier to find because in addition to storing a copy of the image, a database also can store text that identifies and describes the image.

This identifying information is called *metadata*, a term which means "data about data," and it may include elements such as the creator and owner of the image, the subject of the image, the date of the image's creation, the location in which the image was created, and what material or equipment was used to create the image.

Metadata: A set of information about other pieces of information.

Like other types of sources, copies of images can be found on the Internet, in books and journals, and in databases specially designed for image collection, as well as art galleries and museums. Images in books and journal articles may be difficult to find as they are typically not part of the searchable fields in catalogs in databases. You can often find images simply by paging through books and articles that are relevant to your topic. Images are much easier to locate on the Internet and in databases that specialize in collecting images and their metadata. Listed in table 6.5 are some free and subscription-based databases that allow you to access digital copies of images and search for content via metadata.

If you decide to use an image to add depth to your research project, you must make certain to find out as much as possible about its subject and creation. When using images as evidence, you must provide citations just as you would with any other type of source. (See appendix B for more information about citing sources.) However, it is equally as important for you to know all of the image's identifying information so that you can draw accurate conclusions about what the image represents. Consider who created the image and determine his or her purpose in creating it. You should question whether this image was intended simply to provide a realistic record of an event or whether it was intended to sway opinion, draw attention to something, or play upon people's sympathies. You should also consider when it was created in order to determine whether it was produced at the time of an event or whether it is merely a general representation of what something or someone might have looked like at a certain time.

Table 6.5. Databases of Historical Images and Video

Database	Free/Subscription	Description
American History in Video http://ahiv. alexanderstreet.com/	Subscription	Includes historical newsreels, documentaries, and interviews with historians on all eras of American history.
ArtStor http://www.artstor.org/ index.shtml	Subscription	A database of digital images of art and architecture from museums and public spaces around the world.
Critical Past http://www.criticalpast. com/	Free access to low resolution images and streaming film; high resolution clips may be purchased.	Still images and film from the 1980s to the present.
Library of Congress http://www.loc.gov/ pictures/	Free	Digital copies of prints and photographs from the U.S. Library of Congress.
National Archives and Records Administration (NARA) http://www.flickr.com/ photos/ usnationalarchives	Free	NARA makes many of their historical images available at the website Flickr.com.
World History in Video http://alexanderstreet. com/products/ whiv.htm	Subscription	Documentary films covering historical topics from 8000 BC through the 20th century.

Images do not always represent what they seem to. They can be manipulated to make the viewer think a certain thing or feel a certain way. Painted images, photographs, and films by their nature are staged productions and show you only what the creator of the image saw or intended you to see. They can be altered so that the final copy of an image includes something that was not originally there or removes something that was. Joseph Stalin, for example, notoriously erased people from photographs taken with him after they became enemies of the Soviet state. Wartime images that photographer Alexander Gardner took during the Civil War in the United States depict battlefields littered with dead bodies, which were actually live soldiers pretending to be dead; some were actual dead soldiers whose bodies had been moved or rearranged for dramatic effect, with guns and other props added to the scene.[2]

Because of the emotional effect that images can have, and their vulnerability to manipulation, you must consider what value an image adds to your project before including it. You definitely want the image to depict what you think it does. However, even if it represents something less than reality, any image can be useful when it is compared to what is known about historical fact. Though Alexander Gardner staged some of his Civil War photographs after combat was over, it is important to remember that photographs in the 1860s were not instant and the time needed to expose film for an image was longer than would be prudent in the heat of battle.[3] In the 1860s, newspapers depended upon the far more numerous sketch artists to depict action on the battlefield. The photographer's intention probably was not to misrepresent war, but rather to portray its horrors as accurately as possible given the limitations of the medium. Likewise, Stalin's removal of his enemies from photographs speaks volumes about the messages he wanted to communicate to his enemies—and the instability he must have felt as the Soviet leader. Even images that were created intentionally to be flattering toward the subject can provide historians with important context, such as dress style, economic status, and social and cultural aspirations.

FINDING ORAL HISTORIES AND INTERVIEWS

Oral history is the systematic gathering of people's life stories, by way of interview, as they relate to historical and cultural events. Oral histories may be gathered casually from friends and family members or they may be collected by professional historians. They may also be collected from well-known or ordinary individuals. Interviews may be structured and take place within a set time, or they may be informal conversations that take place and are recorded over many years. In a sense, oral histories are recorded every day on radio and television news broadcasts and on various Internet sites.

Oral History: The collection of historical information by way of personal interview.

Although an oral history is a story about events in a person's life, it is not an autobiography. Professionally collected oral histories are directed by trained interviewers who aim to draw specific memories from an individual to support a research project or to answer historical questions. The first step to gathering oral histories is finding interviewees who have relevant stories to tell and who are willing and able to share them. Once candidates are selected, the interviewer prepares for the interview by learning the history of the time, place, and events of interest, and by drafting plenty of relevant questions, even if there may not be time to ask all of them. An interviewer must be prepared to adjust the interview for unexpected reactions from the interviewee and should be particularly sensitive to the emotional state of the interviewee as some stories can be painful and difficult to tell. A good interviewer establishes rapport with the interviewee at the beginning of the session by asking warm-up factual questions, such as date and place of birth or names of parents and siblings, to get the conversation flowing and provide a comfortable setting for the discussion. The interviewer does not ask leading questions to elicit a particular response out of the interviewee, but rather asks open questions that allow a story to emerge naturally. The interviewer should not show bias or judgment during the interview. It is best for the interviewee to converse alone with the interviewer, free from the influences of friends or family members who may try to interject their own perspective on a story or try to correct the interviewee's memories.

While oral histories are enormously useful in the study of history, as a researcher you must exercise a degree of judiciousness when using them in a research project. First, be sure that the person conducting the interview has either a history degree or training in oral history methodology. Because an interviewee's memories may be faulty, the person conducting the interview must verify all facts presented by the interviewee, including names, dates, times, and places. An interviewee may conflate several events, forget details, or ascribe an action or statement to the wrong person, time, or place. Read the interviewer's introduction and notes in order to gain a sense of the professionalism of the interview as well as any limitations or biases of the interviewee. A published interview should include notes about any discrepancies or misinformation offered by the interviewee.

A classic example of faulty human memory is illustrated in an often-quoted story regarding the election of John F. Kennedy to the United States Presidency in 1960. In 1977, Calvin Trillin's article, "Remembrance of Moderates Past," in *The New Yorker* magazine relates the discrepancy between the perceptions of those who claimed to have voted for Kennedy following his assassination in 1963 and the actual voting records:

> John F. Kennedy's assassination not only reshaped Americans' subsequent views of him but even changed how they remembered their earlier perceptions. Although Kennedy was elected with just 49.7% of the vote in the fall of 1960, almost two-thirds of all Americans remembered voting for him when they were asked about it in the aftermath of his assassination.[4]

If you are not certain that facts stated in the interview are correct, you should check them yourself with a historical dictionary or encyclopedia. For more information about using historical encyclopedias and dictionaries, see chapter 4.

Copies of the recordings of oral histories are usually preserved in their original audio or video format at the place where they were recorded or edited. Some repositories of oral history will make the interview available on the Internet in video or audio files. Additionally, transcriptions, which are written or typed copies of the recording, may be included with the audio or video file. You should keep in mind that printed versions of oral histories are almost always edited and may not contain everything the subject said; the transcriber of the interview should make note of this.

Like other types of sources, oral histories may be described in databases by a variety of terms. Synonyms include "transcript," "audio," "video," "podcast," "interview," and "conversation." Other terms found in library catalogs may include "anecdote," "collective memory," "personal narrative," and "reminiscence."

Oral histories can be found in many places but may be located most often in books, databases, newspapers, and on the Internet.

Finding Oral Histories in Books

Oral histories in books are typically collections of interviews. The collections may be transcriptions of many interviews with one person who recounts various parts of his or her life story; or they may be interviews with various people remembering one topic or event. Before following these steps to locate oral histories in books, access your local library's online book catalog and be sure that you are using the Advanced Search or More Options screen. See chapter 5 for more information about accessing a catalog's Advanced Search screen.

- In the Keyword Search box, type the most general descriptive term that relates to your topic on the first line. Examples of general search terms might be "South Africa" or "apartheid."
- On the second Keyword line, type "oral history or personal narrative or interview." Your search should look similar to the one illustrated in figure 6.7.
- Optionally, if the person you are searching for is a native of a country whose language you cannot read, it is a good idea to limit your search to a language you can read as your search may produce results that have not been translated.

When you complete your search you will see a list of books that most likely contain transcriptions of oral histories or interviews somewhere within the book. If your attempt does not produce adequate results, try modifying your search to include one of the other terms mentioned above.

Catalog Advanced Search

all fields(keyword) ▾	South Africa	And ▾
all fields(keyword) ▾	oral history or personal history or interview	And ▾
title ▾		And ▾
subject ▾		And ▾
series ▾		And ▾
periodical title ▾		And ▾
isbn ▾		

[Search] [Reset]

language:	ANY ▾
format (book, cd, etc.):	ANY ▾
location:	ANY ▾
match on:	Keywords ▾
pubyear:	
sort by:	New to Old ▾

Figure 6.7. Advanced Search for Oral Histories. Image courtesy of Dickinson College and SirsiDynix.

Finding Oral Histories in Databases

The number of databases that specialize in preserving transcripts and audio files is small but growing. Some of the sources you may find helpful are listed in table 6.6. Techniques for searching databases are described in chapter 5.

Finding Oral Histories in Newspapers

Newspapers often include transcripts of short or long interviews that can be used as a form of oral history. When searching for an interview published in a newspaper, the easiest way to find them is to search by the person's full name and add the term "interview" to the search. The term "oral history" will likely not be used in newspaper articles to describe a personal interview. If you need to use a printed index to find an interview in a newspaper, you should look up the person by last name and scan the entries for articles that include quotes by the person, as shown in figure 6.8. More information about searching print indexes can be found in chapter 5.

You can also find interviews by searching online newspaper databases. You will first need to access a newspaper database such as Ebsco's Newspa-

Table 6.6. Oral History Databases

Title	Free/Subscription	Description
American History in Video http://ahiv.alexanderstreet.com/	Subscription	Digital videos of historical events and documentaries covering all eras of U.S. history.
Critical Past http://www.criticalpast.com/	Free access to low resolution images and streaming film; high-resolution clips may be purchased.	Still images and films from the 1980s to the present, including interviews with famous historical figures.
In the First Person http://www.inthefirstperson.com/firp/index.shtml	Free	Thousands of personal narratives covering the 17th to the 20th centuries.
Oral History Online http://alexanderstreet.com/products/orhi.htm	Subscription	Audio files and transcriptions of thousands of oral histories in the English language. Covers the 20th century to the present.
Southern Oral History Program http://www.lib.unc.edu/dc/sohp/	Free	Oral history interviews with prominent citizens of the southern United States.

per Source Plus, Dialog's World News Connection, or ProQuest's Historical Newspapers. If your library does not subscribe to one of these databases, ask a librarian to direct you to an alternative newspaper source. After you access a newspaper database, select the Advanced Search option, as described in chapter 5, and simply type the name of the person you are researching on one Search box, and the word "interview" in a second Search box, as illustrated

Greenwich Hospital, Draught of Pensioners, 6 *f* 3 *d*

Grenville, Lord, and the Alien Bill, Interview with the Franch Ambassador, 7 *j* 2 *b*—11 *j* 3 *d* —23 *j* 2 *o*

—— **and M. De Chauvelin's Correspondence between 7 *i* 2 *h*—11 *i* 3 *a*—17 *i* 2 *r*—23 *i* 2 ...**

Figure 6.8. Newspaper Interviews in a Printed Index. Palmer's Index to *The Times* [London], January 1793, scan courtesy of Dickinson College.

ProQuest

Basic	**Advanced**	Publications	🗀 **My Research** 0 marked items

Databases selected: Multiple databases...

Advanced Search   Tools: Search Tips

margaret thatcher		Citation and document text ▾
AND ▾	interview	Citation and document text ▾
AND ▾		Citation and document text ▾

                    Add a row | Remove a row   **Search**   **Clear**

Figure 6.9. Search for Interviews in Newspapers Using ProQuest. Courtesy of Pro-Quest.

in figure 6.9. More information about searching for newspaper articles can be found in chapter 5.

Finding Oral Histories on the Internet

The Internet is a particularly good source of oral histories because of the capability to include the audio or video versions of the interview as well as the transcriptions. Recordings of oral history interviews allow you to hear the emotion in the person's voice or see it on his or her face, and thus perceive which parts of the story were the most memorable and most important to the interviewee. An audio recording or a video of an interview also allows you to discern where the interviewee stumbled over answers and had difficulty recalling details or when he or she speaks most thoughtfully, animatedly, or emotionally of his or her most vivid memories.

Many history websites include links to the audio files or transcripts of oral history interviews. The easiest way to search for this material on the Internet is to create one that combines the most common words associated with oral histories with keywords related to the topic of your search. For example, if you want to find interviews regarding the fall of the Berlin Wall in 1989, you might construct a search using the phrase "podcast OR oral history OR interview" and "Berlin Wall," as illustrated in figure 6.10. A search similar to the one in figure 6.10 should return results similar to those illustrated in figure 6.11.

Note that if you search for the term "oral history" on the Internet without adding a topic, you will likely find information about how to conduct oral histories but not necessarily any actual historical interviews. Table 6.7 provides examples of free oral history collections available online.

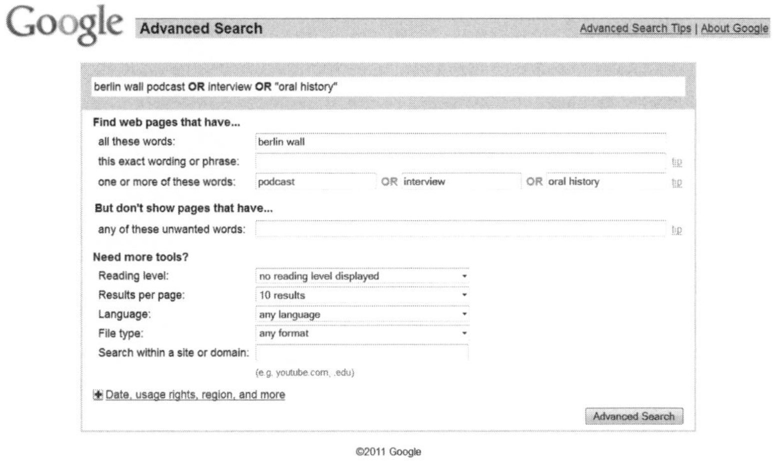

Figure 6.10.   Advanced Google Search for Oral History on the Fall of the Berlin Wall. Courtesy of Google.

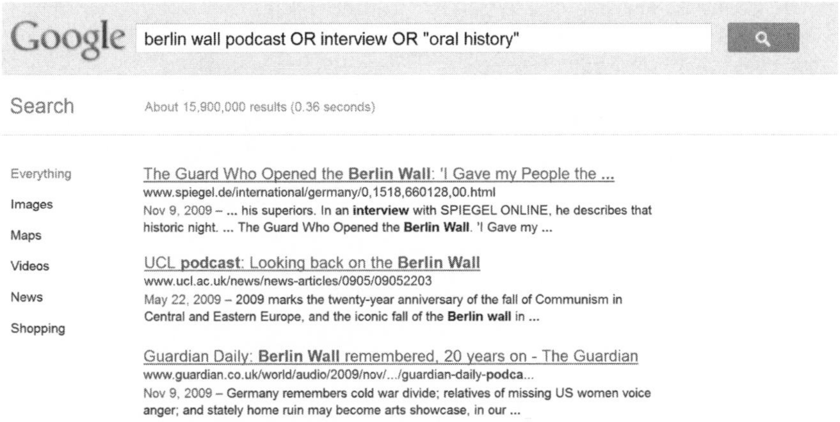

Figure 6.11.   Results of Advanced Google Search for Oral History on the Fall of the Berlin Wall. Courtesy of Google.

After following the techniques recommended so far in this book, you should have a mix of tertiary, secondary, and primary sources that will add breadth and depth to your project. With these sources, you can examine your topic from multiple angles: the tertiary sources will provide you with a broad overview of the topic, the secondary sources will provide you with criticism and analysis of professional historians, and the primary sources will help you understand history from the point of view of those who lived through it. Now

Table 6.7. Free Oral History Collections

Oral History Site	Description
American Folklife Center http://www.loc.gov/folklife/	Around 4,000 collections of recorded songs, stories, and cultural pieces, dating back to the 1800s.
American Memory Project http://memory.loc.gov/ammem/ index.html	Sheet music, song sheets, and digitized sound recording collections.
Baylor Oral History Institute http://contentdm.baylor.edu/cdm4/ index_08buioh. php?CISOROOT=/08buioh	Baylor University has over 1,800 oral history interviews available, as well as 800 memoirs, covering the 19th and 20th centuries.
Columbia University: Oral History Research Office http://www.columbia.edu/cu/lweb/indiv/ oral/	The oldest and largest oral history program in the world, founded in 1948. Contains nearly 8,000 taped memoirs and nearly 1,000,000 pages of transcript. Includes interviews with a wide variety of historical figures.
History Matters http://historymatters.gmu.edu/	A project of the Center for Social History and the New Media and George Mason University. First-person narratives on topics dating from the 16th century to the present.
Matrix: Center for Humane Arts, Letters, and Social Sciences Online http://www2.matrix.msu.edu/category/ oral-history/	Collects folklore, oral history interviews, and songs from various African nations.
National Public Radio (NPR) http://npr.org	The parent of more than 900 independent public radio stations, NPR has recordings, interviews, and recorded programs from politicians, world leaders, and scholars in the arts and sciences.
Oral History Association http://www.oralhistory.org/	A professional organization for oral historians and enthusiasts. The site contains useful links to resources, publications, and standards for oral history.
Public Broadcasting System (PBS) http://www.pbs.org	PBS has video and recorded interviews of groups ranging from Cherokee Indians, veterans, and homeless teenagers.
Rutgers Oral History Archives http://oralhistory.rutgers.edu/home.html	This site preserves oral history interviews from veterans of World War II, the Korean War, and the Vietnam War.
Shirley Chisholm Project on Brooklyn Women's Activism http://shirleychisholmproject.brooklyn. cuny.edu/The_Shirley_Chisholm_ Project/ Archive_%26_Oral_History_Collection. html	Named after the first African-American woman to be elected to Congress, the project is an archive of personal documents relating to Chisholm and social change in New York City, including oral histories.

Oral History Site	Description
Story Corps http://storycorps.org/	StoryCorps archives over 30,000 oral history interviews and allows others to record their own story for the site. It is featured on NPR (National Public Radio) and archived by the American Folklife Center at the Library of Congress.
University of North Carolina: Southern Oral History Program http://www.sohp.org/	More than 4,200 interviews pertaining to the 19th-century history of the American South.
University of Southern Mississippi Civil Rights Documentation Project http://www.usm.edu/crdp/	A bibliography of civil rights oral histories on the courts and law, education, massive resistance, protests, and violence. One must contact the individual university for the transcript or recording.
Veterans History Project http://www.loc.gov/vets/	From the U.S. Library of Congress. Collects, preserves, and makes accessible the personal accounts of American war veterans.

that you have a basic understanding of how to find sources, you can apply what you have learned so far to your research assignments and use the following sections to learn how to search even more efficiently.

NOTES

1. Abraham Lincoln, "Nicolay Copy" of the Gettysburg Address, 1863, Manuscript Division, Library of Congress Digital ID# al0186, 1, http://myloc.gov/Exhibitions /GettysburgAddress/exhibitionitems/ExhibitObjects/NicolayCopy.aspx.

2. Jonathan Mitchell, Producer, "Visualizing the Civil War," Studio 360 Podcast, http://www.studio360.org/2011/apr/08/mathew-brady-and-winslow-homer/.

3. Ibid.

4. Calvin Trillin, "Remembrance of Moderates Past," *The New Yorker*, 21 March 1977, 85. This article has been quoted in: Clifford M. Kuhn, "'There's a Footnote to History!' Memory and the History of Martin Luther King's October 1960 Arrest and Its Aftermath," *Journal of American History* 84, no. 2 (September 1997), 593; Godfrey Hodgson, *America in Our Time* (New York: Random House, 1976), 5; Linda Shopes, "What Is Oral History? Making Sense of Evidence" on *History Matters: The U.S. Survey on the Web*, located at http://historymatters.gmu.edu; and in other sources.

Chapter Seven

Search Tricks

Up to this point, you have learned what kinds of information you need to produce a research project for history, what sources you should use to find that information, and the essential search techniques you should use to draw information from those sources. The sources you will use to research any history topic, whether free or subscription based, print or online, are designed to be easy to use; unfortunately, these sources can be somewhat difficult to navigate, especially if you are a new researcher. Sometimes your first try at searching for sources on a topic may not produce the type of results that you want or need. The results of research on topics that historians have studied extensively for decades may overwhelm you, producing hundreds or even thousands of citations that would take hours or days to review. Alternatively, you may perform a search that produces too few or even zero results.

None of these scenarios should end with you giving up in frustration. Rather, you should try as much as possible to become familiar with the ways in which each research tool works, just as you would familiarize yourself with a new topic by using encyclopedias and dictionaries before you try to find primary and secondary sources about it. Databases in particular are constantly changing and improving the rules and algorithms they use to organize and extract information. This requires all researchers, even experienced ones, to learn special techniques for enhancing the search experience. The strategies offered in this section will help you to learn efficient ways to navigate research tools and show you how to manipulate your search results so that they direct you to even more relevant sources without reconstructing an entirely new search. You will also find that exploratory research in databases can help you refine a topic.

REFINING A TOPIC

If you are starting a project for which you are free to develop your own thesis, you might find the selection of a specific research question to be one of
the most challenging parts of your project. As it is the most important part
of the research process, you must choose your topic with thoughtfulness and
circumspection. Along with your professor or research advisor, you should
always start by assessing the goals of your project. Consider your project's
minimum length requirements and how much time you will need to gather
and read the sources necessary to support your arguments. Your topic should
be one that is focused on a specific question that will sustain your interest so
you can contribute original thoughts to the existing historical literature. You
should be able to support your thesis either directly or indirectly with primary
and secondary sources. Ideally, a good topic should be one that stimulates
discussion and can be examined from multiple points of view. Your topic
should be one that requires you to form an opinion and make scholarly arguments to support it.

Admittedly, topics that fulfill these criteria take time and knowledge to develop, and it can be particularly challenging to write a thesis that will sustain
a large research project if you have limited knowledge of the topic when you
begin. Fortunately, there are various methods you can use to help identify
a topic and to begin the process of developing a thesis. Once you know a
relative area of interest, the best thing to do is start a broad investigation of
your topic by performing some preliminary research. This will help you understand how the topic has been addressed by historians and what questions
are frequently raised about it. Additionally, performing some preliminary
research will save you time in the long run because you will be assured that
you will be able to acquire enough sources to support your own assertions.
You can accomplish your preliminary research easily and relatively quickly
using the strategies listed below.

- Consult historical encyclopedias and dictionaries to make sure you know
  all the pertinent basic facts about the topic. More information about encyclopedias and dictionaries can be found in chapter 4.
- Check your library's catalog for books related to the topic. Read the catalog's summaries or abstracts of those books to make sure they are relevant,
  and examine the books' tables of contents to see what specific aspects of
  your topic are included in the study. You also should skim several chapters
  to see how each book addresses historical arguments. More information
  about searching for books in library catalogs can be found in chapter 5.
- Determine what secondary source databases are relevant to your topic and
  start a broad search for journal articles on your topic. Usually you should

begin your search for articles with either America: History and Life or Historical Abstracts, but other databases more specific to your time period may be useful as well. Skim the results list and read the abstracts of some of the articles. This will help you get an idea of how historians have examined your topic over the years. More information about choosing and searching databases can be found in chapter 3 and chapter 5.

The subscription databases America: History and Life and Historical Abstracts, both described in chapter 5, offer a special feature that may help you develop an idea for a paper topic. The CLIO Notes feature provides brief overviews of major topics in history, lists important historical questions related to the topics, and provides brief biographies of major figures involved, as well as timelines and direct links to journal articles relevant to the topics. Once you have accessed either of these databases, you can get to the CLIO Notes feature by clicking the CLIO Notes button at the top of the screen. After you click on the button, you will see a list of links organized by continent and further subdivided by time period, as shown in figure 7.1.

You can continue to click through the subject links until you reach a set of notes specific to your area of interest. As you read through an encyclopedia entry or CLIO Notes about your topic, you will learn the major questions asked of all historical eras and find out how historians describe and analyze historical events.

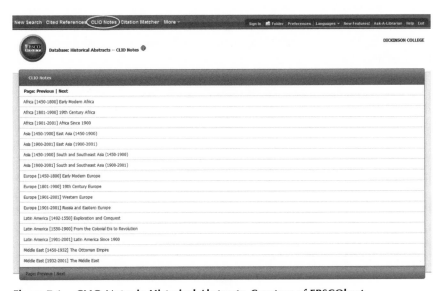

Figure 7.1. CLIO Notes in Historical Abstracts. Courtesy of EBSCOhost.

TERMINOLOGY

Choosing the correct search terms is arguably the most important part of your search. Using invalid terminology in a search will produce few or no results, causing you endless frustration. Using correct terminology not only will help you locate the types of sources you hoped and expected to find, but will likely reveal other unexpected yet valuable sources. If you have only limited knowledge about your topic, you should use historical encyclopedias and dictionaries to learn what words, phrases, and particular spellings professional historians use when discussing the people, places, and events associated with your topic. Historians may not think about your subject quite the same way you might. Background reading will help you search more efficiently because it will give you a good idea of what words or phrases are likely to best describe your topic.

When researching, you must try to identify synonyms for the terms you initially choose and include those terms in your search strategy. A person's personal letters, for example, might be described in a library catalog or database as correspondence; similarly, the word "memoir" may be used in place of the word "autobiography." You must also think of synonyms for the topic itself and how descriptions of that topic have changed over time. For example, a modern researcher seeking sources on freed slaves in the nineteenth-century United States might use the term "African-American" to describe them; however, other terms that have been used throughout history, and certainly in primary sources, include "black," "colored," "Negro," and other words that we now consider to be racist but were nonetheless used by our forebears. Thorough and objective research in history sometimes requires that we face atrocities like slavery and genocide with words that we find to be malicious and offensive.

Remember too that people's names may change over time. Women in particular have been likely to drop their maiden names and use their husbands' last names upon marriage. A person's name may be spelled incorrectly, middle initials may be included or dropped, and nicknames may be used. Some prominent historical figures are referred to by their nicknames, honorific titles, or last names only. George Washington, for example, might be referred to as "General Washington," "The American Cincinnatus," "The American Fabius," or "The Father of His Country." Additionally, people in the nineteenth century often abbreviated their first names in ways that might seem strange to the twenty-first-century reader. For example, Jas. was used as an abbreviation for James and Jno. was used for John.

Immigrants in particular have been known to change their names upon entering a new society. Some of the many possible reasons for this are explained on the website About.com:

Your ancestor may have gone by several different names during his lifetime, and it's also likely you'll find him listed under different spellings as well. Always search for variations of your ancestor's name. You will find that both first names and surnames are commonly misspelled in official records. People were not as well educated in the past as they are today, and sometimes a name on a document was written as it sounded (phonetically), or perhaps was simply misspelled by accident. In other cases, an individual may have changed the spelling of his/her surname more formally to adapt to a new culture, to sound more elegant, or to be easier to remember.[1]

Considering alternative spellings of words also is critical to the research process, particularly when researching in the English language. Spelling in English was not standardized until 1755 when Samuel Johnson wrote *A Dictionary of the English Language*, and British English faded out in America after Noah Webster started to publish his now-famous dictionaries in 1828. Therefore, you have to consider that some words in your search phrases may need to be spelled differently than we do in modern English.

As historians, it is important to remember that terminology for people, places, and things changes over time and that we must learn to think of events in the same terms as those who lived through them did. This is particularly important when searching for primary sources, as both popular and academic literature will change and evolve when the topic is debated and discussed. For example, the Civil War in the United States has been referred to as "the war between the states" and "the war for southern independence." Until World War II, World War I was known simply as "The Great War."

One example of an event that is not described using the terminology you might expect is the Great Depression. The Great Depression is the common name of the event that started in the United States in 1929 with a major stock market crash. The phrase "Great Depression" was popularized by President Herbert Hoover with statements such as "I need not recount to you that the world is passing through a great depression" in a speech delivered to the American Legion on September 21, 1931.[2] The term was later used as the title of Lionel Robbins's book, *The Great Depression*, published in 1934. Even so, "Great Depression" is not a term that is always carried over to databases and library catalogs.

The book shown in figure 7.2, *Rainbow's End* by Maury Klein, is an example of a library catalog record for a book about the Great Depression. You will notice that neither the title of the book nor the book's description uses the phrase "Great Depression." Because it appears nowhere in the record, searching for "great depression" as a keyword or subject would not return *Rainbow's End*, which is about the stock market crash of 1929 that instigated the Great Depression. One way to overcome this problem and locate relevant

Rainbow's end : the crash of 1929

Author:	Maury Klein
Publisher:	Oxford [England] ; New York : Oxford University Press, 2001.
Series:	Pivotal moments in American history.
Edition/Format:	▇ Book : English View all editions and formats
Summary:	"The first major history of the Crash in over a decade, Rainbow's End tells the story of the stock market collapse in a colorful, swift-moving narrative that blends a vivid portrait of the 1920s with an intensely gripping account of Wall Street's greatest catastrophe." "The book offers a picture of a world full of plungers, powerful bankers, corporate titans, millionaire brokers, and buoyantly optimistic stock market Read more...
Rating:	☆☆☆☆☆ (not yet rated) 📖 0 with reviews - Be the first.

Figure 7.2.   Catalog entry for the book *Rainbow's End: The Crash of 1929*. Copyright 2011 OCLC Online Computer Library Center, Inc. Used with Permission. FirstSearch, OCLC, WorldCat, and the WorldCat logo are registered trademarks/service marks of OCLC.

material that might not have displayed on your initial search is to make use of subject headings.

KEYWORDS VS. SUBJECTS

If you carefully examine the advanced search screen of a library catalog or database, you might notice that there are options to search by either keyword or subject. Keywords and subjects are two very different things, and it is important to understand the difference in order to construct a successful search.

Keyword: Any searchable word that appears in the citation or full text of an article or book.

A keyword search is what takes place when you type words in the first search box that is offered on a library catalog, database, or Internet search engine. It is a broad and general search. When you perform a keyword search, the database will provide a list of citations that have your search terms anywhere in any record of any item in the database, including the fields for title, author, subject, and summary.

A subject search, in contrast, is more specific than a keyword search. Subjects also are known as "subject headings," "descriptors," or "controlled vocabulary." A subject heading is a specialized word or phrase used to describe the content of books and journal articles so that they may be easily discovered in indexes or databases. They are applied to books and articles by research professionals who carefully examine each item for its subject content. In a library catalog or database record, subject headings usually are hyperlinked, thus allowing you to click on them and find additional sources to which the same subject descriptor has been applied. When you use subject headings to

Figure 7.3. Subject Headings in Historical Abstracts. Courtesy of EBSCOhost.

search, you make it more likely that you will find relevant material because all books or documents in a catalog or database that address the same topic probably have the same subject headings applied to their records. Usually you must access a database's advanced search screen to perform a subject search.

When you perform a subject search, the catalog or database will provide citations that have your search term listed only in the subject field of each item in the database. By way of example, let us examine the citation for the article "Shopping for Britain" by Maxine Berg, which was published in the journal *History Today* in 2005 and found by searching the database Historical Abstracts. The subject terms applied to Berg's article are illustrated in figure 7.3.

This citation contains both keywords and subject headings. The following words are keywords:

• shopping	• today	• wars
• Britain	• international	• industrial
• Maxine	• trade	• revolution
• Berg	• markets	• commerce
• history	• Napoleonic	• consumerism

The following words and phrases are subject headings, listed in the order in which they appear in the citation:

• Great Britain—commerce	• markets	• Industrial Revolution
• international trade	• Napoleonic Wars, 1800–1815	• commerce
		• consumerism

Notice that all the words appearing in the subject heading list also appear in the keyword list. Thus, a subject heading is always a keyword, but a keyword may not necessarily be a subject heading. A subject search in Historical Abstracts for the phrases "Industrial Revolution" and "Great Britain" would return the "Shopping for Britain" article, whereas a subject search for "shopping" and "England" would not. However, a keyword search for "Industrial Revolution" and "Great Britain" would return "Shopping for Britain." A keyword search for "shopping" and "Great Britain" also would return "Shopping for Britain." A keyword search for "shops" and "England" would not return this article because neither term is used in the book's record.

Most databases default to a keyword search. When you initiate a search in a keyword field, what you are doing is the broadest and least precise search possible. A keyword search often returns hundreds or even thousands of results, many of them irrelevant to the intended topic. A keyword search directs the catalog or database to look for the word or phrase you type anywhere within an item's record no matter where in the record it appears and whether or not it is relevant to your topic. For example, a search on the words "New York" may produce a list of items about New York City, New York State, items that were produced by a publishing company located in New York, or items for which the author may be a corporate or government entity such as the New York State court system or the New York Museum of Modern Art. In cases such as this, it is a good idea to make your search as specific as possible, perhaps by adding a name or event to your query or by limiting your search to materials written in a particular language, printed in a certain format, published in a certain year, or using other available options.

Keyword searches are useful if you are in the early stages of your research and are browsing for available material. In order to make your search more specific, however, you should combine a keyword with other words or phrases. For example, imagine that you are trying to research New York City in the aftermath of the September 11, 2001, attacks on the World Trade Center. A keyword search on the phrase "New York" *may* return items about New York City. It may also return books about New York State. However, such a search is more likely to produce results similar to those in figure 7.4, in which a library catalog keyword search on New York returns more than 150,000 items.

An initial inspection of the list of items returned in the search conducted in figure 7.4 shows that none of the titles appearing on the first page are relevant to the attacks of September 11, 2001, nor do any of them even mention New York in the title. This is the result of searching for the topic by keyword only.

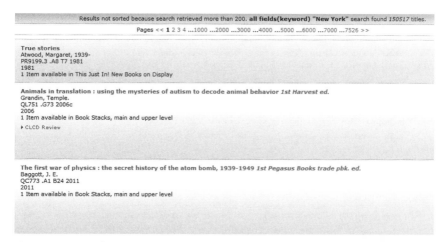

Figure 7.4. Catalog Keyword Search on "New York." Courtesy of Dickinson College and SirsiDynix.

The catalog returned all items that include the keyword in the name of the author or title, in the subject headings, in the name of the publisher, in the book's summary, and any other fields. You can determine why any particular item showed up in your results list by clicking on the button or link that provides additional information about the item. This may be a button labeled Details or More Information, or you may have to click on the book's title.

Let us examine, for example, the book *Beyond Humanity? The Ethics of Biomedical Enhancement* by Allen E. Buchanan, which showed up in the search for New York. In order for this book to have appeared on that list, the term "New York" must be listed somewhere in the book's full record. Clicking on the title of Buchanan's book, for more information, reveals that it was published by Oxford University Press, which has offices in New York, as shown in figure 7.5.

For cases like this one in which your initial search produces such unacceptable results, there are a number of things you can do to improve your search results. One method is to add additional terms to your search if you used only one or two; conversely, you could remove terms from your search if you used more than three or four. You could, of course, try completely different search terms. Another helpful method of improving your search experience is to take advantage of a database's subject heading links.

Subject headings are most useful when you already have an item you know is useful and you would like to find additional items that are similar to it. Let us imagine, for example, that we are doing a research project on the causes

Personal author: Buchanan, Allen E., 1948-
Title: Beyond humanity? : the ethics of biomedical enhancement / Allen Buchanan.
Publication info: Oxford ; New York : Oxford University Press, 2011.
Physical description: xii, 286 p. ; 23 cm.
Series: (Uehiro series in practical ethics.)
ISBN: 9780199587810 (hbk. : alk. paper)
ISBN: 0199587817 (hbk. : alk. paper)
Bibliography note: Includes bibliographical references and index.
Subject: Medical innovations--Moral and ethical aspects.

Figure 7.5.   Detailed Record of a Book. Courtesy of Dickinson College and SirsiDynix.

of the 9/11 terrorist attacks and for class we were assigned to read a book entitled *The Looming Tower: Al-Qaeda and the Road to 9/11* by Lawrence Wright. We now want to find books similar to Wright's. To do this, we would look up Wright's book in a library catalog or WorldCat and click on the title or the Details button to reveal additional information and locate the subject headings, which may be the last part of the book's record. The subject headings assigned to *The Looming Tower* are shown in figure 7.6. One subject heading relevant to our inquiry is "September 11 Terrorist Attacks, 2001." If we click on that link, the catalog would start a new search and return any other books that were added to the library catalog with the same subject heading. In this case, more than ninety additional books resulted from that click.

If you have conducted a search that results in a lot of irrelevant material, it is possible that your search has not in fact been wasted. Even if you find only one item in your initial search that relates your topic, you should take a look at that item's full record and take advantage of the subject links. This may prevent you from having to construct an entirely new search.

Although both library catalogs and databases use subject headings, you should be aware that the subject headings found in library catalogs do not

Personal author: Wright, Lawrence, 1947-
Title: The looming tower : Al-Qaeda and the road to 9/11 / Lawrence Wright.
Edition: 1st ed.
Publication info: New York : Knopf, 2006.
Physical description: 469 p., [16] p. of plates : ill., maps ; 25 cm.
ISBN: 037541486X
Bibliography note: Includes bibliographical references (p. 429-438) and index.
Contents: The martyr. -- The sporting club. -- The founder. -- Change. -- The miracles. -- The base. -- Return of the hero. -- Paradise. -- The Silicon Valley. -- Paradise lost. -- The prince of darkness. -- The boy spies. -- Hijira. -- Going operational. -- Bread and water. -- "Now it begins" -- The new millennium. -- Boom. -- The big wedding. -- Revelations. -- Principal characters.
Corporate subject: Qaida (Organization)
Subject: September 11 Terrorist Attacks, 2001.
Subject: Terrorism--Government policy--United States.
Subject: Intelligence service--United States.

Figure 7.6.   Subject Headings in a Library Catalog for *The Looming Tower*. Courtesy of Dickinson College and SirsiDynix.

necessarily match subject headings found in article databases. Therefore, if you find a subject heading in a book, you should search for that subject only in a library catalog or on WorldCat; conversely, if you find a subject heading in a database, you should search for that subject only in the same database. When you search by subject heading, you must type it exactly as it appears in the original item, or the system may not be able to find matches. Use the subject heading hyperlinks for best results whenever possible.

Using Subject Headings to Find Books

In books, subject headings can be found in two places—either in the book's full catalog record as shown above or on the publication information page in the first few pages of a book. Figure 7.7 illustrates a publication information page with subject headings enumerated below the title.

To return for a moment to our search on books regarding the Great Depression, let us say that we would like to find books similar to *Rainbow's End*. To do this in WorldCat or a library catalog using subject headings, we could construct a subject search by typing the heading "Depressions—1929—United States" in the Subject field as shown in figure 7.8. When you complete this search, you should see quite a few books on the topic of the Great Depression in the United States, some of which probably have titles that do not make the content obvious.

When you initiate a search by typing a subject heading into a search box, remember that you must type the subject phrase exactly as it appears on the book's publication information page. Subject headings for books are selected from specialized thesauruses of terminology created by the Library of Congress and are linked only to books for which the heading specifically applies. If your search does not match a known subject heading, or if your library does not have any other books to which that particular subject heading was applied, you may not see any additional results.

Using Subject Headings to Find Articles in Databases

It is rare for subject headings to be listed in the article's text, as they are on the publication page of a book; therefore, the only place you are likely to find subject headings for articles is in databases. Many databases provide lists of the subject vocabulary used so that you can construct a search by choosing known terms rather than trying to guess at them. Most databases provide lists of subject terms, sometimes referred to as controlled vocabulary, in their help files.

In America: History and Life and Historical Abstracts, you can examine subject terms by clicking on the More button near the top of the search

THIS IS A BORZOI BOOK
PUBLISHED BY ALFRED A. KNOPF

Copyright © 2006 by Lawrence Wright

All rights reserved. Published in the United States by Alfred A. Knopf, a division of Random House, Inc., New York, and in Canada by Random House of Canada, Limited, Toronto.

www.aaknopf.com

Grateful acknowledgment is made to Constable & Robinson Ltd. and Michal Snunit for permission to reprint an excerpt from *The Soul Bird* by Michal Snunit. Reprinted by permission.

Knopf, Borzoi Books, and the colophon are registered trademarks of Random House, Inc.

Library of Congress Cataloging-in-Publication Data
Wright, Lawrence, [date]
The looming tower : Al-Qaeda and the road to 9/11 /
by Lawrence Wright.
p. cm.
Includes bibliographical references and index.
ISBN 0-375-41486-X
1. September 11 Terrorist Attacks, 2001. 2. Qaida (Organization)
3. Terrorism—Government policy—United States.
4. Intelligence service—United States. I. Title.

HV6432.7.W75 2005
973.931—dc22 2006041032

Manufactured in the United States of America
Published August 8, 2006
Reprinted Five Times
Seventh Printing, September 2006

Figure 7.7. Subject Headings on the Publisher's Information Page for *The Looming Tower*. Courtesy of Knopf Publishers.

Catalog Advanced Search

all fields(keyword) ▼		And ▼
author ▼		And ▼
title ▼		And ▼
subject ▼	Depressions - 1929 -United States	And ▼
series ▼		And ▼
periodical title ▼		And ▼
isbn ▼		

Search Reset

Figure 7.8. Subject Search in a Library Catalog. Courtesy of Dickinson College and SirsiDynix.

screen, as shown in figure 7.9, and then clicking Indexes. After you click on the Indexes link, you will see an option labeled Browse an Index. Change this field from the default Select to Headings. Without typing anything, you can then click the Browse button and scan an alphabetically arranged list of all the subject terms used in the database. Alternatively, you can type a term relevant to your topic, such as "Depressions—1929" in the Browse For box, and then click the Browse button to reveal the subject headings that fall in line alphabetically near the term you typed. This Browse For method in America: History & Life is illustrated in figure 7.10. When you complete your search for a subject heading you will see a results list similar to that in figure 7.11.

As illustrated in figure 7.11, the Browse For option provides you with a list of subjects that best match the term you entered, and on the right side of the screen, you will see a records count telling you how many articles in the database have the respective subject applied to it. At this point, you should

New Search Cited References CLIO Notes Citation Matcher More ˅

EBSCO HOST

Searching: **America: History & Life** | Choose Databases »

| in | Select a Field (optional) | ▼ | Search |

AND ▼ | in | Select a Field (optional) | ▼ |

AND ▼ | in | Select a Field (optional) | ▼ | Add Row

Basic Search | Advanced Search | Visual Search | Search History

Figure 7.9. Access to Subject Headings in America: History & Life and Historical Abstracts. Courtesy of EBSCOhost.

Figure 7.10.   Browsing for Subject Headings in Historical Abstracts. Courtesy of EB-SCOhost.

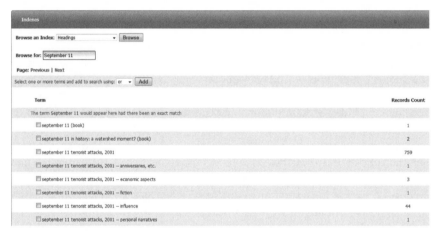

Figure 7.11.   Controlled Vocabulary List in America: History and Life. Courtesy of EBSCOhost.

click the check box next to the subject heading that most closely matches your topic area, then click the Add button above the list of headings, then click the Browse button near the top of the screen. You will be provided with a list of the articles that have the subject heading applied to it. Other databases provide similar subject heading lists and the Help feature on most databases will tell you how to access them.

ABSTRACTS

Sometimes the title of a book or article is not really descriptive of its content. You may find that an item with a title that does not seem useful upon first

Figure 7.12. An Abstract in Historical Abstracts. Courtesy of EBSCOhost.

inspection turns out to be quite relevant to your topic. Or, you may find that a book or article that seems like it should be helpful from its title turns out not to be so once you start reading it. Many library catalogs and databases help to mitigate this problem by providing summaries of each item. These summaries are called *abstracts*. An abstract is a short paragraph summarizing the content of the book or article, including its thesis, evidence, and conclusion. Reading an abstract allows you to determine whether the source has potential usefulness before you access it. This prevents you from wasting time examining materials that prove ultimately irrelevant to your project and helps to lead you directly to those that are relevant. An example of an abstract is shown in figure 7.12.

You should be aware that abstracts are for informational purposes only. Abstracts may be written by the author of the work or the editors of the databases. Generally, there should be no need for you to cite abstracts, but if you do, you must apply the same rules of citation and attribution that you would apply to any other source.

FINDING NONPRINT MATERIALS IN LIBRARY CATALOGS AND WORLDCAT

In addition to books and journals, most libraries collect many other types of materials, such as CDs, DVDs, maps, images, and musical scores. Therefore, you can make your search more efficient by specifying the type of item you want. If you do not do this, the library catalogs will display material in any format as long as the description matches your search terms. Most library catalogs include a search option allowing you to narrow your search by format. For example, if you want the catalog to provide a list of only documentary films about the history of India on DVD but not films in VHS format, books, CDs, or other types of material, you can use the catalog's advanced search screen to ignore everything except DVDs. Figure 7.13 illustrates how to construct a search that will produce documentary DVD films about the history of India using an advanced search screen, and figure 7.14 shows the results of the search.

TRUNCATION SYMBOLS

Truncation symbols are characters used in place of letters that allow you to search for a word that might have spelling variations or plural forms that differ significantly from the singular form. Most databases allow for the use

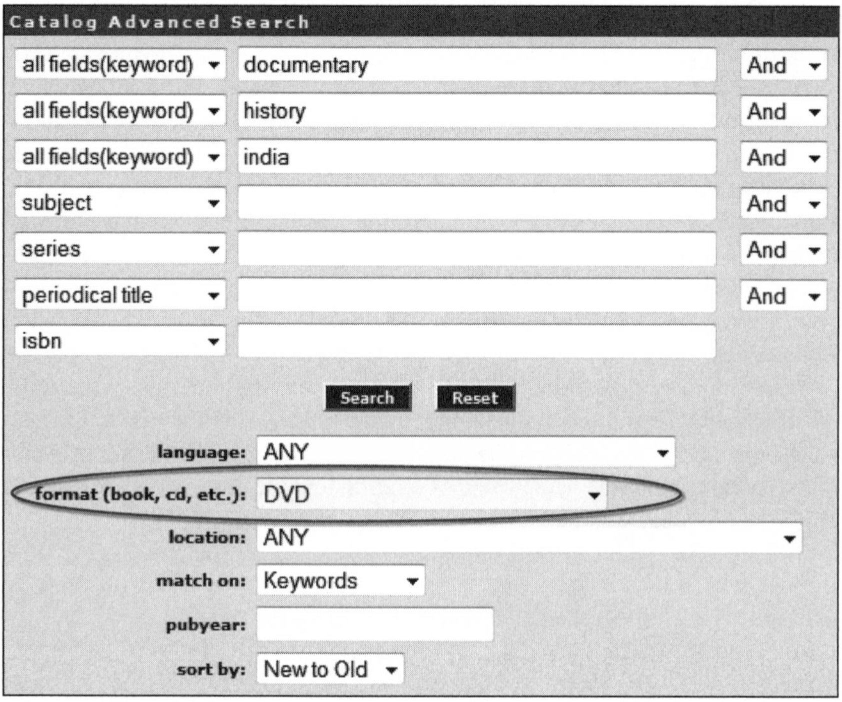

Figure 7.13. Search for DVD Documentary Films on India. Courtesy of Dickinson College and SirsiDynix.

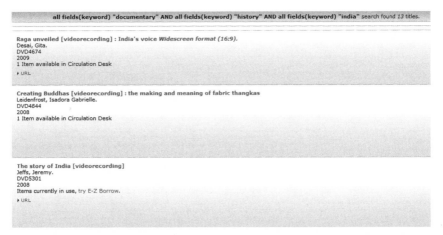

all fields(keyword) "documentary" AND all fields(keyword) "history" AND all fields(keyword) "india" search found *13* titles.

Raga unveiled [videorecording] : India's voice *Widescreen format (16:9).*
Desai, Gita.
DVD4674
2009
1 Item available in Circulation Desk
▸ URL

Creating Buddhas [videorecording] : the making and meaning of fabric thangkas
Leidenfrost, Isadora Gabrielle.
DVD4844
2008
1 Item available in Circulation Desk

The story of India [videorecording]
Jeffs, Jeremy.
DVD5301
2008
Items currently in use, try E-Z Borrow.
▸ URL

Figure 7.14. Catalog Results for DVD Documentary Films on India. Courtesy of Dickinson College and SirsiDynix.

of truncation symbols and most will provide a list of acceptable symbols on the Help page. Some databases may refer to these characters as wildcard symbols.

The alternative to using truncation symbols is to try to think of all the possible different forms of a word, which can make a messy and complicated search. These symbols allow you to keep your search phrases simple and can help you to make sure that you are covering your topic as widely as possible. Three of the most common and useful truncation symbols are the * (asterisk), the ? (question mark), and " " (quotation marks).

* (Asterisk). An asterisk used at the end of a word indicates that you will accept any form of that word with any ending. For example, "industr*" typed into a search box could retrieve the words "industry," "industries," "industrial," or "industrialization," as illustrated in figure 7.15.

? (Question Mark). A question mark used in the middle of a word will replace a single letter. It is useful when you are unsure how a word is spelled or when the spelling of a plural form of a word is significantly different from the singular form. For example, "wom?m" typed into a search box could retrieve the words "woman" or "women."

"" (Quotation Marks). Text enclosed in quotation marks directs the database to retrieve only items that contain the series of words you typed, exactly as you typed them, in the exact order that you typed them, with no additional words allowed in between. You should be careful to avoid misspellings and typos when enclosing a word or phrase in quotation marks, as doing so will direct the database to look for the misspelled word.

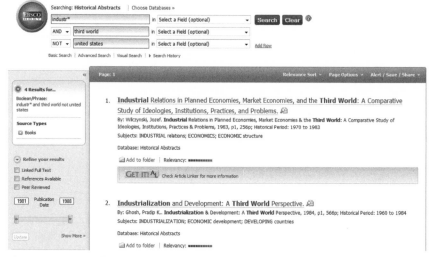

Figure 7.15.   Search Using Asterisk. Courtesy of EBSCOhost.

STOPWORDS

Most databases will ignore commonly used words typed into the search box. Prepositions, articles, question words, pronouns, and some common verbs are considered to be stopwords in many databases. A list of common stopwords is below.

Common Stopwords: a, an, as, at, from, if, in, is, it, its, of, on, out, that, the, these, this, those, to, up, very, what, who, with.

Sometimes a common word is critical to your search. You may, for example, look for a book that begins with a stopword, such as Amy Bass's *Not the Triumph but the Struggle: The 1968 Olympics and the Making of the Black Athlete.* In such cases, you can simply enclose the title in quotation marks to indicate that the stopword is part of your search.

BOOLEAN OPERATORS (AND, OR, NOT)

Boolean operators are conjunctions used within a search phrase to broaden or narrow the results of the search. They are based on mathematical logic. Boolean operators will direct the database either to combine search terms, thereby providing more results, or to exclude search terms, thereby prevent-

Catalog Advanced Search

| all fields(keyword) ▾ | pearl harbor | And ▾ |
| all fields(keyword) ▾ | japan | And ▾ |

Figure 7.16. Catalog Search Using "And." Courtesy of Dickinson College and Sirsi-Dynix.

ing unwanted results from appearing. "And," "or," and "not" are the three most common Boolean operators.

The word "and" combines your search terms, thus directing the database to return only those items in which all of the words or phrases connected by "and" appear somewhere in the record. "And" has the effect of narrowing your search because you are excluding results for which only one of the search terms appears. For example, if you are looking for books concerning Japanese politics and the attack on Pearl Harbor in 1941, you might construct a catalog search similar to that shown in figure 7.16. The search illustrated in figure 7.16 produced twenty-eight titles. In contrast, a search on "Pearl Harbor" alone produced 135 titles, many of which did not directly concern Japan or addressed Japan only marginally.

For many databases, the "and" is implied; in other words, the search will always operate as though you have typed "and" between all your search words and phrases. The Help section of the database you are using will indicate whether or not you need to type the word. Some databases and Google use the plus sign (+) instead of the word "and." Always check the database's Help page to make sure you are using correct terminology and symbols.

Using "or" between search terms tells the database that you will accept results with either word or phrase you enter. The words or phrases around "or" may occur together in the item's record or they may appear alone in the record without the other word or phrase. "Or" has the effect of broadening your search because you are accepting more possibilities in your results list. For example, if you are searching for sources regarding the history of child labor in England, you might add to your search other commonly used terms for that country: Great Britain, which is the geographical term that includes

Catalog Advanced Search

| all fields(keyword) ▾ | child labor | And ▾ |
| all fields(keyword) ▾ | England or Great Britain or United Kingdom | And ▾ |

Figure 7.17. Catalog Search Using "Or." Courtesy of Dickinson College and Sirsi-Dynix.

England, Scotland, and Wales; and United Kingdom, which is a political term that includes England, Northern Ireland, Scotland, and Wales. Figure 7.17 illustrates an example of a search using "or" in a library catalog.

Notice that this search is rather sophisticated in its construction. When you need to perform a search that involves various phrases and the database's advanced search screen provides multiple search lines, you should put separate ideas on different lines, keeping like items on the same line. In figure 7.17, the database is being directed to return any item that includes "child labor," as well as "England" or "Great Britain" or "United Kingdom." At the completion of this search, ten items were returned. In contrast, a search for "child labor and England" returned only four titles.

Using "not" in a search directs the database to exclude results that contain the word or phrase you type after it. "Not" has the effect of narrowing your search because you are rejecting some possibilities from your results list. For example, perhaps you are seeking books or articles on genocide, focusing on countries other than Germany. As would be expected, doing a search on "genocide" would return many articles on the Holocaust in Germany during World War II. Adding "not" to your search will exclude items you know you do not need for the purposes of this particular project. The keyword search illustrated in figure 7.18 using "not" removed more than 100 items from a search conducted without "not." (The library catalog used in figure 7.18 has a drop-down search feature allowing "not" to be added to the search without typing it.) Some databases and Google use the minus sign (–) instead of the word "not." Always check the database's Help page to make sure you are using correct terminology and symbols.

TOO MANY RESULTS

A search that produces too many results usually is caused by using search terms that are not specific enough. When you perform a search that returns many results that are irrelevant to your topic, you probably need to use more specific terminology. A vague search phrase such as "civil war" is likely to

Catalog Advanced Search

| all fields(keyword) ▼ | genocide | Not ▼ |
| all fields(keyword) ▼ | germany | And ▼ |

Figure 7.18.   Catalog Search Using "Not." Courtesy of Dickinson College and Sirsi-Dynix.

produce information about not only the American Civil War, but also about internal conflicts in ancient Rome, seventeenth century England, Revolutionary France, or the Lebanese civil war of the twentieth-century, among others. The results lists are more likely to be shorter and more relevant when you enter search terms that are specific and as descriptive as possible of your topic. If, instead of any civil war, you were actually trying to research the Spanish civil war of the 1930s, you might add terms such as "Spain," "Franco," "Second Republic," or "Spain and Soviet Union."

TOO FEW RESULTS OR IRRELEVANT RESULTS

Sometimes you may perform a search that yields too few results or many results that are irrelevant to your topic. This happens frequently even to experienced researchers, and there are many reasons why it can happen. You may be thinking of your topic in terms that historians do not normally apply to it. Or, you may be making simple errors in your search strategy. When a search produces few or irrelevant results, the problem usually can be attributed to spelling or attempting to perform a search using too many words and phrases.

Spelling

Knowing the correct spelling of names, places, and events is crucial in performing a successful search. Many library catalogs and scholarly databases do not guess at the correct spelling of a misspelled word and offer corrections like Google does. An incorrectly spelled word or phrase often means that no results will appear, and inadvertent typos often are the cause of zero search results. If you are unsure how to spell something, look it up in an encyclopedia or dictionary.

Packing Too Much into One Search

Though it is generally advisable to be specific when constructing a search phrase in a database, it is possible to enter too much information into one search and end up with few or no results. When you need to use more than one term in a search phrase, it is usually best to separate each main idea by typing them on separate search lines if you are using an advanced search screen or by separating each idea with the word "and" if you are using a basic search screen. The reason for this is that some databases will look for the words you type to be in the same field if you do not separate them in some way, ignoring, for example, items in which some of your terms appear in an item's title and some appear in the subject headings. If you start a search using more than two or three terms and your results are limited, try a new search with fewer terms.

NOTES

1. Kimberly Powell, "Top Ten Genealogy Mistakes to Avoid: Don't Limit Yourself to Just One Spelling," About.com Genealogy, http://genealogy.about.com/od/basics/ss/mistakes_7.htm.

2. Herbert Hoover, "Address, September 21, 1931," *The Depression Papers of Herbert Hoover*, edited by Myles B. Williams, http://hhpapers.org/paper19310921.html.

Chapter Eight

Case Study

This book provides you with an introduction to basic methods in historical research, though it would be impossible to include in these pages examples of every possible research scenario. The advice in this book is designed to ground you in transferable research skills that can be applied in any research setting and for any research project. As with any other skill, though, research takes practice before it becomes second nature; indeed, even well-seasoned researchers must periodically relearn research techniques when the available tools change and improve, as they inevitably will.

This case study you are about to read demonstrates how the research methods recommended in this book can be put into practice to retrieve information that can then be used to weave a historical narrative. The author of the following case study was by no means a research expert. On the contrary, at the beginning of this project, the author was a junior in college who was not a history major and had never engaged in historical research. Yet by putting this book's methods into practice, he uncovered material that allowed him to produce an original and impressive essay. Though many research projects at the college level may not involve the months of research and travel that this one did, you will see in this case study practical demonstrations of some of the many possible methods and avenues of research that you may need to follow during the course of your own project. You will also see illustrated in this essay how the various pieces of information the author collected connect to one another and build upon each other. Finally, you will see how a historical question can change focus and emphasis during the course of research.

INTRODUCTION TO THE CASE STUDY

The subject of the following essay, John A. J. Creswell, was a graduate of Dickinson College's Class of 1848 and proved to be an intriguing figure who has not received as much attention in historical literature as he perhaps deserves. The search for information on Creswell led to many different kinds of research material, including library catalogs and databases, books and articles, and free and subscription sources, as well as interesting locations such as the Library of Congress, the National Archives, and the Historical Society of Cecil County in Maryland. During the search, we uncovered tertiary, secondary, and primary sources in print and online, all of which had to be thoroughly analyzed for their accuracy and provenance. Prior to reading early drafts of this book, the primary author of this essay had no formal instruction in historical research methods nor did he have any familiarity with John A. J. Creswell. Nevertheless, he was able to piece together a more complete biography of Creswell than any of those previously published, as well as answer some of the questions about Creswell's life and career that other historians had not yet addressed. This case study was researched and written by W. John Monopoli, Dickinson College Class of 2011. It was further researched and edited by Colin Macfarlane, Dickinson College Class of 2012.

JOHN A. J. CRESWELL

When Representative John A. J. Creswell fervidly advocated for the Thirteenth Amendment in January 1865, invoking images of the Crusades and condemning slavery as effectively murder, he confirmed his status as a distinguished public servant. Indeed, his comparison of the struggle against slavery to "a holy crusade for country and for freedom" and his argument that the system "could not endure save for wanton homicide" indicated a congressman confident enough to vehemently promote his beliefs. These qualities are even more impressive when one considers that Creswell represented a border state (Maryland) and advocated his position while the Civil War raged outside. This confidence contributed to Creswell's successful career not only as a congressman, but also as postmaster general for President Ulysses S. Grant and as a lawyer in his home of Cecil County, Maryland. Other than his speech in Congress supporting the Thirteenth Amendment, he is most known for developing the postcard and reforming the mail system as postmaster general of the United States, all while remaining a local icon in Cecil County.

As a state legislator, congressman, senator, and presidential cabinet member, one could say that Creswell was a political man. Despite these distinc-

Figure 8.1. Hon. John A. J. Creswell, MD. Courtesy of the National Archives and Records Administration.

tions, there is one detail about his life that biographies and encyclopedias have not addressed: Creswell apparently changed his middle names, likely sometime in the early 1860s. Records in Archives and Special Collections at Dickinson College, his alma mater, indicate that his full name was "John Andrew Jackson Creswell" throughout college. An official list of the class of 1848 and the Commencement program from that year both list that version of his name in handwriting, probably that of the college secretary. Although most biographical entries and journals neglect to address his name change and simply abbreviate his middle initials as A.J., the *Dictionary of American Biography* called him "John Angel James" in 1929.[1] In addition, the *Biographical Dictionary of the U.S. Congress* refers to him as Angel James on its website.[2] One would think that any summary of the man's life would include at least a sentence or two about why he wanted to change his name or even the fact that he did so at all. The name change is particularly curious considering that Andrew Jackson, a Democrat, was elected president on November 3, 1828, fifteen days before Creswell was born. How often does a member of Congress share a name with a president, only to rid himself of it? Indeed, an exchange of "Allan Jacob" for "Angel James," would have been less remarkable. Natural speculation may point to politics as a reason for the switch—Creswell was initially a member of the Whig party before joining Jackson's Democrats, and then became a Republican in Congress—but the evidence so far uncovered was merely circumstantial. Discerning when he changed his name and the reasons behind it are the main reasons for this case study and the efforts that accompanied it.

Name change aside for the moment, one can say that Creswell enjoyed a successful career. He is somewhat of a secondary historical figure, meaning that he played an important role in politics from 1855 to 1875, but was not a president or a famous, long-tenured senator. His status as a notable, but not central, character in history is important in this research project because merely searching for him on the Internet or in a library catalog did not yield much information. For example, the first result of a Google search for Ulysses S. Grant provides detailed information from Wikipedia on different aspects of his presidency as well as his army career. In contrast, a search on John A. J. Creswell does not yield many results at all. One finds a few short biographical entries, references to a few nineteenth-century *New York Times* articles, and a link to the summary of the Library of Congress's collection of

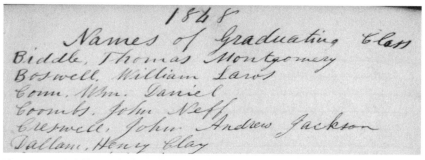

Figure 8.2.   Dickinson College Class of 1848 Graduation List (detail). Courtesy of Archives and Special Collections, Dickinson College, Carlisle, PA.

his personal documents. The first two pages also include a short Wikipedia article and a link to a paragraph on Cecil County's website that summarizes his professional life. A Google search for "John Andrew Jackson Creswell" yields most of the same results, with the addition of a biographical entry listed under that name by Dickinson College's online Civil War project, *House Divided*. This summary was essentially the same as the others from the websites of the Dickinson College Archives and Special Collections and the U.S. Congress. Results for "John Angel James Creswell" were slightly different, with links to the Questia Online Library and to Encyclopedia.com. There was also a link to purchase a copy of a speech he made honoring fellow Marylander and congressman Henry Winter Davis after his death in 1865. However, copies of that eulogy exist in other archival collections and can be accessed at no cost, as we will see.

In short, the Internet allows us to develop a basic outline of our figure's life. John A. J. Creswell was born on November 18, 1828, in Elkton, Maryland, and graduated from Dickinson College in Carlisle, Pennsylvania, twenty years later. He married the former Miss Hannah Richardson in 1857, and the couple had no children. Creswell joined the Maryland bar in 1850, practiced law for a few years and engaged different political perspectives. He was originally a Whig, then a Democrat following the Whig party's dissolution in 1856. He served a two-year term in the Maryland legislature beginning in 1861 and, in the midst of the Civil War, was elected to the U.S. House of Representatives in 1863 as a Republican. He served there for two years until assuming the deceased Thomas Hicks's chair in the Senate in 1865. In both sessions, he represented his home state of Maryland. President Grant appointed him postmaster general in 1869 and he presided over reforms that were revolutionary for the time. Creswell resigned from Grant's cabinet for unstated reasons in 1874 to return to Elkton and died of complications from pneumonia in 1891.

From this initial search we know about his career in Congress and as a member of Grant's cabinet. We do not yet know that he changed his name sometime after graduating from college or that he changed political affiliations twice during his career. It is clear that in-depth research on specific aspects of his career, especially the personal and professional factors that led to a mysterious name change, calls for much more. It requires searching for old journals and biographical books and in archival collections and newspapers from that era. Research entails patience and focus, carefully noting what each source provides (or does not provide) and following up on more sources later.

Because Dickinson College is Creswell's alma mater, I first visited the archives there. When researching specific aspects of an individual's life—his or her associates, thinking process, or elements of personal life such as a name change and the factors that contributed to it—primary sources are especially helpful. I examined Creswell's documents from college records and some alumni books from the late nineteenth century that profiled him. I hoped to find papers that Creswell may have signed, any documents representing important aspects of his college career, and any other information I might use in context with other primary or secondary sources.

Searching "John A. J. Creswell" in the library's catalog provided a few hints about material that might be helpful. Results included a speech he gave to Congress defending the Thirteenth Amendment, a copy of a public oration he gave as a student at Dickinson College entitled "Italy Under Pius IX," and U.S. Senator James B. Groome's eulogy of him in 1892. Visiting the archives afforded the first glimpses into his personal life and also highlighted elements of his career. Typically, collections of personal documents consist of seemingly random parts of a person's life as well as the parts that made him or her significant, and this is the case with Dickinson's collection on Creswell. For example, there is a letter he wrote to his friend Andrew H. H. Dawson after President Grant's death that elaborates on his relationship with the former president. Creswell wrote that he "knew Grant intimately," and spoke of his "gentleness, self-control, purity, and inaffected simplicity," and how the former president "finished his work nobly in every detail."[3] Creswell added that he was at Grant's bedside when he passed away, so his fulsomeness on the president's life and career comes as no surprise. Creswell's comments on Grant's legacy and his presence at his deathbed reflect their close friendship, and a researcher might question why Creswell resigned in the middle of his presidency. Perhaps there were pressing family issues in Maryland, or maybe he wanted to leave at the height of his career. Regardless, any thought was merely speculation at this point. It seems reasonable to assume that informing his close friend, President Grant, about his decision to resign in the middle of a term must have been the product of some internal conflict, and I would bear this in mind as I explored other sources.

The Dickinson College Sophomore Class Listing of 1845, illustrated in figure 8.3, shows, curiously, that the person recording the names of students wrote "Andrew" as Creswell's first name, only to cross that out and replace it with "John A." Other pieces of the Archives' collection included a property list and account book, as well as a record of his membership in the Belles Lettres, one of the college's two main literary societies at the time where Creswell likely learned the arts of public speaking and debate. There was additional correspondence from several Maryland lawyers to then-President Benjamin Harrison encouraging him to nominate Creswell for a vacancy on the United States Supreme Court in 1889. A. P. Barnes, an attorney in Worcester County, Maryland, wrote that Creswell was a "jurist and states-

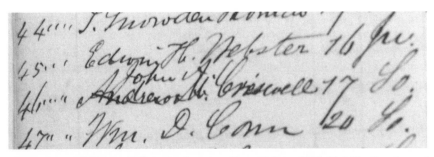

Figure 8.3. Dickinson College Sophomore Class Listing, 1845 (detail). Courtesy of Archives and Special Collections, Dickinson College, Carlisle, PA.

man" and that he would make an excellent justice.[4] A copybook in the collection contained more than 150 pages of letters that praised him in similar ways, although President Harrison instead nominated David Josiah Brewer, a judge on the United States Court of Appeals for the Eighth Circuit.

Perhaps the most interesting piece in the Archives was a copy of Creswell's aforementioned speech to Congress in January 1863 supporting the proposed Thirteenth Amendment. The speech is often cited in the few scholarly articles and biographies that exist on him, but seeing it in its entirety is a different experience than merely reading about it. The tertiary and secondary articles and biographies note that Creswell is well known for the speech, but that in itself does not capture its significance. In piercing language, Senator Creswell addressed religion, the contribution of African-American soldiers to preserving the Union, and indolent landowners in arguing why slavery should be abolished. Referring to African-Americans' participation in the Union Army, he said, "from this galling servitude . . . there was no deliverance? Such a slave couldn't be granted his liberty?" He mocked the slave owners by saying "helplessness hits masters more! Gracious heaven, how shall we get along? We've never worked a day in our life!"[5] He declared that history would note the North's noble cause in defeating the Confederacy, comparing it to a religious crusade:

> When men despaired because they could discover no solution of the dreadful enigma which slavery propounded; when even the churches quailed before it and prostituted the Bible to the propitiation of the monster, God came to the rescue, and solved the riddle by destroying the sphinx. If God is nowhere else recognized in the Constitution, nevertheless, He will speak in every word of this amendment.[6]

Different questions arise from actually reading the speech instead of seeing references to it in the few scholarly articles that exist on Creswell. One wonders how his fire was perceived among the less-radical senators and how a speech like that impacted his relationship with others. Was Creswell's emotional display typical in the Senate, or was that speech an exception and a product of the divisive issue? Creswell's consistent references to religion, specifically Christianity, are also interesting. He addressed the "Christian virtues" of the "Negro soldiers" when arguing why they should enjoy freedom. To what extent was Creswell religious, and how might that have factored into his career? If time had permitted us to pursue this question, additional primary sources might have been helpful. A researcher might look for personal correspondence to family and friends in which Creswell discusses Christianity or written opinions on controversial topics that contain references to religion.

However, the overarching question remains the same: what motivated this senator from a border state to make such vehement comments against an institution that was hundreds of years old, in the context of the Civil War? Although Maryland did not secede from the Union, it had its share of Confederate supporters and was literally in the middle of the raging struggle over slavery. Slavery had its supporters and detractors in Maryland, but it is astonishing that a politician as significant as Creswell embraced opinions that were certainly viewed by some of his peers as extremist. Creswell was well respected among his contemporaries, and there is nothing to indicate he was perceived as anything other than that from his time at Dickinson through his tenure as postmaster general. Though beyond the immediate scope of this project, additional research using secondary sources may have been able to help answer this question.

Although Dickinson's archives contain perhaps the most important aspect of Creswell's career in the Senate, other information found there was relatively unimportant to the research question at hand. His property and account book, class notes, and his commencement speech may be fascinating to examine as 150-year-old artifacts, but for a historian inquiring about his political career and specifically his name change, they do not reveal anything significant. Further, for a researcher starting with limited background on Creswell, gaining a comprehensive view of his professional and personal career from an archival collection can be difficult. Archives may contain a list of holdings on one individual, but a researcher must examine each one to judge its relevance. For example, a listing of "letter from John A. J. Creswell to President Grant" may pertain to Creswell's profound thoughts about retirement or may be a note regarding lunch plans. The only way to know is to find the note, read it, and analyze how it relates to other items in the archives or the character's position at that time. In this manner, searching an archival database is analogous to piecing together a large puzzle—and sometimes all of the pieces are not there. Subscription databases usually reveal more general information than the primary sources found in archives, and exploring them constituted an appropriate follow-up. Some databases lead to collections of primary sources such as newspapers, but I was interested in moving on from primary to secondary sources. Just like in the archives, identifying relevant secondary source material amidst a sea of potential sources was difficult, and this could be attributed to Creswell's status as a minor historical figure.

Like other colleges and universities, Dickinson has a quite a few research databases, many of which pertain to history or the humanities or social sciences in general. Such databases include ProQuest, JSTOR, and Humanities Full Text, but none appeared to have any useful information. For a project such as this one, searching various forms of Creswell's name and hoping to find results, or searching by trial and error, appeared to be the only option. A situation such as this one called for professional guidance, and a librarian suggested the database America: History and Life. Searching Creswell's name in the database revealed an article written in 1969 entitled "John A. J. Creswell of Maryland: Reformer in the Post Office," published in the *Maryland Historical Magazine*. Dickinson College subscribes to that journal, so retrieving the article entailed a short walk to the print journals section in the library. The author, Robert V. Friedenberg, wrote a ten-page overview of Creswell's life and analyzed his career, the type of summary a researcher would find interesting when beginning a project. Friedenberg discusses Creswell's election to the House of Representatives in 1863, his Thirteenth Amendment speech, and his appointment to the Senate to fill the seat left vacant by Maryland Senator Thomas Hicks's passing. However, he writes in depth for most of the article about Creswell's stellar career as postmaster. He notes Creswell's considerable influence in developing the postcard, which accrued sales of over $300,000 in 1873, the first year they were available. Accounting for inflation, that translates to more than $5 million today.[7] In addition, Creswell was instrumental in increasing the efficiency of mail bound for overseas destinations, reaching agreements with European countries about reducing the cost of postage. Friedenberg cites the annual postmaster's report from 1871, stating that the total cost of steamship service for mail decreased by just under $150,000 that year, corresponding to a 10 percent increase in the amount of mail sent overseas. Committed to increasing revenue, Creswell led a successful campaign to eliminate the often-abused franking privilege, which allowed certain government officials to send mail free of charge. Unequivocally dedicated to service, the postmaster strived to appoint the most competent men to local postmaster jobs around the country, causing consternation among the incumbents. Frustrated with those who visited him in Washington in the hopes of retaining their jobs, Creswell sent a clerk to inform them that by traveling to see him, they had wasted time that otherwise could have been spent at work. Friedenberg's research supports the notion of Creswell as a strong leader and innovative individual.

Although Friedenberg's summary was helpful in drawing a more complete picture of Creswell's life, he did not speculate about why a name change occurred or why Creswell switched political parties. Despite knowing much more about the height of his career in President Grant's administration, the answer to the question behind this investigation remained elusive. Not only was no answer in sight, but nothing I had read so far even alluded to Creswell's name change. However, Friedenberg cited numerous sources, including newspaper articles published in the 1860s from the *New York Times* and the *Baltimore American*, old postmaster general reports, primary sources from the Library of Congress, and Elizabeth Grimes's master's thesis at Columbia from 1939. If Friedenberg integrated enough information from these sources to write a coherent article, tracing them seemed like a suitable next step. But an interesting development occurred while I reviewed the footnotes—Friedenberg wrote in one of them that "the spelling of Creswell has frequently caused confusion, though he consistently spelled his name with one 's.' Creswell's middle initials have been considered abbreviations for both 'Angel James,' and 'Andrew Jackson.'"[8] Strangely, Friedenberg's footnote added yet another complication to this search: Creswell's name is again misspelled and the exact statements read ". . . Creswell's middle initials have been considered abbreviations for . . . Angle James . . . ," and ". . . the *Dictionary of American Biography* use[s] 'Angle James . . .'" Although that seemed to be a simple typesetting error, both variations of Creswell's name warranted further examination.

With these added twists, I continued by searching the online full-text version of the *New York Times* available at Dickinson College, which provides full-text copies of articles dating back to 1851. Having already scoured the archives and read a comprehensive summary of Creswell's career, I thought a different type of primary source would add context to the project. Newspaper articles could help me envision Creswell as the media saw him and maybe discuss coverage of political events in which Creswell may have been involved. Keeping in mind Friedenberg's note about the name spelling, I was sure to search all possible forms of his name. In 1865, a *New York Times* article listed him as a member of the 39th Congress.[9] An article on March 6, 1869 critiquing President Grant's cabinet nominations reported that "great disappointment and profound regret prevails in the consequence of these selections" but that the "selection of ex-Senator Creswell, of Maryland, for Postmaster-General probably gives more general satisfaction than any other name on the list."[10] Given our knowledge of his tenure as postmaster, this assessment seems especially prescient 150 years later. Other results include summaries of Congressional activity, occasional reports of reforms to the postal service, and briefings about political events. The *Times* also published Creswell's response to a congratulatory letter from the president of the executive committee of colored Republicans, George Myers. He wrote, "I value highly your congratulatory note of 6th last, and am happy to have your assurance that the colored men . . . approve of my appointment to . . . the cabinet of our illustrious president."[11] Considering Creswell's support of the Thirteenth Amendment, seeing an indication of his support from African-Americans was affirming. Less serious items included a briefing from July 29, 1869, reproduced from the *Baltimore American* of two days prior, that described how Creswell positioned his chair too close to the edge of his father-in-law's porch and fell off, but sustained "no serious injury."[12] Although the *Times* reported that he was in a significant deal of pain, he would return to Washington for work within days.

The *Times's* review of Grant's nominations gave further context to Creswell's career, but like much of the material in the archives, many of the articles seemed interesting but relatively insignificant as they related to the overall investigation. However, reviewing the *Times* did raise additional questions, which validated my efforts. For example, one has to wonder how

Figure 8.4. John A.J. Creswell (center, seated) and Other Members of U.S. Grant's Cabinet. Image from the *Cecil Democrat*, courtesy of the Historical Society of Cecil County.

President Grant managed to choose an exceptional character like Creswell when the rest of his cabinet selections were considered mediocre, at least in the view of the editors at the *New York Times*. Perhaps Creswell's success as postmaster means that he worked independently of mediocrity's influence, but we would not know this without doing more research on Grant's cabinet.

Another aspect to consider when searching in Dickinson College's Historical Newspapers database was variations on the spelling of Creswell's name. As Friedenberg suggested, "Creswell" and "Cresswell" appeared to be used interchangeably, further clouding the name confusion. This reinforces the need to fully explore sources by searching all forms of his name. It is important to note here that slight variations in the search query can uncover different articles. Before moving on, I was committed to researching more forms of Creswell's name.

Heeding a librarian's suggestion to investigate additional tertiary sources, I searched the library's catalog for biographical dictionaries and found that they used different versions of his name. As a bonus, they contained comprehensive summaries of his life that provided new information, unlike the biographical summaries I found online. The *Dictionary of American Biography*'s entry on John Angel James Creswell told of his marriage to Hannah J. Richardson, who was a "woman of considerable wealth."[13] Before reading this, I had seen nothing in the Dickinson Archives, the *Times*, or in any online summary about Creswell's wife. The article also reinforced information I already knew in reporting that his Thirteenth Amendment speech gave a "strong impression" and that his changes to the post office were "sweeping, reformatory, and constructive."[14] The *Dictionary* reported that Creswell called the franking system the "mother of frauds,"[15] leading to his campaign to abolish it. The article also described how in 1871 Creswell was appointed counsel for the Alabama Claims Commission, which was established to seek compensation from Great Britain for its material support of the Confederacy.

Another encyclopedia, *Appleton's Cyclopaedia of American Biography*, titled the entry after the usual form of Creswell's name (John A. J.) and addressed his attendance at various political conventions in the 1860s. Creswell attended the National Union Convention that nominated President Lincoln in Baltimore in 1864, again when it was held to support President Andrew Johnson in Philadelphia in 1866, and at the Border States Convention in Baltimore in 1867. That meeting was held by representatives of southern states advocating for universal suffrage, which eventually came when Congress passed the Fifteenth Amendment in 1870. Given Creswell's identity as a Republican and advocate for former slaves' rights, reading of his attendance was no surprise.

In the final biographical dictionary I investigated, I found relevant information regarding Creswell's political history in the 1860s and his career after retiring as postmaster in 1874. The *National Cyclopedia of American Biography*, published in 1897, reported that he consistently voted with the Democrats until the Civil War's outbreak. That "brought out a secession feeling for the Maryland Democrats, and Creswell, who was naturally a Union man, cut loose from them and declared himself in favor of the Union."[16] The entry also called him a "citizen of reputation and importance," pointing to his work with the Citizens National Bank in Washington and the National Bank of Elkton, Maryland, both in the 1880s. This instance represented the first time I felt satisfied with the investigation's progress: I could now form a plot of Creswell's life, starting with his education at Dickinson and filling in the years between his tenure as postmaster and his death in 1891. Each of the biographies contributed different pieces of information that other sources did not disclose. However, none of the biographies even alluded to a name change, although the *Dictionary of American Biography* spelled out Angel James rather than abbreviate it as A. J. The *National Cyclopedia*'s suggestion that Creswell severed ties with the Democratic Party based on their advocacy for Maryland's secession supports the idea he would no longer want "Andrew Jackson" in his name, but that remains just a theory.

Having studied personal documents, articles from the *New York Times*, and old biographical dictionaries, my resources at Dickinson seemed exhausted. However, careful use of research method ensured that I made the most of them. Each of the sources added different pieces of information, and I faced a challenge in finding them and fitting the parts together. The variations of Creswell's name—from A. J. and Angel James to Cresswell and Angle—alerted me to the need for caution and attention to detail when searching any database or journal. At this point, with a fairly complete picture of his life, I was ready to completely focus on the name change that no historian had apparently noticed, much less discussed. This called for visits to the Library of Congress and National Archives in Washington, DC.

The biggest library in the United States, the Library of Congress houses millions of personal documents, photographs, manuscripts, and other research material. Recalling that one of my Google search results was a link to the Library of Congress's summary of Creswell holdings, I examined that first. The collection summary is entitled "John A. J. Creswell Papers: A Finding Aid to the Collection of the Library of Congress, Manuscript Division," and summarizes the overall collection, the scope of the documents, how they are arranged, and the contents of each container. Though entitled "John A. J. Creswell Papers," this finding aid lists the creator of the collection as "Creswell, John A. J. (John Angel James), 1828–1891" and also refers to him as "John Angel James Creswell" in the content note.[17]

According to the website, the Library of Congress has twenty-one boxes of general correspondence, account books, and letter books concerning his career in law, tenure in Congress, and the 1867 Maryland Constitutional Convention. Most of the material is from 1862 to 1865. Despite the collection's vastness, the content was disappointing because a day's worth of research revealed little new information. The papers qualify as personal documents, but most are letters to Creswell or his assistant concerning his law practice, hence none provide any insight into his political beliefs, attendance at political conventions, tenure as postmaster general, or most importantly, his name change. Most of the letters appeared to regard the office's activities in cases that were surely of interest to a client in 1862 but were not helpful for the purposes of my investigation. One item that added credibility to the information I already gathered was an incomplete personal biosketch that Creswell had written to an unknown recipient in November 1863.[18]

One unsigned letter originating from "Elkton, Cecil County, MD," and written in 1861, as shown in figure 8.5, caught my attention because of the salutation, which read "Dear Andrew."[19] This was strange because I thought

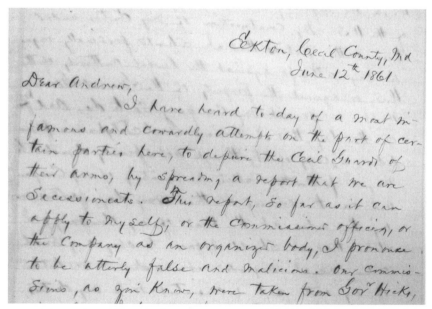

Figure 8.5. Letter to John A. J. Creswell, Sender Unknown. Courtesy of the Library of Congress.

Creswell had abandoned that name in the 1850s and because most of his business correspondence was addressed to "Hon. Creswell" or "Mr. Creswell." The letter is written by a man who appears to have been part of a militia or pro-Union group that was facing accusations of being secessionist. The man denounces the rumor as "false and malicious" and professes his allegiance to the "old flag, without a stripe erased or polluted" before asking for a favor. He requested that Creswell speak with Thomas Hicks, then governor of Maryland, to assure him that the group was pro-Union. Unfortunately, the letter is not signed. Which of Creswell's acquaintances might have called him "Andrew" in the 1860s? Seeing this letter only exacerbated my disappointment with the library's collection because it contained no letters that Creswell wrote, so finding his response could be difficult. We must wonder how he would have responded to an unsigned note anyway—perhaps the sender was a good friend whom he would know just from reading the document. At this point, the only way to investigate the sender's identity would be to find records of Maryland militia members and soldiers, and explore each individual's possible connection to Creswell. At this point, there was nothing further to find in the Library of Congress.

My experience at the Library of Congress raises an important point about research at a major institution. Information on the volume of collection and a basic summary of its contents is almost always available online, but determining its relevance to your project is difficult without seeing the actual items. The Library's website accurately reports that the Creswell collection consists of letter books, account books, and general correspondence, but does not delve into detail. As a result, I was not aware until arriving there that much of the collection was composed of letters to him regarding routine business.

My next stop in Washington, DC, was the National Archives and Records Administration (NARA). Other than its allure as a tourist attraction, I did not know much about the National Archives. However, the Internet can inform a researcher in less than ten minutes, and it proved valuable here. I started the research process there by logging onto its website and reading a review of how to start researching, from determining a research topic to what to do upon arriving in Washington. Like the Library of Congress, the National Archives encourages researchers to look for records on their topic prior to arriving, so I searched the various forms of Creswell's name in the catalog. Unlike the library though, the results are organized in a type of Google-style where one link represents one document or one piece of collection. Results for Creswell were curious, but unremarkable: the page showed a few links to "photographs and other graphic materials" at the Archives' College Park, Maryland, branch, and details of a few Congressional documents stored in Washington, DC. Once I gained my researcher's card and entered the reading room, I found out that these included basic information on the 38th and 39th Congresses, of which Creswell was a member, as well as material mainly relating to the proceedings and issues of the legislative branch. For example, the *Congressional Globe: Debates and Proceedings of Different Senates, 38th Congress, 2nd Session*, contained a copy of his famous speech supporting the Thirteenth Amendment and summaries of senators' dialogue that followed. There also was the text of Creswell's eulogy of his good friend Henry Winter Davis, a representative from Maryland. After spending some time looking for it, one of the archivists at the National Archives produced Creswell's Senate credential, the document that authenticated his entry into the United States legislature.

What I did not find in Washington, after two days of work, despite online descriptions of more than 6,000 items in the Library of Congress alone, was the expected additional documentation concerning reforms to the post office or aspects of his political life, such as the factors that led him to switch party affiliation. It is conceivable that Creswell discussed his changing political views or possible disillusionment with the Democratic Party in business correspondence, although no such letters were to be found in Washington, DC. At the conclusion of this trip, I was left to continue pondering these issues along with the letter from the Maryland militia member that began with the perplexing salutation "Dear Andrew."

At this juncture, I had exhausted all of Dickinson's resources, scoured available tertiary and secondary sources, and visited two of the largest research institutions in the United States. Although I had gained a fair amount of information, I felt the project had begun to overemphasize the business and professional perspective of Creswell. Specifically, I thought that a personal touch was lacking because most of my information pertained to his political career rather than the finer details of his personal history prior to his tenure in Washington. In order to change the investigation's frame, I had to think critically about where to find new sources. By this time I knew Creswell had been born and raised in Elkton, but besides knowing that the Maryland state line is a short drive from Dickinson College, I was unsure about the town's precise location. However, I thought the Elkton area must have a local historical society, and considering Creswell's importance to the town, it seemed reasonable to think that some of his papers and other information would be there. I searched Google for local information, found the phone number for the Cecil County Historical Society in Elkton, Maryland, and talked with a historian familiar with the area. He reported that they had a variety of Creswell papers, including information on family history, comprehensive biographies, and old articles from two now-defunct newspapers, the *Cecil Whig* and the *Cecil Democrat*. Upon hearing I was from Carlisle, the historian encouraged me to visit and suggested that the two-hour drive would be justified given all of their material. This interaction illustrates one of the benefits of researching at local societies: you receive individualized attention from someone, sometimes a volunteer, who is passionate and knowledgeable about local history. In addition, positive interpersonal experiences make research more enjoyable as well as more fruitful.

After spending a few hours in Elkton one afternoon, I left with a feeling of satisfaction—and curiosity—that my time in Washington failed to evoke. During my time there, I consulted sources that provided me with a more complete picture of Creswell's life, especially personal history that occurred outside of Congress. We knew he joined the Maryland bar in 1850, and the *Cecil Historical Journal* reported in an article from 2003 that he joined Col. John C. Groome's law office, which the Democrat dubbed Elkton Law School, as a junior member. He worked with Col. Groome for four years until opening his own practice with George Earle, Esq., in 1854. During those four years, he would have gained experience as a lawyer while cultivating his political interests. The 1897 edition of the *Portrait and Biographical Record of Harford and Cecil Counties, Maryland*, which I found at the Historical Society, addressed Creswell's initial political status as a member of the Whig party in reporting that he cast his first presidential vote for Gen. Winfield Scott in 1852.[20] The *Portrait and Biographical Record* reported that, when the Whig party dissolved in 1856, Creswell became a Democrat and attended the 1856 convention at which delegates nominated fellow Dickinson alumnus James Buchanan for president.

Creswell likely remained a Democrat until the sentiments of Southern secession boiled over and led to war's outbreak in 1861, as the *Cecil Democrat* reported, "when slavery demanded disruption of the Union, Creswell renounced his allegiance to that party."[21] The *Cecil Democrat* was quite disparaging of Creswell for his support of black suffrage. In an 1867 article, the editors of the *Cecil Democrat* repeatedly used his full name "John Andrew Jackson Creswell," clearly in a mocking way, to speculate that Creswell supported black suffrage merely to gain votes for his Senate position.[22] This article raised an interesting question: could the taunts of the *Cecil Democrat* and the editors' intimations that Creswell was disingenuous in supporting the union, freeing slaves, and black suffrage have been his motivation to change his name?

Reading about this phase of Creswell's life finally enabled me to connect the parts of his young adulthood: he sharpened his law skills under Col. Groome's supervision and changed political parties two times under different circumstances. If Creswell split with the Democrats in around 1861, it makes sense that he would have abandoned the name Andrew Jackson around the same time. Why would he have distanced himself from a Democratic president prior to his departure from the party? Many possible reasons exist, but the possibility that Creswell highlighted the end of his Democratic tenure with a personal name change is a reasonable inference given the current information.

Among the summaries of Creswell's political life in the 1850s, I found a few other interesting items in Elkton that shed light on his status as an important local figure. For example, the *Biographical Record* stated that the family owned several acres of land in northeast Maryland, pointing to an upper-class upbringing.[23] When Creswell died, James B. Groome—Col. Groome's son—reported that a man approached him on the street and inquired about reports of Creswell's illness. The man spoke of the postmaster's office as the "ablest and most useful our country has ever had" when it was under Creswell's supervision.[24] Pointing to his lasting legacy, the Maryland Historical Society erected a marker on the location of his family's mansion, which was destroyed by fire in the twentieth century.

One piece of information I found in Elkton proved to be the most curious, and yet most maddening, aspect of the project. James B. Groome represented Maryland in the U.S. Senate in the 1880s. The article in the *Biographical Record* suggests that he admired Creswell and looked to him as a political mentor. Creswell had worked for his father between 1850 and 1854, and it is reasonable to think he enjoyed a personal relationship with the Groome family. Groome even served as a pallbearer at Creswell's funeral. All of this is important because Groome felt qualified to write in 1892 that "after some seeming hesitation [Creswell] severed his connection to the Democratic party."[25] What might the basis of that hesitation have been, and how was he personally affected by switching political parties for the second time in a decade? Finding the answer to that question would be especially difficult considering that I had investigated seemingly all of the relevant sources, but exploring related questions about the context of this history would be worthwhile. For example, did most Whigs become Democrats after their party dissolved? What percentage of Democrats realized an intense desire to preserve the Union, even if they agreed with their party on other issues? Could this issue have been restricted to the border states? In all, how many Democrats switched parties, and what were their sentiments when doing so? Deliberate research could point to some possible answers.

Aside from the local, state, and federal political settings in which Creswell excelled, we still have yet to consider the factors that might have influenced his parents in giving him the name of a Democratic president who happened also to be a wealthy slave owner. Perhaps one or both of Creswell's parents were passionate Democrats who wanted their son to share his name with the president. How might having political parents affected the trajectory of his personal and professional life? This hypothesis would gain more or less validity if we could research his parents' political attitudes, but this information lay outside the scope of this project.

Visiting Elkton was a worthwhile experience that illuminated new facts and sparked more curiosity. The *Portrait and Biographical Record* and the *Cecil Historical Journal* were excellent sources for gathering details that neither Dickinson College's Archives and Special Collections nor the Library of Congress had on record. I learned of Creswell's early professional development in his work under Col. Groome, discovered that he was active in local events, noted a small amount of information concerning his family history and upper-class upbringing, and affirmed information regarding his party allegiances.

At this point, I was nearing the end of the time I had to complete this project, but I decided to make one final check for Creswell. At the suggestion of one of Dickinson College's history professors, I decided to search the papers of Ulysses S. Grant to see if Creswell was mentioned anywhere in his presidential records, which would make sense considering that Creswell was an important member of Grant's cabinet. While pursuing this lead, I uncovered three additional intriguing sources.

The first was a mention of Creswell in the transcription of the murder trial of John H. Surratt, which is available on Google. A former Confederate soldier, Surratt was arrested in 1866 on charges of colluding with John Wilkes Booth to kidnap Abraham Lincoln. His trial took place in June of 1867. During the trial, Stephen F. Cameron, a witness for the defense, was being questioned when the following exchange took place:

Q: "Do you know Mr. Creswell?"

A: "I know John Andrew Jackson Creswell."

Q: "The Senator?"

A: "I believe he is."

Later in the testimony, Cameron goes on to say that he had lived in Elkton, Maryland, and knew Creswell from his time spent there.[26]

The second reference to Creswell was in a short article published in a Maryland newspaper in 1869. The unnamed reporter describes an interview he conducted with Creswell, during which Creswell described his appointment to the postmaster general position in President Grant's cabinet. During the interview, Creswell recounted the following exchange:

> [Grant] called me aside and said, "Mr. Creswell, let me see; what are your initials, J.N. is it not?" "No," said I; "John Andrew Jackson Creswell." General Grant took a pencil from his pocket and wrote the name in full on a scrap of paper.[27]

Finally, a letter from President Grant dated July 12, 1873, formally addressed to "Honorable John Andrew Jackson Creswell" appears in a volume of *The Papers of Ulysses S. Grant*. This letter invites John and Mrs. Creswell to spend a week at the beach with President and Mrs. Grant.[28]

All of this information brought me tantalizingly close to an answer regarding the question forming the project's basis, especially Senator Groome's statement about "a great deal of hesitation," but produced no definitive answers. It is peculiar—and perhaps telling—that so much information would exist on his family background and career without addressing a name change, especially if it was linked to a change in political party. This project illustrates a frequent trajectory in the study of history—that it is difficult, and perhaps even wrong, to search for definite conclusions. Rather, we search for influences in the development of events and assess their importance in the appropriate context. Perhaps Creswell's name change was quiet, reflected only in a few personal documents that have escaped preservation in an archive, or perhaps it was just the result of a skilled politician's ability to keep personal matters private. Could it be that a 30-something-year-old Creswell entering politics attempted to change his name in order to distance himself from the slave-owning president but that critics in his home state would not let it catch on? Perhaps the truth is that Creswell never actually changed his name at all, and that the entry of "Angel James" was some unfortunate error on the part of a recording secretary that has been perpetuated in tertiary sources for more than 120 years. Regrettably, Creswell had no direct descendants who may have preserved his personal papers and could possibly have been contacted and interviewed for this project. All we know for certain is that our esteemed postmaster general entered Dickinson College as "John Andrew Jackson Creswell" in 1844 and that colleagues, friends, and detractors used that name, and not "Angel James," as late as 1861. Moreover, available evidence explicitly suggests that in his dealings following the Civil War with this friend and chief executive, Ulysses S. Grant, he was called "John Andrew Jackson Creswell."

I had accomplished a great deal over the course of a few months: viewing archival records and matching them with current knowledge about our Creswell, finding the only known journal article regarding his tenure as postmas-

Figure 8.6. John A. J. Creswell. From *Portrait and Biographical Record of Harford and Cecil Counties*, courtesy of the Historical Society of Cecil County.

ter general, discerning personal history in old biographical dictionaries, and uncovering new information that likely exists only at the Cecil County Historical Society. On a broader level, I developed a framework for the process of historical research—the sources to consult, the appropriate questions to ask, and how to analyze information ranging from 200-year-old documents to more recent journal articles. Investigating and pursuing sources cited in these journal articles and in any biographical entry is also critical. In terms of the general goal of research to accumulate as much information as possible and to generate new and thoughtful questions, I consider the endeavor a success.

The final component of this research that warrants mention is professional guidance from a librarian. I started the project with essentially a clean slate—I knew nothing of Creswell, his accomplishments, or his importance in mid-nineteenth century history. Visiting the Dickinson Archives constituted an appropriate first step in the research process, but guidance proved especially helpful in assisting me with the second and third steps. I was puzzled about how to use the information I gained at the archives, and a librarian facilitated my search for scholarly articles in journals relevant to the topic. Without this assistance, I may have eventually found more information, but only by trial and error and after floundering for a great deal of time. A professional also emphasized the research process and sharpened my focus regarding how to analyze information. This reinforced the overarching theme that I was not looking only at the material itself, but also at its sources and how I might access them. I accomplished all of the research cited and analyzed in this essay, but professional guidance can enhance the process and facilitate a smoother course.

JOHN A. J. CRESWELL BIBLIOGRAPHY

"Accident to Postmaster General Creswell." *New York Times*. 29 July 1869, 1.

Barnes, A. P. Snow Hill, MD to "The President of the United States" [Benjamin Harrison], 16 April 1889 (from letter copy book), MC2010.2, Archives & Special Collections, Dickinson College.

"Creswell." *The Cecil Democrat*. 13 July 1867, 2.

Creswell, John A. J. *John A. J. Creswell Papers*. Washington, DC: Library of Congress, Manuscript Division, 1819–1885.

Creswell, John A. J. "Speech of Hon. John A. J. Creswell of Maryland on the Proposed Amendment to the Constitution of the United States." Delivered in the House of Representatives, 5 January 1865. Washington, DC: Printed by L. Towers.

Creswell, John A. J. Washington, DC to Andrew H. H. Dawson, 16 August 1885, MC2010.2, Archives & Special Collections, Dickinson College, Carlisle, PA.

Dunlap, Lloyd A. and Sherralyn McCoy. "John A. J. Creswell Papers: A Finding Aid to the Collection of the Library of Congress, Manuscript Division." Washington, DC: Library of Congress, 2002.

Fisher, George F., Presiding. *Trial of John H. Surratt in Criminal Court.* 2 vols. Washington, DC: Government Printing Office, 1867.

Friedenberg, Robert V. "John A. J. Creswell of Maryland: Reformer in the Post Office." *Maryland Historical Magazine* 64, no. 2 (1969): 133–143.

Groome, James Black. "Tribute of Former U.S. Senator James B. Groome to the Memory of John A. J. Creswell, Delivered at a Meeting of the Cecil County Bar Association, January 5, 1892." Elkton, MD: Cecil County Bar Association, 1892.

"How One of the Members of the Cabinet was Appointed." *Rockland County Journal.* 10 April 1869, 1.

Portrait and Biographical Record of Harford and Cecil Counties, Maryland. New York: Chapman Publishing Company, 1897.

"The Postmaster General and the Maryland Colored People." *New York Times.* 11 March 1868, 1.

Simon, John Y, ed. *The Papers of Ulysses S. Grant.* Carbondale: Southern Illinois University Press, 2000.

"Special Dispatches to the *New York Times*." *New York Times.* 6 March 1869, 1.

"The Thirty-Ninth Congress." *New York Times.* 4 December 1865, 1.

NOTES

1. *Dictionary of American Biography*, s.v. "Creswell, John Angel James."

2. "Creswell, John Angel James," *Biographical Directory of the United States Congress*, http://bioguide.congress.gov/scripts/biodisplay.pl?index=C000904.

3. John A.J. Creswell, Washington, DC to Andrew H.H. Dawson, 16 August 1885, MC2010.2, Archives & Special Collections, Dickinson College, Carlisle, PA.

4. A.P. Barnes, Snow Hill, MD to "The President of the United States" [Benjamin Harrison], 16 April 1889 (from letter copy book), MC2010.2, Archives & Special Collections, Dickinson College.

5. John A.J. Creswell, "Speech of Hon. John A. J. Creswell of Maryland on the Proposed Amendment to the Constitution of the United States," delivered in the House of Representatives, 5 January 1865 (Washington, DC: Printed by L. Towers), 11.

6. Ibid., 16.

7. This figure was calculated using the conversion tools at MeasuringWorth.com.

8. Robert V. Friedenberg, "John A. J. Creswell of Maryland: Reformer in the Post Office" *Maryland Historical Magazine* 64, no. 2 (1969), 133.

9. "The Thirty-Ninth Congress," *New York Times*, 4 December 1865, 1.

10. "Special Dispatches to the *New York Times*," *New York Times*, 6 March 1869, 1.

11. "The Postmaster General and the Maryland Colored People," *New York Times*, 11 March 1868, 1.

12. "The Accident to Postmaster General Creswell," *New York Times*, 29 July 1869, 1.

13. *Dictionary of American Biography*, Centenary Edition, s.v. "Creswell, John Angel James."

14. Ibid.

15. Ibid.

16. *National Cyclopedia of American Biography*, vol. 4, 19, 1897.

17. Lloyd A. Dunlap and Sherralyn McCoy, "John A.J. Creswell Papers: A Finding Aid to the Collection of the Library of Congress, Manuscript Division" (Washington, DC, 2002).

18. John A.J. Creswell to unknown recipient, 17 November 1863, John A. J. Creswell Papers, Box 3 – General Correspondence, Manuscript Division, Library of Congress, Washington, DC.

19. Unknown sender, Elkton, MD to John A.J. Creswell, 12 June 1861, John A. J. Creswell Papers, Box 1 – General Correspondence, Manuscript Division, Library of Congress, Washington, DC.

20. *Portrait and Biographical Record of Harford and Cecil Counties, Maryland* (New York: Chapman Publishing Company, 1897), 121.

21. "Creswell," *The Cecil Democrat*, 13 July 1867, 2.

22. Ibid.

23. *Portrait and Biographical Record*, 119–120.

24. James Black Groome, "Tribute of Former U.S. Senator James B. Groome to the Memory John A.J. Creswell, "Delivered at a Meeting of the Cecil County Bar Association, January 5, 1892," 7.

25. Ibid., 4.

26. George P. Fisher, Presiding, *Trial of John H. Surratt in Criminal Court*, vol. 2 (Washington, DC: Government Printing Office, 1867), 765.

27. "How One of the Members of the Cabinet Was Appointed," *Rockland County Journal*, 10 April 1869, 1.

28. Ulysses S. Grant to John Andrew Jackson Creswell, Long Branch, NJ, 12 July 1873. In *The Papers of Ulysses S. Grant*, ed. John Y. Simon, vol. 24 (Carbondale, IL: Southern Illinois University Press, 2000), 165.

Appendix A

Bibliographies

A bibliography is a list of sources, formatted according to a particular set of stylistic rules, made up of all the sources consulted in preparation for a research project. All items that helped inform the project, even those that are not directly quoted, should be included in the bibliography.

The act of compiling a bibliography serves a number of purposes. It familiarizes you with terminology you can use to conduct effective searches and will help you to form original opinions about the subject. It will help you learn about the historical arguments surrounding your topic and will lead you to discover the leading historical experts and most important writings about it. If your audience wants to know more about your topic, the bibliography will direct them to the sources you found informative. Perhaps most importantly, building a bibliography will help you avoid plagiarism. When you supply a bibliography, you demonstrate to your audience, whether that is your professors, fellow students, or readers of a publication in which your work is included, that you invested time conducting thorough research and that you consulted the best available primary and secondary sources to support your arguments. Your citation list demonstrates that you have synthesized the sources to form your own opinions about the topic and that you are using them effectively and persuasively at appropriate points in your narrative.

CREATING CITATIONS ACCORDING TO THE CHICAGO MANUAL OF STYLE

The information provided in a bibliography must be presented in a manner that is acceptable to your intended audience and understandable to readers of your work. Usually, you will use a citation style that is required or recommended by your institution, employer, or publisher. There are numerous styles of bibliography, including the Modern Language Association (MLA) style, which is normally associated with literature and other disciplines in the humanities; and the American Psychological Association Style (APA), which is often associated with the study of psychology and other sciences. Most publishers of history books and journals and, by extension, most college and university history departments, follow citations as described in the *Chicago Manual of Style*. The Chicago style is simply a set of rules that lays out in what order and what format the bibliographic information should appear. It has been used to cite sources throughout this book.

A bibliography is made up of individual citations. Each citation in the bibliography is a description of the essential elements of each work consulted. Citations are constructed using fairly strict rules regarding punctuation, text format, and paragraph indentation. Bibliographies written for history papers must be formatted according to the Chicago style even if the catalog or database in which you found sources does not format citations according to Chicago rules. Researchers using historical resources could be studying any number of topics besides history, such as art, literature, religion, and politics, and not all of those disciplines use the Chicago rules for citing. Because they are used by a variety of academic disciplines, library catalogs and databases do not provide citations in any particular format; rather, they most often list the title of the item first instead of the author, which is normally the first element of a Chicago-style citation.

The *Chicago Manual of Style* is available both in print and online versions. You should check your library's catalog or consult with a librarian to find a copy in your library. If you plan on studying history as a college major and your library does not have access to the online version of the manual, it is a good idea to invest in a personal copy of this important reference. More information about the Chicago style of citing can be found at http://www. chicagomanualofstyle.org/home.html.

The *Chicago Manual of Style* is a comprehensive source that provides rules and examples for citing any type of source you might use for a research project. All of the Chicago rules cannot be reproduced here, but provided below are the most basic rules for citing.

• The bibliography is arranged in alphabetical order by authors' last names. If an author is not listed, arrange the item alphabetically according to the first main word of the title.

- The author is always the first element of a citation. Single authors are written with the last name listed first, followed by a comma, followed by the first name. Names of any additional authors are written naturally, with the first name listed first and the last name listed second. For four or more authors, the abbreviation "et al." ("and others") is used after the name of the first author.
- Second and all subsequent lines of a citation are always indented approximately half an inch from the beginning of the first line.
- Capitalize the first letter of all main words in the titles of books, journals, and article titles.
- Include the country or state of publication only if the city is not well known. States and countries do not need to be included for publishers in well-known cities such as New York, Boston, or London. When a state must be included, use the U.S. Postal Service's two-letter abbreviation without periods.
- Encyclopedias and dictionaries are normally not included in the bibliography; rather, they should be cited in footnotes only if necessary to clarify a discrepancy or explain a point that would otherwise interrupt the flow of the main text.
- Illustrations and tables are usually cited in footnotes or a caption, rather than in a bibliography.

The Chicago style provides specific rules for citing a book.

- A book citation must always include author(s) and/or editor(s), title and subtitle, city of publication, publisher, and date of publication. Other necessary elements, if applicable, are translator(s), edition numbers, revision notes, series title, and volume number.
- Book titles are always italicized.

The Chicago style also provides these specific rules for citing journal articles.

- An article citation must always include the author(s), title and subtitle of article, title of journal/magazine, date of publication, volume and/or issue number, and all inclusive page numbers on which the article can be found.
- Titles of articles are always enclosed in quotation marks.
- Titles of journals are always italicized.

Following are samples of some of the most common types of citations.

BOOK WITH TWO AUTHORS

Shapin, Steven, and Simon Schaffer. *Leviathan and the Air Pump: Hobbes, Boyle, and the Experimental Life*. Princeton: Princeton University Press, 1989.

In this example, Steven Shapin and Simon Schaffer are the authors of the book, *Leviathan and the Air Pump: Hobbes, Boyle, and the Experimental Life*, which was published in Princeton, New Jersey, by Princeton University Press in the year 1989.

Book with an Editor in Addition to an Author

Roosevelt, Theodore. *Theodore Roosevelt's Letters to His Children*. Edited by Joseph Bucklin Bishop. New York: Charles Scribner's Sons, 1919.

This type of citation is most often used when citing a collection of published primary sources. Theodore Roosevelt is the author of the book's content, while Joseph Bucklin Bishop, the editor, selected the letters for inclusion in the book and prepared them for publication. The book was published in New York City by the publisher Charles Scribner's Sons in 1919.

Edited Book

Marston, Daniel P., and Chandar S. Sundaram, eds. *A Military History of India and South Asia: From the East India Company to the Nuclear Era*. Westport, CT: Praeger Security International, 2007.

This format is used when you are using multiple chapters from a book in which each chapter is written by a different author. If you are citing a single chapter in a book for which each chapter is written by a different author, use the Chapter in an Anthology example below.

Chapter in an Anthology

Coatesmith, John H., and William R. Summerhill. "The New Economic History of Latin America: Evolution and Recent Contributions." In *The Oxford Handbook of Latin American History*, edited by Jose C. Moya, 407–423. New York: Oxford University Press, 2011.

This format is used when you are citing a single chapter in a book for which each chapter is written by a different author. If you are citing several chapters in a book for which each chapter is written by a different author, use the Edited Book example above.

Journal Article (Scholarly)

Brown, Elizabeth. "The Tyranny of a Construct: Feudalism and Historians of Medieval Europe." *American Historical Review* 9, no. 4 (1974): 1063–1088.

In this example, Elizabeth Brown is the author of the article, "The Tyranny of a Construct: Feudalism and Historians of Medieval Europe" is the title of the article, and *American Historical Review* is the title of the journal in which the article was published. The volume number is 9 and the issue number is 4. The article was published in 1974 and 1063–1088 represents the page numbers on which the article appeared.

Magazine Article (Nonscholarly)

Ellison, Jesse. "Did Britain Wreck the World?" *Newsweek* 154, no. 8/9 (24–31 August 2009): 78.

Nonscholarly journals are usually published more often than scholarly journals and may not have volume or issue numbers. The complete date of publication including days is therefore crucial to the citation.

Newspaper Article with No Author

"Senatorial Contest in Illinois—Speech of Mr. Lincoln." *New York Times*. 16 July 1858, 4.

In this example, no author or byline was noted. "Senatorial Contest in Illinois—Speech of Mr. Lincoln" is the title of the article, which was published in the *New York Times* newspaper on July 16, 1858. The article appeared on page 4 of that issue.

Newspaper Article When City Is Not Included in the Title

"Clear Creek Gold! Three Important Strikes in Old Mining Districts." *The Daily Mining Record* [Denver, CO]. 7 September 1893, issue 9, col. A.

When the official title of a newspaper gives no indication of its city of origin, include the city in the citation by enclosing it in brackets immediately after the newspaper's title.

Video

Ward, Geoffrey C., Ric Burns, and Ken Burns. *The Civil War*. 5 discs. DVD. Directed by Ken Burns. Burbank, CA: PBS Home Video, 2004.

In this example, Geoffrey C. Ward, Ric Burns, and Ken Burns are the writers of this documentary film series. If you are using a videotape, substitute VHS for DVD.

Website

Pinsker, Matthew, and John Osborne, eds. "Conway, Moncure Daniel." *House Divided: The Civil War Research Engine at Dickinson College*. Last modified 2011. http://housedivided.dickinson.edu/.

When citing a website, you should include as much information about the specific page you use as possible. The main title is italicized and the subtitle appears in quotation marks. Keep the web address as short as possible, avoiding long strings of code.

CITATIONS IN LIBRARY CATALOGS AND DATABASES

You should be aware that library catalogs, WorldCat, and other databases, including databases exclusive to history, will not present citations in the style you are required to use. Library catalogs, WorldCat, and other databases will normally present the title and author of an item on separate lines and may scatter the other citation information on separate lines that are not organized to conform to any particular style. General purpose databases, and even many history databases, have the potential to be used by researchers studying many different subjects, whose citation style may differ significantly from Chicago. Therefore, you cannot simply cut and paste citation information from the catalog into your project without editing it for style. It is your responsibility to rearrange the citation information you use according to the Chicago rules, whether manually or by using one of the bibliographic management programs mentioned in chapter 2. Always consult the *Chicago Manual of Style* to make sure your citations are correct.

The order of the citation information that you see onscreen will vary by database. In a library catalog, you will likely see the title of the item first, followed by the author or editor and call number. Other identifying information would come next, such as publisher, year of publication, and city of publica-

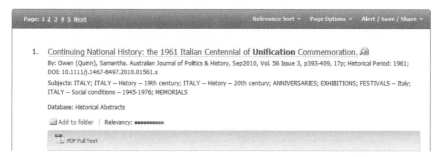

Figure A.1.   Sample of Results in Historical Abstracts. Courtesy of EBSCOhost.

tion. Sometimes you will have to click on the item's title or a Details button to get the complete citation information.

Articles in America: History & Life and Historical Abstracts normally appear with the title of the article first, followed by the author(s), journal title, volume, issue, and page numbers. The results of a search in Historical Abstracts for "Italy" and "unification" are illustrated in figure A.1.

In this example, "Continuing National History: The 1961 Italian Centennial of Unification Commemoration" is the title of the article and *Australian Journal of Politics and History* is the title of the journal in which the article appears. Samantha Owen (Quinn) is the author of this article, which was published in September 2010. The year 2010 was designated as volume 56 for the journal, and in September, issue number 3 was published. The article appeared on pages 393–409.

To format for the Chicago style, the citation information for the article illustrated in figure A.1 would be rearranged to look like this:

Owen (Quinn), Samantha. "Continuing National History: The 1961 Italian Centennial of Unification Commemoration." *Australian Journal of Politics and History* 56, no. 3 (September 2010): 393–409.

Other databases may use different arrangements for citations. It is important to familiarize yourself with the layout of database screens so that you may quickly and efficiently read them for the information you need.

Appendix B

Notes

As with bibliographies, there are numerous formats you can use to tell your audience where you obtained a specific quote or other piece of information you reference in your writing. For history projects, this is usually done by making notes. Notes are short, numbered, explanatory citations or sentences that give credit to a source of information, or add an explanation to the main body of the text that is crucial to understanding the material but would otherwise interrupt the flow of the narrative. Notes refer the reader to the original source of information when a direct quotation is made, when the author paraphrases material, or when inconsistencies require further explanation. They indicate what specific words and phrases are borrowed from another source and should be used whenever another author's work is paraphrased or directly quoted.

Historians usually create notes according to the rules of the *Chicago Manual of Style*, which recommends the use of either footnotes or endnotes when citing. Whether you use footnotes or endnotes, the presence of a note is indicated in the text of your writing by a small superscript number immediately following the quote or phrase to which it refers. This number corresponds to a complete note appearing either at the bottom of the page on which the quotation appears if the footnote method is used, or at the end of the chapter or work if the endnote method is used. Your professor should indicate whether footnotes or endnotes are required for your class; often for class papers footnotes are preferred, while endnotes may be preferred for longer works with chapters.

Examples of endnotes in the Chicago style can be found throughout this book. Figure B.1 is an example of a page in a journal using the footnote convention.

Finally, we have the honor of publishing Barbara Harris's "Defining Themselves: English Aristocratic Women, 1450–1550," which is based on her 2009 presidential address to the North American Conference on British Studies. In an essay that complements and enhances the arguments and evidence of her most recent article in this journal, Harris offers another innovative study of women's tombs and other types of funerary monuments.[2] Here, she shows how aristocratic women between 1450 and 1550 fashioned themselves in stone and glass. They were demonstrating a sense of self, she argues, in contradistinction to scholars who implicitly or explicitly suggest that "selfhood" is a more modern phenomenon. As this evidence suggests, this sense of self was one deeply defined by the integration of women into families in a patriarchal society. Harris thus makes an innovative use of visual evidence to contribute to a wider debate. She shows how women negotiated among competing family claims and attempted to define themselves as they shaped their own commemoration after death.

Our next issue will include an article by the late David Underdown on civic pageantry and charivari in early seventeenth-century Somerset, as well as articles on early Stuart Puritanism; the representation of the army on the early eighteenth-century London stage; the debates surrounding the Gin Acts of 1736 and 1751; religion and politics in northern Ireland and Britain in the long nineteenth century; modernist culture and architecture in early twentieth-century Cambridge; and British sexual culture in the 1940s and 1950s.

1 Blair Worden, "The Commonwealth Kidney of Algernon Sidney," *Journal of British Studies* 24, no. 1 (January 1985): 1–40.

2 Barbara J. Harris, "The Fabric of Piety: Aristocratic Women and Care of the Dead, 1450–1550," *Journal of British Studies* 48, no. 2 (April 2009): 308–35.

Figure B.1.   Footnotes in a Scholarly Journal. Courtesy of University of Chicago Press.

CREATING FOOTNOTES ACCORDING TO THE CHICAGO MANUAL OF STYLE

It is a good idea to take advantage of the automated feature for creating notes available in most word processing programs. These tools help you automatically number and situate your notes and keep your notes in the correct order if you add, delete, or move any while editing your text. The automated feature is particularly helpful when creating footnotes, as it ensures that the footnote stays on the same page as its referring text even if the text moves to a different page. Your word processor's help file will provide instructions for creating notes. Following are the most basic rules for creating notes according to the Chicago style:

- All authors' names are written naturally with no punctuation between the first and last names: First name Last name. For four or more authors, the abbreviation "et al." (meaning "and others") is used after the name of the first author.
- The first line of a note should always be indented approximately half an inch from the beginning of the second and subsequent lines.
- When using footnotes, you can use the abbreviation "Ibid." (Latin for "the same place") along with a page number when repeating the same source that is used immediately before it, e.g., Ibid., 63.

Following are samples of some of the most common types of notes.

Note for a Book

[1]Steven Shapin and Simon Schaffer, *Leviathan and the Air Pump: Hobbes, Boyle, and the Experimental Life* (Princeton: Princeton University Press, 1989), 285.

The note for a book contains the same information as its bibliographic entry, with the addition of the specific page number on which the quote or paraphrase appears. Otherwise, only the formatting of the publication information is different.

Note for a Journal Article

[2]Elizabeth Brown, "The Tyranny of a Construct: Feudalism and Historians of Medieval Europe," *American Historical Review* 9, no. 4 (1974), 1071.

The note for an article contains the same information as its bibliographic entry, except that the specific page number from which a quote was taken is noted instead of the entire range of pages on which the article appears. Otherwise, only the formatting of the publication information is different.

Note for a Nonscholarly Journal Article

[3]Jesse Ellison, "Did Britain Wreck the World?" *Newsweek* 154, no. 8/9 (August 24-31, 2009), 78.

The note for a nonscholarly article contains the same information as its bibliographic entry, except that the specific page number from which a quote was taken is noted instead of the entire range of pages on which the article appears. Otherwise, only the formatting of the publication information is different.

Note for a Newspaper Article

[4]"Clear Creek Gold! Three Important Strikes in Old Mining Districts," *The Daily Mining Record* [Denver, CO], 7 September 1893, issue 9; col. A.

The note for a newspaper article contains the same information as its bibliographic entry. Only the formatting is different.

Note for a Map

[5]John Mitchell, "A Map of the British and French Dominions in North America" [1757] case map, David Rumsey Map Collection, http://www.davidrumsey.com/.

John Mitchell is the creator of the map, which is housed in the David Rumsey Map Collection. "Case map" indicates that this is a single map, not part of an atlas.

Note for an Image

[6]Mathew Brady, *Hon. John A. J. Creswell, MD, ca. 1860–ca. 1865,* Still Picture Records Section, Special Media Archives Services Division (NWCS-S), National Archives at College Park, MD, http://arcweb.archives.gov/arc/action/ExternalIdSearch?id=528721.

Usually, images are described only in captions, but in cases where they need to be included in a note, include the its creator, brief description, year created, and the source in which you found it.

Note for a Tertiary Source

[7]*Dictionary of American Biography*, Centenary Edition, s.v. "Creswell, John Angel James."

Tertiary sources normally are cited only in notes, not in the bibliography. If you must cite a tertiary source in a note, only the title of the book, the edition number if not the first, and title of the entry are necessary. The abbreviation "s.v." (subverbo, meaning "under the word") is used when the entry you are referencing is arranged alphabetically in the volume.

Note for a Video

[8]Geoffrey C. Ward, Ric Burns and Ken Burns, *The Civil War*, episode 9, disc 2, directed by Ken Burns (Burbank, CA: PBS Home Video, 2004), DVD.

If a video is released in a set of tapes or discs, the note should include only the disc from which the quote or clip was taken. Otherwise, the note for a video contains the same information as its bibliographic entry. Only the formatting of the publication information is different.

Note for a Website

[9]Pinsker, Matthew, and John Osborne, eds., "Conway, Moncure Daniel," *House Divided: The Civil War Research Engine at Dickinson College*, last modified 2010, http://housedivided.dickinson.edu/.

Other than punctuation and indenting, the note for a website is much the same as its bibliographic entry.

USING NOTES TO PROVIDE EXPLANATION OR COMMENTARY

In addition to citing direct quotes or paraphrased statements, notes also can be used to further explain a point or provide commentary about a topic when that text would otherwise interrupt the flow of the main passage. For example, in the article "John A. J. Creswell of Maryland: Reformer in the Post Office" by Robert V. Friedenberg, which was published in the *Maryland Historical Magazine* in 1969 and was cited in this book's case study, the following statement appears:

> The *New York Times* believed that the "selection of Ex-Senator Cresswell [*sic*] of Maryland for Postmaster-General probably gives more general satisfaction than any other name on the list."[2]

The number 2 in superscript refers to the following footnote at the bottom of the first page of the article:

> [2]*New York Times*, March 6, 1869. The spelling of "Cresswell" has frequently caused confusion, though he consistently spelled his name with one "s." Creswell's middle initials have been considered abbreviations for both "[Angel] James," and "Andrew Jackson." Henry Powell's *Tercenary History of Maryland* and the *Dictionary of American Biography* use "[Angel] James." However all government documents and the *Biographical Dictionary of the American Congress: 1774–1961* use "Andrew Jackson."

This footnote provides context to the confusion about Creswell's name and establishes the author's spelling preference for the rest of the article. It also provides the reader with additional material that can be used to further research Creswell and to verify the author's claims about the sources of Creswell's apparent name change. More subtly, the author is telling the reader that anyone researching John A. J. Creswell should use a number of different variations on his name, including John Angel James Creswell, John Andrew Jackson Creswell, and Senator Creswell, as well as possibly using the misspelled "Cresswell" with John Angel James and John Andrew Jackson.

Appendix C

Academic Presses and Scholarly Journals for Historians

There are many reputable, scholarly presses that publish history books. A sample of some American and English book publishers you may be likely to use for a history research project are listed in table C.1. You can get information about these publishers on their websites by searching for them on Google or another search engine. If you identify a book on a publisher's page that you want to read, check your library's catalog or WorldCat to obtain a copy, as explained in chapter 5.

There also are many scholarly journals available for your research needs. A sample of some journal titles you might use for a history research project is in table C.2. You can get information about the journals on their websites by searching for the titles on Google or another search engine. To obtain the full text of the articles contained within the journals, you must access them by way of the subscriptions available through your library's website, as described in chapter 3.

Table C.1.   Scholarly Book Publishers for History

Alfred A. Knopf
http://knopf.knopfdoubleday.com/
Ashgate Publishing Group
http://www.ashgate.com/
Bedford St. Martin's Press
http://www.bedfordstmartins.com/
Catalog/discipline/History
Brepols Publishers
http://www.brepols.net/Pages/Home.
aspx
John Wiley & Sons, Ltd.
http://www.wiley.com/WileyCDA/
Section/id-350748.html
Cambridge University Press
http://www.cambridge.org/us/
Columbia University Press
http://cup.columbia.edu/
Cornell University Press
http://www.cornellpress.cornell.edu/
Duke University Press
http://www.dukeupress.edu/

Farrar, Straus & Giroux
http://us.macmillan.com/fsgadult/
categories/General/History
Harvard University Press
http://www.hup.harvard.edu/

McFarland & Company, Inc.
http://www.mcfarlandpub.com/

I. B. Tauris & Co., Ltd.
http://www.ibtauris.com/
New York University Press
http://nyupress.org/
Oxford University Press
http://www.oup.com/us/catalog/general/
subject/History/?view=usa
Princeton University Press
http://press.princeton.edu/

Routledge
http://www.routledge.com/history/

Rowman & Littlefield Publishing Group
https://rowman.com/
Stanford University Press
http://www.sup.org/
University of California Press
http://www.ucpress.edu/
University of Chicago Press
http://www.press.uchicago.edu/index.
html
University of Pennsylvania Press
http://www.upenn.edu/pennpress/

W. W. Norton & Company, Inc.
http://books.wwnorton.com/books/
subject-detail.aspx?tid=264
Yale University Press
http://yalepress.yale.edu/yupbooks/
browselist.asp?cat_id=5

Table C.2. Scholarly Journals in History

American Historical Review
http://www.indiana.edu/~ahrweb/

British Journal for the History of Science
http://journals.cambridge.org/action/
displayJournal?jid=BJH

Comparative Studies in Society and History
http://journals.cambridge.org/action/
displayJournal?jid=CSS

Diplomatic History
http://www.wiley.com/bw/journal.
asp?ref=
0145-2096

English Historical Review
http://ehr.oxfordjournals.org/

Ethnohistory
http://www.ethnohistory.org/journal/

Historia
http://www.steiner-verlag.de/Historia/

Historian
http://www.wiley.com/bw/journal.
asp?ref=0018-2370

Historical Methods
http://www.tandf.co.uk/journals/titles/
01615440.asp

History and Memory
http://muse.jhu.edu/journals/ham/

History of Science
http://www.shpltd.co.uk/hs.html

History Today
http://www.historytoday.com/

International History Review
http://www.tandf.co.uk/journals/rinh

International Review of Social History
http://journals.cambridge.org/action/
displayJournal?jid=ISH

Isis
http://www.jstor.org/action/showPublica
tion?journalCode=isis

Journal of Modern History
http://www.jstor.org/action/
showPublication?
journalCode=jmodernhistory

Journal of Religious History
http://www.wiley.com/bw/journal.asp?
ref=0022-4227&site=1

Journal of Social History
http://chnm.gmu.edu/jsh/

Journal of Women's History
http://www.press.jhu.edu/journals/
journal_of_womens_history/guidelines.
html

Kritika
http://www.slavica.com/journals/kritika/
kritika.html

Medieval Studies
http://www.pims.ca/publications/
journal.html

Journal of Modern History
http://www.jstor.org/action/
showPublication?
journalCode=jmodernhistory

Journal of Religious History
http://www.wiley.com/bw/journal.
asp?ref=
0022-4227&site=1

Modern Intellectual History
http://www.rairo-ita.org/action/
displayJournal?jid=MIH

Oral History Review
http://ohr.oxfordjournals.org/

Past and Present
http://past.oxfordjournals.org/

Public Historian
http://ucpressjournals.com/journal.
asp?j=tph

Renaissance Quarterly
http://www.rsa.org/?page=RQ

Renaissance Studies
http://www.wiley.com/bw/journal.
asp?ref=
0269-1213

Russian Review
http://www.russianreview.org/

Table C.2. (*Continued*)

Journal of African History http://journals.cambridge.org/action/ displayJournal?jid=AFH	**Seventeenth Century** http://www.manchesteruniversitypress. co.uk/ journals/journal.asp?id=5
Journal of American History http://www.journalofamericanhistory. org/	**Sixteenth Century Journal** http://www.sixteenthcentury.org/ journal.shtml
Journal of Cold War Studies http://www.fas.harvard.edu/~hpcws/ journal. htm	**Slavic Review** http://www.slavicreview.illinois.edu/
Journal of Colonialism & Colonial History http://www.press.jhu.edu/journals/ journal_ of_colonialism_and_colonial_history/	**Slavonic and East European Review** http://www.ssees.ucl.ac.uk/seer.htm
Journal of Contemporary History http://jch.sagepub.com/	**Speculum** http://medievalacademy.org/speculum/ speculum.htm
Journal of Interdisciplinary History http://www.mitpressjournals.org/loi/jinh	**Viator** http://www.cmrs.ucla.edu/publications/ viator.html
Journal of Medieval and Early Modern Studies http://jmems.dukejournals.org/	**War in History** http://wih.sagepub.com/
Journal of Military History http://www.smh-hq.org/jmh/jmh.html	

Appendix D

How to Tell the Difference between an Online Article and a Website

Journal articles that are available online should not be confused with websites. Different types of sources are published on the web just as they are on paper, but digital format can make it difficult to distinguish between a website and an online book, journal, or newspaper article. However, the distinction is important. You need to know the format of your material in order to cite it properly and also so that you can determine whether it is likely be a reliable, scholarly source. As mentioned in previous chapters, each type of source has its defining characteristics. An online scholarly journal, for example, should include elements such as an author with credentials in the field of study, a reputable academic publisher, a table of contents, a volume and/or issue number, and the date of publication. A website may include some of these characteristics, but not all. The website The Avalon Project, illustrated in figure D.1, is an example of a scholarly website that is not a journal.

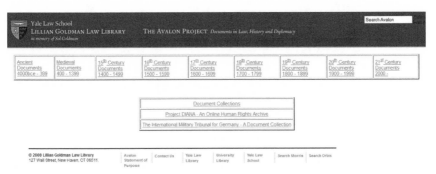

Figure D.1.   The Avalon Project as an Example of a Scholarly Website. Courtesy of the Yale Law Library.

1 This charter, granted by Charles II to William Penn, constituted him and his heirs proprietors of the province, which, in honor of his father, Admiral Penn, (whose cash advances and services were thus requited,) was called Pennsylvania. To perfect his title, William Penn purchased, in August, 1682, a quit-claim from the Duke of York to the lands west of the Delaware River embraced in his patent of 1664. Back

" Charter to William Penn and Laws of the Province of Pennsylvania passed between the Years 1682 and 1700, preceded by Duke of York's Laws in force from the year 1676 to the year 1682, with an appendix, containing Laws relating to the organization of the Provincial Courts and Historical matter. Published under the direction of John Blair Linn, Secretary of the Commonwealth. Compiled and edited by Staughton George, Benjamin M. Nead, Thomas McCamant. Harrisburg: Lane S. Hart, State Printer. 1879. " 614 pp.

2 The portion in brackets is found in the original copy, in the Public Record Office, London, Bundle 388, Privy Seals and Signed Bills (Chancery) 33 Charles the Second. See a certified copy in MS. from the Assistant Keeper of Public Records, London, September 25, 1878, in the Historical Society of Pennsylvania. Back

Source:
The Federal and State Constitutions Colonial Charters, and Other Organic Laws of the States, Territories, and Colonies Now or Heretofore Forming the United States of America
Compiled and Edited Under the Act of Congress of June 30, 1906 by Francis Newton Thorpe
Washington, DC : Government Printing Office, 1909.

Figure D.2.   Detail of "Charter for the Province of Pennsylvania—1681" from the Avalon Project. Courtesy of the Yale Law Library.

Although The Avalon Project shares some attributes with a journal, it is not a journal. A journal would likely include a volume and/or issue number and the date of the most recently released issue. Though the editors may periodically add new documents to the site, The Avalon Project does not have entire issues added on a consistent schedule. Perhaps the most obvious clue that this site is not a journal is that it does not provide secondary source articles; rather this page provides links to copies of historical primary sources only.

While The Avalon Project may not be a journal, it is a scholarly source. This is evidenced by its hosting site, Yale University, and by the notes and citations included with each document, as shown in figure D.2.

More information about scholarly journals and websites can be found in chapter 3. If you find potentially valuable research material on the Internet and are unsure what type of source it is, or whether it is acceptable to use, ask a professor or a librarian for advice.

Appendix E

How to Scan Secondary Sources for Content

Although it is critical to read all your sources carefully before actually using them for a research project, it is not necessary to read each entire book or article you find when you are making an initial determination about whether the item might be useful. By following the steps below, you should be able to make an informed decision relatively quickly about whether an item is relevant to your research.

FOR A BOOK

- Read the summary if available in the library catalog or WorldCat. You might also find summaries of a book on the Internet or on the book's cover.
- Read a few reviews about the book. Instructions for finding book reviews can be found in chapter 4. A book review will not only give you a summary of the book, but also provide another scholar's opinion of it.
- Examine the table of contents to see what major topic areas are addressed in the book.
- Read the introduction and/or preface to find the author's thesis statement. Here the author will tell you what he/she set out to accomplish with the writing of the book and how he/she proposes to accomplish it.
- Read the last chapter of the book to find a summary of the author's conclusions.
- Examine the index. This will tell you specifically which people, places, and events are addressed in the book, and approximately how prominently they figure in it.

- Scan the bibliography and footnotes or endnotes to see what sources the author used when researching the book. These may also lead you to additional helpful sources, including books, articles, and primary and secondary works.
- Read any extended explanatory footnotes. The author may use the footnotes to describe alternative arguments, omissions, or additional citation information.

For articles

- Read the summary if one is available in a database.
- Read the introduction or first few paragraphs to find the author's thesis statement.
- Read the last few paragraphs to find a summary of the author's conclusions.
- Scan the bibliography and footnotes or endnotes to see what sources the author used when researching the book. These may also lead you to additional helpful sources, including books, articles, and primary and secondary works.
- Read any extended explanatory footnotes. The author may use the footnotes to describe alternative arguments, omissions, or additional citation information.

Index

About the Author

Christine Bombaro is the associate director for Information Literacy and Research Services for the Waidner-Spahr Library at Dickinson College in Carlisle, Pennsylvania. She teaches research methods to history, English, and art majors and supervises the college's information literacy program. Her previous work on research pedagogy has been featured in journals such as *The History Teacher* and *References Services Review*, as well as in books such as *Practical Pedagogy for Library Instructors*, edited by Doug Cook and Ryan Sittler, and *The Role of the Library in the First College Year*, edited by Larry Hardesty. She also presents regularly at information literacy conferences and workshops. Christine graduated from Dickinson College with a bachelor's degree in history and secondary teaching certification, and from Drexel University with a master's degree in library science.